Home Is Where
the Hurt Is

Home Is Where the Hurt Is

Media Depictions of Wives and Mothers

SARA HOSEY

McFarland & Company, Inc., Publishers
Jefferson, North Carolina

This book has undergone peer review.

ISBN (print) 978-1-4766-7198-7
ISBN (ebook) 978-1-4766-3736-5

Library of Congress and British Library
cataloguing data are available

© 2019 Sara Hosey. All rights reserved

No part of this book may be reproduced or transmitted in any form or by any means, electronic or mechanical, including photocopying or recording, or by any information storage and retrieval system, without permission in writing from the publisher.

Front cover: Essie Davis and Noah Wiseman in *The Babadook*, 2014 (IFC Films/Photofest)

Printed in the United States of America

*McFarland & Company, Inc., Publishers
Box 611, Jefferson, North Carolina 28640
www.mcfarlandpub.com*

For Jess, John, and Julian

Table of Contents

Preface and Acknowledgments   1

Introduction   5

PART I: HURT

1. Housebound: Horror Begins at Home   19
2. At Home in Patriarchy: Girly Moms and Worldly Girls in *Gilmore Girls, Parenthood* and *Teen Mom*   37
3. "Some kind of monster": Fraught Motherhood in *Twilight* and *The Hunger Games*   55
4. The Real Housewives of Post-Industrial USA: Hysteria and Toxic Discourse   71
5. "When did he stop treating you like a princess?" Domestic Violence in *Enough* and *Waitress*   90

PART II: HOPE

6. "Little boys don't get to go around anymore hurting little girls": Evolving Depictions of Domestic Violence   109
7. "You're so epic": Matrophilia in Indie Films   124
8. "No wrong way to make a family": Hope and Home in *Tully* and *The Handmaid's Tale*   142

9. "You're such a good mom": Transparenthood, Pain and Privilege — 160

Conclusion: "Un poco mas doloroso": *Jane the Virgin* and the Home as a Little Less Painful — 177

Chapter Notes — 187

Works Cited — 200

Index — 219

Preface and Acknowledgments

A few years before the #MeToo movement took off, around the time I began work on this book, I attended a conference at which I chatted with a colleague about what shows we were watching. I was embarrassed to admit that I'd gotten pretty emotionally invested in a couple of MTV reality series.

I remarked that as a white anti-racist feminist, I had often wrestled with the difficulty of trying to reconcile enjoying media that conflicted with my political convictions. My white male colleague seemed surprised and responded that he had never had that problem, that the media he consumed, of course, aligned with his values.

I'd like to believe that my colleague tossed that remark off without considering it rather than believe that he had no problem whatsoever with much of mainstream media's depictions of various groups, including women, people of color, the disabled, the fat, the elderly, and the poor. He wasn't, as far as I could tell, a particularly hateful person, a white supremacist or an MRA (men's rights activist). Instead, I think he simply hadn't noticed that so much television and film broadcasts casual contempt for individuals in many of these groups—or ignores them completely.

Many of us cannot afford not to notice. Growing up in the late 20th century, I consumed plenty of media that treated women as irrelevant, disposable, or annoying, if it didn't suggest that we only exist for men's comfort, pleasure, and/or titillation. My interests then and now were diverse and I loved science fiction (I was big into *V* and *Star Wars*), but I also enjoyed comedy and action and drama (I loved Richard Adams' novel *Watership Down* and its TV movie adaptation, I knew most of the lines to John Hughes' *Sixteen Candles,* and the *Rocky* series was a favorite of mine for a long time) and I was totally on board with more traditionally feminine media such as soap operas (I was very serious about *General Hospital* and *Beverly Hills, 90210,* for many years).

As I look back now, however, I see that a lot of my childhood and teenage favorites didn't include many women or people of color; they also didn't feature many old folks or individuals with impairments. They often relied heavily on racist and sexist stereotypes, particularly about what certain kinds of women were like as well as what certain kinds of women deserved. Sadly, rape or the threat of rape lurks somewhere in each of these texts, sometimes as a plot device, sometimes as a prelude to romance, sometimes as a joke. I didn't notice these things when I was a child or a teen, but I certainly internalized them.

That is, I was only vaguely aware of the sexism that saturated our culture, just as I was only vaguely aware of the racism in so much of what I enjoyed. That is one reason why coming to feminism in the '90s was so life-altering: it provided me with the critical equipment I needed to makes sense of what I saw onscreen, to identify what I found troubling or offensive or even, more fundamentally, to begin to be able to articulate to myself *that* I found something troubling or offensive. Reading feminist zines and connecting with feminist mentors and friends also introduced me to a treasure trove of feminist-friendly media, demonstrating that although they weren't necessarily mainstream, there were other stories and other ways of telling those stories; I just had to look for them.

In part, this book arose from the complicated feelings I continue to have about popular media. That is, there is still so much I enjoy, even if it I find a text's messages troubling or upsetting. I've come to terms with being able to recognize that often, as the title of a wonderful but now-defunct Tumblr puts it: "Your fave is problematic." There are texts and authors and filmmakers that I choose not to support or engage with, but frankly—and this is what I wish I had told my male colleague—if I didn't sometimes consume media that ran counter to my feminist, anti-racist values, I really wouldn't have that much to watch or listen to or read at all.

That is changing, however. And tracing that change is one of the overarching projects of this book.

One of the shifts that has been most interesting to me personally has been in the depictions of motherhood. While I've been engaged with analyses of motherhood for a long time, it was after becoming a mother myself, an event which occurred during an uptick in media attention to mothers more generally, that brought into focus for me the importance of these discussions. As a result, the first chapters of *Home Is Where the Hurt Is* examine texts that do focus on women's stories and the issues that disproportionately affect wives and mothers, such as single parenthood and intimate partner violence. I argue in these chapters that popular media is responding to feminist thinking and the calls for more nuanced representations of women's lives. These texts explode the myth that the home and marriage are inherently good and safe for women, instead suggesting the perils of the domestic. However, in looking closely at these narratives, I also found that they often reify postfeminist thinking, holding up patriarchy as inescapable or maybe just not all that bad.

Later chapters of this book, however, discuss media that, for me, at least, are cause for hope. That is, these texts, many of which are produced, directed or written by women, continue to identify the injuriousness of outmoded ideas about motherhood, the home, and romance, but also point us toward a feminist future in which women's stories are celebrated and our concerns are amplified.

Thus it is easier for me these days to consume media that aligns with my values. Although perhaps no show or movie is perfect, some of them come, for me, pretty close: I am thrilled to engage with social justice issues as presented from a feminist perspective on *Orange Is the New Black*, to see feminist debates take place on the small screen on *Transparent*, to watch young feminist women grappling with romance in *Girls* and *Insecure*, and to see mothers and older women treated with love and respect on *Jane the Virgin* and in *Obvious Child* and *Grandma*.

It's also been my great delight to not only enjoy this media, but to have the opportunity to share my thoughts and reactions with a like-minded feminist community.

On that note, I extend thanks to my colleagues and friends who have shared their time, expertise and interest with me, both in hallway chats and more formal discussions: thank you to Barbara Horn for her consistent support and mentorship and to Francesco Pupa, who not only provided me with astute feedback, but also often recommended the work of philosophers who wound up significantly informing my project. Frank has also been one of my favorite people to talk with about movies and TV shows. I am also indebted to my writing partner, Elizabeth Abele, who not only read and critiqued every chapter, but who, on demand, could generate an exhaustive list of media on a variety of topics. Google could learn a thing or two from you, Elizabeth.

I've also enjoyed talking about many of these issues with students in my women's and gender studies classes as well as students in NCC's WSA. I am grateful to them not only for sharing their pop culture expertise with me, but also for sharing their energy and enthusiasm for activism. As discussed in this book, the term "mom" has become a compliment young people extend to women who function as mentors and role models; I'm much older than most of you, but you're still "moms" to me.

Thanks to Nassau Community College for providing a sabbatical during which I began the research for this book. Thank you to NCC's librarians and, in particular, David Crugnola, who consistently went above and beyond to secure the materials I needed. Additionally, I will always be grateful to NCC's Children's Greenhouse Childcare Center and, especially, Greenhouse director Janet Walsh, who, in caring for my children so expertly, made much of my work possible. The Children's Greenhouse is a model of what high-quality daycare can be if it is supported by a larger community: affordable, flexible, and nurturing of both child and parent. Many homes would be happier if all parents who desired it had access to childcare like that provided at the Children's Greenhouse.

Thank you to the two peer reviewers whose insights have helped to strengthen my thinking here. Thank you to *Feminist Formations*, which published a version of Chapter 3 ("Canaries and Coalmines: Toxic Discourse in *The Incredible Shrinking Woman* and *Safe*," *Feminist Formations*, vol. 23, no. 2, September 2011, pp. 77–97). Thank you to Derek Davidson at Photofest for his help gathering the images that, I hope, enrich my readings of the texts. Layla Milholen at McFarland has my endless gratitude: thank you for your wisdom and support.

Finally, special thanks to my partner Jess, whose patience, good humor, and love have made our home a happy, hopeful one.

Introduction

We Should All Be Feminists?

Several books with titles qualifying or renouncing feminism—most notably Roxane Gay's *Bad Feminist* (2014), Jessa Crispin's *Why I Am Not a Feminist* (2017), and Andi Ziesler's *We Were Feminists Once* (2017)—have appeared in recent years, contributions to an important and longstanding tradition of feminist self-scrutiny. Each seeks to draw boundaries, to define feminism, to suggest where the movement has gone wrong and where it may be going right.[1] They've appeared during a decade in which young women in particular are increasingly comfortable identifying as feminists (Weiss) at the same time as, according to some critics, many Western women's feminism is itself relatively content-less: a neoliberal endorsement of consumer capitalism justified as women's self-care or, as Crispin puts it, "a fight to allow women to participate equally in the oppression of the powerless and the poor" (xiii).[2] According to some, rather than an expansive term accommodating diverse women's needs and interests, feminism has been hollowed out, a flimsy shell used to cover over misogyny, injustice, and internalized self-hatred. When women as diverse as Beyoncé, bell hooks, Taylor Swift, Sarah Ahmed, Lindy West, Hillary Clinton, Alicia Garza, and Ivanka Trump are each perceived as having an equal claim to the label "feminist," perhaps the term has been exhausted.[3]

And yet, each of these women exists in a world in which the influence of feminist thinking and activism is undeniable. Even conservative women who disavow feminism, such as former U.S. representative Michele Bachmann or critic and commentator Ann Coulter, are themselves beneficiaries of women's hard-fought right to public speech and argument. As the title of Jo Reger's 2012 book suggests, feminism is "everywhere and nowhere" or, as Jennifer Baumgardner and Amy Richards declare in *Manifesta: Young Women, Feminism, and the Future* (2000, 2010), feminism is "like fluoride … it's simply in the water" (17).

As a result of its pervasiveness, diversity, and continuous evolution, feminism's influence on U.S. popular culture has produced complex and often confusing messages about gender, sex, family, and the home.[4] This study offers an ideological analysis of contemporary popular culture texts with an eye to their engagement with feminisms and the social changes resulting from feminist movements. More specifically, *Home Is Where the Hurt Is* argues that depictions of motherhood and the domestic indicate a larger cultural ambivalence about women's status and changing roles that has arisen, in part, from the growing awareness of the perils of home and the domestic for women. This study is primarily concerned with how mass media, specifically film and television, has responded to feminist activists' and researchers' demands that we attend to the ways in which domesticity can be fraught, difficult, and dangerous.

That is, after two hundred years of propaganda aimed at convincing women that the safest place was the home, our popular media is catching on to the idea that the home is one of the most perilous places for a woman to be.[5] This shift is crucial because mass media depictions have long shored up injurious myths that discouraged women from venturing into public spaces or beyond the domestic. American media often contradicts our lived realities. For example, despite anxiety about "stranger rape," the home is in fact more dangerous than the dark alley: according to the Rape, Abuse, and Incest National Network, most women know their rapists (or rather, most rapists know the person they attack); further, 28 percent of perpetrators are the victim's "intimate partner" while 7 percent are victim's family members ("The Offenders"). In addition to the message that the world beyond the home is hostile and dangerous, women are inundated with media suggesting that the attainment of (heterosexual) romantic love is the only true path to a woman's happiness. At the same time, however, according to the National Coalition Against Domestic Violence, a staggering one in five women has been the victim of "severe" violence at the hands of her partner ("What Is Domestic Violence?"); as a result, the title of 2018 United Nations Press Release declares the home "the most dangerous place for women." Finally, despite representations of the home as a woman's haven, or even simply as a site in which a woman is in control, some researchers associate the almost 50 percent increase in cancer rates between 1950 and 1990 with the introduction of thousands of new chemicals into consumer, commercial, and industrial use during that time period, many of which may be found in cleaning products, household furniture, and cosmetics (Knopper 40).[6] The home, then, is potentially poisonous, especially for women.

This study argues that media is catching on. Thus, although authentic and complex portrayals of relationship and intimate partner violence are still too rare in our popular culture, at least we are no longer presented with films that depict a man's violence against his wife as humorous and/or justified (such as in the famous opening of the 1940 film *The Philadelphia Story*). While motherhood is still idealized, the mothers we see in our mass media are no longer the unchanging, ever-smiling automatons of television past (see June Cleaver or Carol Brady). And while romance and motherhood remain the dominant storyline in women-focused literature and film, "married with children" is no longer always presented as the answer, the prize, or the safe haven for women that it once was.

This book attends to the ways that media capitalizes on, defuses, and contributes to feminism's development. Thus, engaging with media such as the series *Teen Mom, Gilmore Girls, Parenthood,* and *American Horror Story,* the movies of filmmakers including Noah Baumbach, Lena Dunham, Tyler Perry, Todd Haynes, Rebecca Miller, Michael Apted, Jennifer Kent, Lee Daniels, and Jason Reitman, and streaming series *Orange Is the New Black, Transparent,* and *The Handmaid's Tale,* I contend that although many contemporary depictions continue to circulate damaging stereotypes, they also begin to acknowledge aspects of women's lives, including caregiving and the performance of heterosexual womanhood, as inherently political activities which intersect with other important identities and practices.

I focus primarily on media in and from the United States; this is my most immediate context and is an important site of media influence globally.[7] Additionally, I focus on media at the turn of the 20th/21st century, although at times my analyses begin with earlier texts that I argue are influential or otherwise crucial for understanding a larger representational tradition. *Home Is Where the Hurt Is* is organized thematically, each chapter anchored by an "issue" which predominantly affects women, such as intimate partner violence, relegation to the domestic, or negotiation of motherhood, and the book is broken into two parts: "Hurt" and "Hope." The first six chapters discuss texts that are primarily transitional, in that they are narratives that address troubling realities at the same time as they fall back on outmoded, limiting understandings of gender roles; these texts often identify sites of gender inequity only to conclude that such injustice is insurmountable, thus naturalizing women's oppression. Others within the "Hurt" section epitomize neoliberal postfeminism, suggesting that women must struggle silently and alone against the forces that oppress them. The texts discussed in "Hope," (Chapters 6, 7, and 8, as well as the Conclusion) continue to identify contemporary contradictions and limitations surrounding gender roles, but also present women and mothers as individuals deserving of dignity and safety. These utopic texts identify the injuriousness of outmoded ideas about motherhood, the home, and romance, and also point us toward a feminist future in which women's voices and concerns are amplified and respected.

Feminism, Postfeminism and Contemporary Media

While resisting adherence to the formula described by Charlotte Brunsdon in her critique of the "feminist Ur-article," in which the critic identifies a problematic text and discovers its feminist possibilities, I maintain the value of feminist analyses of depictions of women in popular culture ("Feminism").[8] That is, I follow Kim A. Loudermilk in her contention that attending to how recent film and television represent traditional feminine roles such as "wife" and "mother," we can better understand women's changing roles as well as how "media contains and recuperates feminist politics" (13).

In "Popularity Contests: The Meanings of Popular Feminism," Joanne Hollows and Rachel Moseley provide an overview of the ways in which feminist critics have approached the relationship between feminism and popular culture. They write, "many studies retain an implicit or explicit assumption that popular culture could still benefit from a 'proper' feminist makeover.... This reproduces the idea that the feminist has good sense and therefore the moral authority to legislate on gendered relations, and also reproduces hierarchical power relations between 'the feminist' situated outside the popular and the 'ordinary woman' located within it" (11). While Hollows and Moseley raise excellent points regarding the shortcomings of an oversimplified feminist analysis, perhaps some pop culture texts would, in fact, be improved by a "proper" feminist makeover. That is, much of our popular culture continues to erase and/or circulate harmful stereotypes regarding women, people of color, people with physical and intellectual impairments, older people, and poor people. While many feminist critics would rightly disavow a "moral authority" to cast judgment on popular texts, what is the point of feminist criticism of popular culture if not to attempt to identify and describe representations that promote or undermine understandings of all individuals as valuable, complex, and deserving of dignity and autonomy?

Further, Hollows and Moseley argue that the insider/outside dichotomy is a false one, an important point I want to emphasize here. An analysis of popular culture with a focus on the relationship between cultural narratives and feminist movements and thinking would not reinforce insider/outsider dynamics if the analysis takes into account that feminist "insiders" are working in popular culture and that feminist "insiders" are also "ordinary women." For example, discussing the Amazon streaming series *Transparent*, showrunner Jill Soloway asserts that art is, in fact, "propaganda": "I'm like, cis-hetero patriarchy has been making propaganda forever.... I had to grow up watching fucking white dudes act like women should be competing for them on the basis of their financial success—that's propaganda. So I'm gonna make my propaganda until it's all equal" (Jung). Soloway is at once a feminist, a consumer of media and a creator of media, so their remarks draw attention to the ways in which heterosexist, racist, exclusionary narratives are often framed as neutral. As a feminist, then, one might feel that some representations are "better"—more just, more expansive, more feminist—than others.

However, as Melissa Ames and Sarah Burcon observe, not only is pop culture becoming "increasingly didactic" (4), much of it "exists as a type of funhouse mirror constantly distorting the real world conditions that exist for women and girls and magnifying the gendered expectations that they face" (5).[9] Further, as critics including Rosalind Gill, Yvonne Tasker, and Diane Negra have argued, mass media often uncritically shores up neoliberalism and postfeminism, ideologies imbricated in their shared framing of empowerment as a consumer choice.[10] Angela McRobbie argues that in a postfeminist context,

> Elements of feminism have been taken into account, and have been absolutely incorporated into political and institutional life. Drawing on a vocabulary that includes words like "empowerment" and "choice," these elements are then converted into a much more individualistic discourse, and they are deployed in this new guise, particularly in media and popular culture, but also by agencies of the state, as a kind of substitute for feminism [*Aftermath* 1].

As these authors observe, postfeminist ideology at once reassures us that progress has been made and equality accomplished at the same time that individuals themselves must redouble their efforts to alter, improve, and correct themselves. That is, for women, empowerment becomes a consumer category; feminist history and activism tools that enable individual women to "have it all," when having it all means a productive job, a family, and a home to care for.

A 2013 advertisement for the Swiffer mop is emblematic of the postfeminist age: in a visual allusion to Rosie the Riveter, herself not an unproblematic feminist icon, a woman clutches her mop defiantly (Figure 1). An inversion of Rosie's call for women's employment beyond the home—"We Can Do It"—is here applied to combatting dirty floors.[11] The ad's cooption of what has become a feminist icon suggests that it is precisely because the goal of normalizing women's paid labor outside the home has been achieved that Rosie can be playfully invoked in this way. Perhaps despite itself, the ad reflects many dissonant realities: women still do the bulk of household cleaning at the same time they are told—impelled even—to work outside of the home; women are still often politically and economically disenfranchised at the same time they are told that they have unprecedented power.[12]

And yet, the original Rosie image is not an uncomplicated feminist artifact either. Created in 1942 by J. Howard Miller, the picture was designed to "boost morale" for white women employed in wartime factories. In "Feminist Protest Assemblages and Remix Culture," Red Chidgey points out that although the image has become associated with second wave feminism, it was not until

Figure 1. "Get a Deep Clean" Swiffer advertisement: A visual allusion to Rosie the Riveter (Swiffer advertisement, Swiffer Bissel, 2013).

the 1980s that the image of Rosie became popularly circulated: it was "simply not available for public consumption or activist reuse in the 1960s and 1970s" (200). Additionally, Rosie's call to empowerment in the form of employment may not resonate with the many poor women, women of color, and immigrant women who have never *not* been working in the U.S.

Significantly, another Rosie reboot appeared in 2014: superstar Beyoncé Knowles posted a picture to Instagram that featured her posing as Rosie, the words "We Can Do It" in a bubble behind her. This Rosie 2.0, embodied by an astoundingly successful African American woman, potentially presents a message of inspiration and empowerment; Beyoncé, for many, is the epitome of female personal and professional success.[13] In addition, Beyoncé claims Rosie as part of her own black feminist inheritance. Chidgey writes that Beyoncé's staging "isn't just a remix … she is calling upon the layered elements of cultural memory associated with this image (as patriotic symbol, as 'ordinary woman,' as worker, as feminist icon) and reworks these components through her own celebrity assemblage—crucially, also remixing the whiteness of dominant mainstream feminism and historical Rosie representations" (201). In inhabiting Rosie, Beyoncé, who Britney Cooper says has "spread the gospel of feminism to the masses" (31), both revitalizes and revises this complicated feminist figure.[14]

As these recent homages to Rosie suggest, feminist iconography is palimpsestic, with layers that may at once enrich and revitalize as well as conceal or distort each other. In addition, they may also exist as readily recognizable and monetizable. On the one hand, these Rosie-revisions demonstrate that the feminism that appears in popular culture may be watered-down, misleading, or even sexist. On the other hand, some manifestations of feminism suggest an expansiveness and inclusivity; Beyoncé's image, for example, may function as an invitation.

As Beyoncé's deployment of Rosie suggests, women are increasingly participating in the creation of cultural texts; again, feminist critics and activists have been instrumental in insisting not only that our media present more nuanced representations of women's lives, but also in raising awareness about who is creating cultural texts as well as calling for more diversity "behind the camera." In fact, as suggested above, during this recent "golden age of television," writers, directors and producers are increasingly participating in feminist discourse. In *Stealing the Show: How Women Are Revolutionizing Television*, Joy Press writes, "For most of TV history, broadcast networks had focused on series that could deliver a mass audience to advertisers, with particular emphasis on eighteen-to-thirty-four-year-old-guys," but that as the competitive landscape changed, "cable and digital executives grew more receptive to programming that appealed to niche populations, and anxious broadcast networks took a few more risks in response" (2). Streaming services in particular are producing overtly feminist content, including series such as *Orange Is the New Black* (Netflix), *Insecure* (HBO), and *Transparent* (Amazon). While we must continue to call for more diverse representations of women, people of color, disabled folks, LBGTQ+ and other marginalized groups, for many of us, the aforementioned programs present exciting opportunities to see our group identity, political commitments, and values reflected in mainstream media. Discussing the pleasure of consuming media that aligns with her values, critic B. Ruby Rich avows, "I'm never happier than in those rare times when my own interests, the films I love, the interests of a community to which I belong, and the larger society's attention all converge. I live for those moments still" (xxix).

As discussed in the chapters in the "Hope" section of this study, these moments are becoming more common. Radner and Stringer point out that media generally, and film in particular, "has become much more self-conscious in its treatment of gender ... movies in the twenty-first century are aware of their role in the social production of gender, and commonly represent, and deliberately reflect upon, the dilemmas that face the contemporary subject" (Rader and Stringer *Feminism* 4). These dilemmas, I argue in the chapters that follow, include a profound ambivalence about women's relationship to the home.

Chapter Breakdown

Part I, "Hurt," investigates mass media that diminishes women and mothers, that suggest the inevitability of patriarchy, and that depict the home as a site of captivity and pain for women. Chapter 1, "Housebound: Horror Begins at Home" examines women's relationship to the physical home, looking specifically at "horror" narratives (I use the term expansively) including the first season of the television series *American Horror Story* (2011), and the films *The Babadook* (2014) and *Precious* (2009). In each of these narratives, the mother is either unable or unwilling to leave the home. I argue that these texts function on an allegorical level to suggest the impossible position of many contemporary mothers, who are at once aware of a cultural imperative to public life at the same time as they find themselves unable to extricate themselves from the demands of the private. The home is a trap and, in the films *The Babadook* and *Precious*, homeboundness itself threatens to turn the mother into a monster.

Extending the discussion of the threat of the single mother, Chapter 2, "At Home in Patriarchy: Girly Moms and Worldly Girls in *Gilmore Girls*, *Parenthood* and *Teen Mom*," focuses on the presentation of young single mothers as inept and emotionally stunted but also conventionally attractive and "hot," revealing an idealization of the girl (rather than the woman). I argue that the increasing prevalence of "girly moms" happens in tandem with the rising popularity of the sophisticated teenager, what I term the "worldly girl." Beginning with *Gilmore Girls* (2000–07), a program often lauded for its positive representations of female figures, and continuing through other primetime comedies and "dramedies" such as *Parenthood* (2010–15), I suggest that the glorification of the girly mom reaches its nadir in the MTV reality series *16 and Pregnant* (2009–14), *Teen Mom* (2009–2012, 2015–present), *Teen Mom 2* (2011–present) and *Teen Mom 3* (2013). Taken together, these programs reveal a troubling collapse between the identities of woman and girl, daughter and mother, adult and child. Consistent with politically disempowering neoliberal and postfeminist thinking, these narratives reassert the naturalness and inevitability of patriarchal family and social structures.

In Chapter 3, "'Some kind of monster': Fraught Motherhood in *Twilight* and *The Hunger Games*," I argue that these young adult franchises go even farther in divesting mothers of power and relevance and that the ostensible insignificance of the mother-figure in *The Hunger Games* and *Twilight* is directly related to the larger devaluation of mothers in our culture.[15] Drawing on Adrienne Rich's concept of "matrophobia," I argue that in the *Twilight* and *Hunger Games* movies and books, the mother-character is represented as peripheral to the daughter's development and, in fact, rejection of the mother is depicted as necessary for the protagonists' transition to adulthood. At the same time, however, these books and films shore up the "motherhood mandate"[16] or notion that motherhood is the necessary and most desirable conclusion of a woman's narrative or life.

Chapter 4, "The Real Housewives of Post-Industrial USA: Hysteria and Toxic Discourse," further considers depictions of wives and mothers who are dismissed, discredited, and devalued. However, looking at movies from three decades, *The Incredible Shrinking Woman* (1981), *Safe* (1995) and *Consumed* (2015), this chapter traces media responses to increased concern regarding pollution and toxicity and I argue that the films discussed in this chapter reveal not only a profound uncertainty regarding the integrity of our homes and bodies, but also a skepticism of the solutions offered by scientific and technological advances. Further, these texts foreground the obstacles confronting women who attempt to challenge the social and scientific status quo. As women more vigorously lay claim to various forms of political, scientific and expert authority, we increasingly see depictions of women who are silenced and ignored, despite the legitimacy of their complaints. These films, then, not only depict the dangers of the domestic, but the challenge of sexist epistemic injustice.

The two chapters that follow investigate a threat that emerges from within the home itself: intimate partner violence. Chapters 5 and 6 turn to depictions of domestic violence and, in particular, how women are depicted as responding to violence. I trace the evolution of representations from a postfeminist version of empowerment through embrace of the masculine and the acceptance of economic rescue, to depictions which celebrate women's resourcefulness and the possibilities of community. In "'When did he stop treating you like a princess?' Domestic Violence in *Enough* and *Waitress*," I review depictions of intimate partner violence in two early 21st century films in order to identify how these depictions engage in larger public discourse about heterosexual romance and the roles of wife and mother. While both films reveal the influence of feminist thinking about the intolerability of wife-battering and thus present domestic violence as unacceptable, they nevertheless present unsustainable and potentially injurious "happy endings," achieved through capitulation to patriarchy.

The second chapter on domestic violence extends this investigation, but also functions to set up the second half of the book, "Hope." In Chapter 6, "'Little boys don't get to go around anymore hurting little girls': Evolving Depictions of Domestic Violence," I argue that despite attempting to depict the complex realities of intrafamilial violence, many films nevertheless recirculate antifeminist agendas, suggesting that victims who avail themselves of legal channels, social safety nets or even the label "victim" are weak, corrupt, or in part to blame for their own victimization. At the same time, the narratives discussed, including *Personal Velocity* (2002), *Madea's Family Reunion* (2006), and *Big Little Lies* (2017), not only indicate a legitimate skepticism of governmental and legal agencies, but move away from over-simplified solutions and introduce alternatives to a surrender to patriarchy, including an embrace of the restorative possibilities of sustaining female community.

Chapter 7 turns to positive—and at times even idealized—visions of mothers and motherhood's potential. In "'You're so epic': Matrophilia in Indie Films," I again draw on Adrienne Rich's thinking in order to identify representations of the dauntingly successful mother in selected independent films, including *Margot at the Wedding* (2007), *Tiny Furniture* (2010), *Obvious Child* (2014) and *Grandma* (2015). I argue that while a differentiation from—or outright rejection of—the mother is still presented as necessary in many coming-of-age narratives, these films depict children grappling with their desire for and admiration of the mother. Thus, rather than matrophobia, the children in these films suffer an excess of matrophilia: they fear failing to meet the mother's standards and achievements. Insisting that adulthood depends in part on an honest assessment of both the self and the mother, these films move away from Hollywood clichés and toward more nuanced, sophisticated depictions of this fundamental relationship.

Chapter 8, "'No wrong way to make a family': Hope and Home in *Tully* and *The Handmaid's Tale*," discusses how the aforementioned texts engage with recent debates surrounding the employment of paid female labor to perform domestic and reproductive tasks traditionally associated with women. I argue that each narrative is instantiated by a crisis in resources and depict the problems surrounding increased exploitation as a means of maintaining the patriarchal status quo. Although both *Tully* and *The Handmaid's Tale* remain fairly grim in tone and content, they nevertheless gesture to the necessity of resisting patriarchy and reimaging the domestic. Both texts, I argue, suggest the untenability of patriarchy as well as the possibilities of sustaining family structures beyond the heteronormative.

New family formations are also central to the discussion in Chapter 9, "'You're such a good mom': Transparenthood, Pain and Privilege," which argues that recent streaming services have allowed for more complex depictions of parenthood. In particular, mass media depictions of trans folks who are parents *before* they transition allow for both investigations of the ways in which traditional gender roles remain naturalized in mainstream culture, as well as the ways in which parenting roles can be flexible enough to accommodate and to change with an individual over a lifetime. Two streaming series, Netflix's *Orange Is the New Black* and Amazon's *Transparent*, explore the ways in which transitioning changes one as a parent and how being a parent might impact one's transition. In each of these shows, the trans character is a father before she transitions. Crucially, in each series, parenthood is deployed at times as a device through which trans characters find themselves confronted with their past or current sexism, allowing them an opportunity to reflect on their actions and to reconcile who they are now with who they once were.

In what follows, I provide a sense of the fundamental shifts in understandings of family and the domestic that have taken place in U.S. society and media in the past three decades, as well as the areas in which even ostensibly politically enlightened media retreats to entrenched positions and solutions to the problems posed by gender inequities. For example, in several of the texts discussed here, a patriarch (re)emerges in order to somehow save or redeem the otherwise-independent protagonist. In addition, women are still often depicted as reluctant activists; concern for her family's health is consistently used as justification for a woman's participation in public life. Finally, despite attempts to depict motherhood with compassion, complexity, and humor, over and over again mothers are depicted as, if not actually bad mothers, unable to *feel* like good mothers.

In "Unhitching from the 'Post' (of Postfeminism)," Mary Douglas Vavrus reviews the response to Wharton School professors Betsey Stevenson and Justin Wolfers' (2009) study "The Paradox of Declining Female Happiness," in which the authors suggest that women's reported decrease in happiness since the 1970s may in part be attributable to feminism. Vavrus writes, "Even while acknowledging other potential explanations for this trend, such as the dramatic increase in income inequality in the United States since the early 1980s (which is the majority of the period of Stevenson and Wolfers' analysis), they abandon the examination of these and instead lay the blame mainly at the feet of the women's movement for raising women's expectations above a psychologically sustainable level" (224). Stevenson and Wolfers' work—which received significant media attention—functions to draw attention to the problems and complications that have arisen from women's rising participation in public life without scrutinizing the persistence of systemic sexism. Much of the media discussed here provides a similarly myopic picture of what ails women: overwhelmed mothers can strive to "have it all" as long as having it all does not include radically challenging the tradition of the nuclear family, or critiquing its gender dynamics or even simply demanding state-sponsored high quality childcare. Thus, on the one hand, many depictions reveal the ways in which feminism can no longer be denied in popular culture at the same time as those depictions deliver a watered-down version of what gender equity might look like.

I follow Tasker and Negra in their commitment to feminist critique, especially "at a time when women face significant challenges to their economic well-being, hard-won reproductive rights, and even authority to speak, while popular culture blithely assumes that gender equality is a given" (12). Through analyzing and responding to cultural representations of the struggles faced by wives and mothers, *Home Is Where the Hurt Is* thus contributes to a growing field of feminist media studies which promotes better understanding of the position of women, as well as calls for more nuanced, just, and expansive understandings of women as wives, partners, and mothers.

Part I : Hurt

1
Housebound: Horror Begins at Home

The 2012 film *What to Expect When You're Expecting* follows several women in their journeys toward parenthood.[1] One figure, Jules (Cameron Diaz), is presented as a fitness guru along the lines of Jillian Michaels, a reality star host of a weight-loss program. Jules self-righteously refuses to allow pregnancy to slow her down; she travels and is filming a live segment in which she ambushes and harangues a former show contestant about his eating habits (launching into lunges to demonstrate to him how it's done), when she suddenly gasps and falls to the ground. A few scenes later, Jules is shown ordered on bed rest. She exhibits her tenacity and can-do attitude, arguing with a doctor, "I climbed Everest, okay? I'm pretty confident that I can keep this baby in until I get home. I can do that, okay? I can do it" (*What to Expect When You're Expecting*). The doctor answers solemnly, "No, you can't. You need to stay in bed. Honestly? You don't have a choice."

This narrative thread functions to chasten Jules, as well as to naturalize the concept that pregnant women do not "have a choice." That is, the health of the fetus is presented as the mother-to-be's unquestionable priority. Not unlike the epistemic injustice perpetrated against women charged with "hysteria" described in Chapter 3 of this study, in *What to Expect When You're Expecting*, a woman who is an ostensible expert on health is revealed as no longer an authority on her own body or capability. Ultimately, Jules is put in her place: she must remain in the home and, in this extreme case, the bed itself. That Jules reconciles herself to this imperative and is depicted as adjusting and learning how to allow others to care for her suggests that this particular challenge has been good for Jules, humbling her and improving her relationship with her partner. In *What to Expect*, pregnancy and motherhood are consistently presented as revealing to women their true domestic natures.

If the film's title is to be used as a guide, a mother-to-be can "expect" to discover that she is comically unprepared for pregnancy and parenthood. In particular, the film revels in revealing the shortcomings of those women—Jules, and another character, Wendy—who are ostensibly *too fit* to parent. Significantly, both Jules and Wendy must surrender to doctors, relinquishing their intellectual and emotional conceptions of their own pregnancies as well as their physical autonomy to a medical establishment that knows better than they what is good for them and, of course, for their unborn children.[2] Their storylines enact the description of alienation in pregnancy and birthing described in Iris Marion Young's 1983 essay "Pregnancy and Embodiment: Subjectivity and Alienation": "Pregnancy does not belong to the woman herself. It is a state of the developing fetus, for which the woman is a container; or it is an objective, observable process coming under scientific scrutiny; or it becomes objectified by the woman herself as a 'condition' in which she must 'take care of herself'" (46).

The disempowerment of the pregnant women and of mothers is common in much popular media and depictions are often contradictory, at once suggesting that a woman has no choice but to surrender to "experts" including doctors, social workers, and other institutional representatives, at the same time as those institutions are often presented as flawed and their delegates obtuse and ineffective. Such ambivalence signifies larger cultural uncertainty as women are at once encouraged to construe pregnancy and parenthood as deeply personal and empowering conditions at the same time as they may experience pregnancy as unnervingly public (as strangers feel entitled to comment on or even touch a pregnant woman's torso) or disempowering (such as when a woman is subject to a hospital's mandatory drug-testing policies or a stranger's intrusive parenting advice).

In this chapter I argue that this ambivalence is emblematized in the narrative of the housebound woman in three generically disparate "horror" narratives: the "Murder House" season of FX's *American Horror Story* (2011), the horror film *The Babadook* (2014), and the award-winning social drama *Precious* (2009). In each, the mother's confinement to the home is the stuff of nightmares and the intrusions of medical and social authorities only serve to exacerbate already dangerous situations. Exploring the intersection of two conflicting ideas—that women should remain at home and that confinement in the home is injurious to the mother and those around her—these narratives reveal that neither the public nor the private provides a woman with safety or legitimate control. Thus, although the home figures differently in each text, all of the narratives discussed below contain a suggestion that home-boundedness breeds dysfunction, as well as a skepticism of the ability of patriarchal authorities to comprehend—and at times, contain—the mother's power.

American Horror Story: *"I am not a house"*

Only recently has the visibly pregnant body become publicly acceptable, an attitude that reflects the belief that the expectant mother belongs at home. Kelly Oliver writes in *Knock Me Up, Knock Me Down: Images of Pregnancy in Hollywood Films* that "From the mid-nineteenth century until the late twentieth century, pregnancy was considered a medical condition that should be hidden from public view.... When not pathologized, the pregnant body was hidden from view because it was considered ugly, even shameful. Women were advised to 'lay-in,' which meant not leaving their homes or even their beds" (Oliver 1).[3] Further, despite superficial acceptance of pregnancy and maternity, contemporary media depictions nevertheless often shore up the notion that pregnant women, in the words of Jules' doctor in *What to Expect*, "don't have a choice" with regard to their physical movement or lifestyle choices.

This is true in the "Murder House" season of *American Horror Story*, a "horror anthology franchise" (Janicker 1), which traces mother Vivien's victimization and disempowerment at the hands of pro-natal patriarchal culture. Clearly participating in the Gothic tradition, the show includes a haunted house, a trapped woman, and a demonic insemination. In her introduction to *Reading* American Horror Story: *Essays on the Television Franchise*, Janicker argues that *AHS* is "an intricate, self-reflexive and ever-expanding universe of horror scenarios derived from, and entrenched within, a long history of popular culture that seeks to make sense of the world by grappling with terror and gore" (2). The season's most obvious narrative forebear is Roman Polanski's 1968 *Rosemary's Baby*. In both, despite superficial trappings of empowerment, the pregnant woman is overwhelmed and instrumentalized by powerful nefarious forces. Further, in both, the "terror" and "gore" are often located in the vicissitudes of the maternal body.

Connie Britton plays Vivien, the mother-figure in "Murder House." The casting of Britton, an actress who, for many, embodies "the possibility of beauty and vibrancy and sexuality over 40," and whose celebrity "fundamentally challenges the polished, safe, postfeminist vision of female stardom that currently dominates" (A.H. Petersen), further reflects the series' meta-textual engagement with media, gender constructs and women's roles. In addition, Vivien's narrative trajectory dramatizes the postfeminist tension between the idealization of home and the need to escape the dysfunctional domestic. In an early scene, Vivien visits a doctor in order to discuss conceiving after a miscarriage. The doctor uses a house metaphor in order to try to convince Vivien to take a fertility-enhancing drug: "your body is like a house. You can fix the tiles in the bathroom and the kitchen, but if the foundation is decaying, well, you're wasting your time" ("Pilot"). Vivien resists, telling the doctor, "I am not a house" and explaining to him that she is simply "trying to get control over my body again after what happened." She presents as informed and confident about decisions regarding what she chooses to injest and is firm in her objections. But the doctor persists, asking Vivien what she's "afraid of"; a subsequent scene shows Vivien carrying a bag of prescriptions, indicating that she will take the drugs after all.

This scene presents a critique of a patriarchal medical establishment that naturalizes the surrender of women's bodily autonomy in pursuit of the postfeminist ideal of youthfulness. The doctor's dismissal of Vivien's concerns further suggests that her perspective, her attempt to "get control" over her own body is of little importance to him. Like Jules in *What to Expect When You're Expecting*, despite a woman's claim to self-education and her reasonable objections, the medical figure is presented as the final authority on the woman's body. It is notable that in his pitch, the doctor several times repeats the promise that the hormone treatment will make Vivien look and feel younger, side effects ostensibly unrelated to the drugs' intended result, but nevertheless supposedly attractive to Vivien.

Not only does the doctor implicitly connect fertility, physical vitality, and female beauty, his use of a house metaphor objectifies women's bodies, suggesting that they are—like homes apparently—constantly in need of repair and renovation. In keeping with postfeminist ideology, the woman is presented as responsible for vigilance in her unending improvement project. However, Vivien's initial rejection of the doctor's metaphor, "I am not a house," articulates resistance to the myth of medical interventions for women as safe, easy, and necessary. Her ultimate capitulation thus suggests the inescapability of a medical-patriarchal complex that insists on women surrendering their power and personal values.

Over and over again, Vivien's storyline foregrounds the ways in which women are stripped of autonomy and choice. Raped by an evil ghost, Vivien becomes pregnant with twins, thus unwittingly "housing" demon spawn and serving as a vehicle for someone else's agenda. It is only later in the pregnancy that Vivien and her husband Ben discover that each twin has a different father. Perhaps because she is already six months pregnant or perhaps because of an assumed risk to the fetus biologically related to Ben, abortion is never presented as an option, further suggesting that Vivien has very little choice or "control."

Further, after Vivien is assaulted at home, she tells Ben that she wants to move. He replies that they can't afford to do so, to which Vivien responds, "you're telling me that we have no *choice*?" (emphasis added, "Murder House"). A common trope in haunted house narratives, the family's economic inability to cut their losses and relocate is at once a plot device that permits the narrative's forward movement, but also, as several critics have pointed out, addresses anxieties surrounding the American dream of home ownership in times of recession and instability.[4] Further, that Ben cannot financially support his family signals a crisis in patriarchal authority. The possibility of Vivien working in order to contribute financially is never presented; although not explicitly discussed, it seems that the fragility of Vivien's pregnancy is what prevents her from seeking employment. The season thus implicitly positions the pregnant woman's proper place as "in the home," regardless of the woman's own desires or the family's best interests.

In addition to the economic barriers (to which her pregnancy contributes), Vivien's pregnancy also functions to keep her housebound in several other respects. First, Vivien's obstetrician declares, "no moving while you're pregnant" and further suggests that Vivien is responsible for maintaining a healthy pregnancy: "We don't want any CRH, corticotropin-releasing hormone, wreaking havoc in there. High levels could lead to a spontaneous abortion" ("Murder House"). Second, because of the supernatural forces at work, Vivien becomes ill whenever she leaves the house, a situation that Vivien's doctor interprets as a form of hysteria, stating, "Maybe it's your body's way of telling you to stay home" ("Open House"). While perhaps the doctor cannot be faulted for the misdiagnosis, on a metaphorical level, the doctor's misunderstanding might represent the failures of well-meaning but out of touch medical professionals. In fact, Charlotte Perkins Gilman's feminist indictment of patriarchal misconstrual of women's needs, "The Yellow Wallpaper," is explicitly referenced in another episode ("Rubber Man").

These various plot devices function as an allegorical depiction of women in a postfeminist world: at once urged to leave the home and perhaps anxious to work and to maintain active social and political lives, a woman's immediate conditions, including economic constraints, the messages and directives of the larger society, and the ostensible precariousness of her physical and emotional well-being, may make meaningful departures from the home impossible. For example, women continue to experience pregnancy discrimination; in particular, that a woman's work is often underestimated when she is visibly pregnant (Correll, Benard, and Palik), reveals entrenched skepticism of mothers' competence and their commitments to their careers. Then, despite increased acceptance of women maintaining careers once they are mothers, the prohibitively high cost of childcare may make working an irrational or even impossible economic choice for many women ("Child Care Is Fundamental").[5] Those who choose and are able to work may be made to feel guilty that they are not participating in "intensive"-enough mothering (Douglas and Michaels 5). All of these factors contribute to the practice of what Linda Seidel terms "neoliberal mothering" and further includes an expectation of maternal "emotional self-sufficiency" (xv). In short, many mothers who might have chosen otherwise find themselves at home, alone, with a child.

Thus, Vivien's story of an increasingly narrow field of choice crystallizes the micro and macro-aggressions faced by many women in their so-called childbearing years. Furthermore, although one's death is an event that no one truly controls, it is notable that for Vivien, even this moment is dominated by men (most notably her husband and a ghost-doctor). The scene of her death yet again suggests that Vivien is unable to assert herself or to advocate for her own well-being. Hemorrhaging after the birth of the twins, Vivien sees her daughter Violet (who is herself already a ghost). Violet assures her mother that she can "let go," to which Vivien responds, "I don't think I have a choice" ("Birth"). Thus, throughout, Vivien's reproductive, maternal, and even end-of-life decisions are all beyond her control and again and again, despite her stated early desire to "get control" of her own body, she is depicted as increasingly disempowered.

And yet, despite all of the horror, Vivien is presented as quite content in the series' conclusion. In the last episode, the Harmon family is a picture of domestic bliss: now ghosts, Violet, Ben, and Vivien (who holds one of the newborn-ghost babies), congregate around a Christmas tree with Moira, the erstwhile maid, who is ultimately de-sexualized and functions as a doting aunt.[6] Formerly sullen teenager Violet smiles widely; Ben announces: "I didn't think it was possible for me, Vivien, but I'm happy" ("Afterbirth"). Vivien and Ben will remain forever young-ish and conventionally attractive. Although watched through a window by the "bad" ghosts who are excluded from the

Figure 2. As ghosts, the Harmons seem to have a lovely Christmas. Shown from left: Taissa Farmiga, Dylan McDermott, Connie Britton, Frances Conroy (*American Horror Story*, FX, season 1, 2011).

domestic dream, the Harmon's conclusion is itself an endorsement of a middle class ideal of the nuclear family.

Dawn Keetley astutely observes in her investigation of the "entropic" movement of the series that "In its multiplication of twins, including the striking ... way in which almost every major character dies to become his or her own clone, *American Horror Story* evokes and transforms a staple trope of the Gothic—the 'double'" (98). However, while Keetley sees this conclusion as suggesting a "regression of the human to a spent, useless state" (92), I suggest that the ending of the series is a postfeminist fantasy. On the one hand, Vivien's life-after-death does not seem so different from her actual life. She is still confined at home, hanging around with the housekeeper. And while some of her marital problems seem to have resolved, she is still literally haunted by the ghost of her husband's former lover, just as she was in life. On the other hand, not unlike the vampires in the *Twilight* movies (discussed in Chapter 6), the Harmons in death present as more attractive, better versions of their living selves.

In fact, from the perspective of patriarchal medicine's goals, Vivien may now represent the ideal. Young has argued that the failures of patriarchal medical models with regard to the female body are a result of the assumption that "the normal, healthy body is unchanging"; Young points out that "Health is associated with stability, equilibrium, a steady state" (57). Rather than an aging house in need of constant upkeep, Vivien has now achieved an "unchanging" state. She is incorporeal but nevertheless visible and active, capable of having sex and enjoying relationships. While she can no longer bear children, she is the parent to an eternal infant. The family unit too, earlier imperiled by infidelity, miscarriage, and economic instability, is no longer subject to earthly vicissitudes. Thus, relegation to the private is presented as the pinnacle of the American dream. Vivien, whose name, of course, means "life," is most at home in death.

"You can't get rid of the Babadook": Maternal Rage and Repression in The Babadook

Like *American Horror Story,* Jennifer Kent's 2014 horror movie *The Babadook*[7] features a mother who has lost control and who is unable to leave her haunted house. In addition, also like *American Horror Story,* the mother-figure's body is identified with the house itself: in *The Babadook,* the home's basement comes to represent a dangerous, haunted site, as well as the literal and metaphorical location for that which the maternal figure needs to repress, conceal, and manage. Unlike *American Horror Story* however, *The Babadook* does not conclude with a cheerful surrender to the domestic and embrace of stasis. Instead, in its exploration of the ways in which even a "good" mother might become unfit, *The Babadook* proposes isolation and homeboundedness as injurious to the mother and, by extension, the child. In *The Babadook*, home really is where the hurt is. Patriarchal authorities are incapable of truly comprehending the depths and profound dangers of maternal rage; it is only through an honest confrontation of her ambivalence about the home and motherhood—including her feelings of frustration and anger—that the mother can hope to overcome the monster.

The film introduces Amelia (Essie Davis), a widow whose husband was killed in a car accident while driving Amelia to the hospital to deliver their son, Samuel (Noah Wiseman). When the film opens, six-year-old Samuel is presented as an anxious oddball and Amelia is somber and harried. Samuel spends time constructing elaborate weapons with which to fight off a supposedly imaginary monster he calls "the Babadook," a character from an eerie and mysterious pop-up book. The book warns that "you can't get rid of the Babadook" and that "the more you deny ... the stronger I get" (*The Babadook*). Amelia puts the book in the trash, but it reappears and, when she reads through it, she sees that it features images of a woman murdering her dog and child before killing herself. The movement towards death is presented as ineluctable. Then, one night, the Babadook enters Amelia through her open mouth when she screams in terror. The remainder of the film traces the battle between the Babadook, Amelia, and Samuel. Possessed by the monster, Amelia becomes an imminent threat to Samuel and to herself. The film concludes with Samuel and Amelia vanquishing the monster and the Babadook is relegated to the home's basement.

Even before her possession, Amelia struggles to be a "good" mom. That is, Amelia is presented as a mother-on-the-edge, unhappy and overwhelmed; Paula Quigely writes that early in the film, "Amelia's sense of physical and emotional entrapment is palpable" (62). Amelia appears to cherish time without Samuel, as suggested by a scene in which she skips out of work to sit alone on a bench and enjoy an ice cream cone. There is a price for this small freedom, however, and she discovers that her sister, who has been watching Samuel, has been struggling with him and has been calling her cell phone. "Where have you been?" her sister demands when Amelia arrives to pick Samuel up, demonstrating that Amelia's life, where she goes and what she does, are always in relation to Samuel (*The Babadook*). As a single parent, Amelia bears sole responsibility and must be physically and emotionally available at all times or risk categorization as a bad mother.

Although Amelia desperately needs distance from Samuel, the film traces how they are thrown ever more together: Samuel is suspended from school and, having no one else to care for him, Amelia must stay home from work. The bulk of the film takes place in the creepy house that the two rarely leave.

In an interview, director Jennifer Kent acknowledges how Amelia and Samuel's lives become circumscribed in the film: "Gradually the film becomes just the house. But the house is alive, it's a reflection, an extension of what's going on for Amelia—and for Sam, but mostly for Amelia" (Sélavy). Briony Kidd suggests that "If the house is a metaphor for Amelia's psyche, then there are many hidden and potentially shameful aspects to who and what this woman is—all of which, it's implied, can be exploited by the Babadook for his own nefarious purposes" (Kidd 10).

The possession is possible because of Amelia and Samuel's isolation; their confinement effected by a monster who fills the vacuum left by the absent patriarch. That is, without a partner and without a supportive family or community, there is no one but Samuel to witness Amelia's increasingly erratic behavior. Because of Samuel's strangeness and her own decomposition, Amelia seems compelled to stay at home; however, the one time the two leave, the Babadook interferes and causes Amelia to have a car accident. Thus housebound, Amelia's authority is unchecked even as she becomes more dangerous to Samuel. In this way, *The Babadook* capitalizes on anxieties about the fatherless home, a notion underlined on the occasions that the Babadook takes the form of Amelia's late husband. It is when the son himself exercises male authority, physically dominating and subduing his mother, that Amelia can begin to reclaim her own power.

In addition to capitalizing on the single mother's vulnerabilities, the Babadook monster functions as an embodiment of the negative feelings such as resentment and rage that many parents disavow but nevertheless may appear "in a word ... or in a look," and which may grow stronger if they are not managed (*The Babadook*). That is, impatience, annoyance, and frustration with her son already exist within Amelia, whose sister observes, "You can't stand being around him yourself." These feelings, perhaps like the Babadook, may only grow "stronger" the more they are denied. Mekado Murphy writes in the *New York Times* that "the book is a metaphor for the demons that lurk in the mother's psyche and that she must confront." Paula Quigley writes, "virtually all of the critics and reviewers of the film have read the Babadook as embodying the 'return of the repressed'—that is, as the uncanny manifestation of Amelia's repressed state" (58).

While these assessments are accurate, none of the criticism takes into account that part of the horror of the film is the way in which Amelia's behavior so closely resembles the behavior of many abusive, substance-addled, or untreated mentally ill parents.[8] Over the course of the film, Amelia becomes increasingly unpredictable, nasty, and violent. The single mother operating in the extra-patriarchal home becomes predator rather than protector. The home, rather than a safe haven, becomes a danger zone. Unwell, sleep-deprived, and later, possessed, Amelia verbally excoriates and threatens her child. When Samuel says he is hungry and informs her that there is no food in the kitchen, Amelia nastily declares that he can "eat shit." When Amelia discovers that Samuel has reached out to a neighbor for help, she takes a knife and cuts the phone wire. Amelia kills the dog (as predicted in the book), calls Samuel a "little pig" and then tells him, "I just want to smash your head against a brick wall until your fucking brains pop out" (*The Babadook*).

That Amelia intermittently seems to come to her senses and apologizes renders the depiction even more chilling as it may resonate with the experiences of many abused children who have witnessed parent's unpredictable mood swings, including rage and regret (Heitler). Of course, Samuel is able to reassure himself that Amelia is not to blame and, when he fights back against the Babadook, he exclaims, "You're not my mother!" (*The Babadook*). While this moment functions within the logic of the film, it too has extrafilmic connotations and perhaps leads a viewer to wonder how often an abused child might fantasize or rationalize that a parent's bad behavior is not an accurate reflection of his or her true feelings.

The film thus explores the slippage between the categories of fit and unfit parent, brought into focus when Amelia and Samuel interact with outsiders. While Amelia and Samuel are presented as cut off from community, those authorities that Amelia does communicate with are either obtuse or threatening themselves: Samuel and Amelia are opaque to school administrators and, when Amelia visits a police station, she is at first dismissed and then threatened. The world that Samuel and Amelia inhabit is beyond the reach and comprehension of the authorities.

In addition, a scene in which social services comes to the home brings into focus how Amelia and Samuel's dysfunctional dynamic appears to outsiders. As Samuel's agitation about the Babadook intensifies, his behavior becomes increasingly eccentric at the same time as Amelia increasingly presents as an abusive parent. One afternoon, in the kitchen, Amelia discovers a roach infestation in the kitchen. She pulls off wallpaper to reveal a vagina-shaped hole out of which the roaches pour. She is cleaning frantically when representatives from the "department of community services" arrive at the home to check on Samuel.

This scene capitalizes on the dramatic irony of a situation in which Amelia appears, to these government representatives, as unhinged and potentially unfit to parent, a state made worse when Samuel declares, "I'm a bit tired from the drugs mom gave me" (a doctor had prescribed pills to help Samuel sleep at night). The home is in disarray and Amelia disheveled. The male social worker tells Amelia, "We've caught you at a bad time.... We're required to come back in a week to talk about your options." His statement suggests that perhaps Samuel will be removed from Amelia's care. The viewer is acutely aware that if the social workers suspect that Samuel should be removed from the home, they are not incorrect. Amelia is not only incapable of protecting Samuel, she is herself a threat to her child. However, perhaps like many "real life" dysfunctional families, it is truly the parent who is in need of rescue. Yet, social services are not remotely equipped to deal with Amelia's problems. The scene thus depicts social services designed to support families as, at their best, irrelevant and, at their worst, insidious. Social workers cannot get rid of the Babadook, but they can further disrupt an already precarious situation.

Healing, in the film, has to come from within the family and arises specifically from the child's redemptive love, which enables the mother to reclaim her right position. In this respect, then, the ending, in which Samuel activates his mother's strength, may also function as a wish-fulfillment, telling a very specific story about how child-love can save the abusive parent, snatching her back from the claws of dysfunction and violence. Samuel, who physically overcomes and restrains Amelia, says "I love you, mom. And I always will." His words evoke the kind of unconditional love usually expressed by a parent; here, however, the child articulates this unwavering, timeless commitment, an assertion he "always will" love Amelia suggests forgiveness or a love regardless of her misdeeds. Notably, Samuel declares this love after stabbing his mother, knocking her unconscious and tying her up.

Through Samuel's love, Amelia can become a fit mother again. Still not subdued, Amelia is able to escape Samuel's binds and she tries to strangle him. However, he gently strokes her face and it appears that this tender gesture enables Amelia to overcome the Babadook. Her subsequent reaction evokes a perverse or reverse-birth: Amelia thrashes and groans before vomiting black liquid onto the floor. Thus Amelia became a mother at first when she pushed Samuel from her body; she becomes a mother again when she expels the Babadook. Redeemed, Amelia's behavior more closely aligns with ideals of maternal love and her murderous violence is redirected to a more appropriate subject. As Aviva Briefel points out, Amelia confronts the monster by "deploying a language of authority and possession, in reference to both herself and her property: 'This is my house!… You are trespassing in my house! If you touch my son again, I'll fucking kill you!'" (Briefel 17). Amelia thus reclaims control over her home and her maternal self.

However, the Babadook is not fully vanquished as, of course, "you can't get rid of the Babadook" (*The Babadook*). That is, the Babadook may be managed, but Amelia and Samuel will never be free of its presence. At the film's conclusion, Amelia and Samuel are at last depicted outside, enjoying their garden and each other, an indication that they are no longer housebound. They interact with their neighbor and discuss plans for a birthday party, suggesting freedom from isolation and a return to the community. However, the Babadook remains in their basement and, playing a "quasi-maternal" (Quigley

Figure 3. At the conclusion of *The Babadook*, Amelia (Essie Davis) and Samuel (Noah Wiseman) are finally free to be outdoors (*The Babadook*, Entertainment One/Umbrella Media, 2014, directed by Jennifer Kent).

75) role in relation to the monster, Amelia creeps down to soothe it and feed it worms. Amelia's negative or murderous emotions must be sustained, but not allowed free rein.

In addition to resonating with abused children, *The Babadook* may also present moments that are disconcertingly familiar to many parents, such as when an overwhelmed parent says something she regrets to her child. In this way, the film explores a fear that exists for many parents: that there is a badness within them that is always only barely kept in check. Along these lines, the idea that Amelia herself is the author of the pop-up book that seems to catalyze the haunting further suggests that the monster already existed within Amelia; it only emerged when the conditions were right. The film thus explores the mundane challenges of parenthood, echoed in Amelia's sister's words "You can't stand being around him yourself!," as well as the more insidious, potentially murderous possibilities, echoed in Amelia's threat to "smash" Samuel's head against a wall, that can fester in conditions of isolation and homeboundedness.

Precious: The Maternal Vampire

Lee Daniels' *Precious* (2009, based on the 1996 novel *Push* by Sapphire), although generically quite different from *The Babadook*, reflects a similar anxiety about disorder in the matriarchal home. In particular, single mother

Mary Jones' (Mo'Nique) behaviors resemble those exhibited by Amelia when she is possessed in *The Babadook:* Mary rarely leaves the home and she is verbally and physically abusive toward her daughter Precious (Gabourey Sidibe), who is also a mother. According to Precious, Mary's routine is "watch tv, eat, watch tv, eat again," leaving only to "play her numbers" (*Precious*). Mary does little to maintain the home (Precious cooks and cleans), yet she economically exploits Precious, collecting welfare payments for the care of Precious and, fraudulently, for Precious' disabled daughter.

While not a "horror" narrative in the same sense as the other texts discussed in this chapter, *Precious* is nevertheless a deeply disturbing film, which Armond White called a "sociological horror show" (qtd. in Lee).[9] Stephen Pimpare takes issue with *Precious,* writing that it "reaffirms in every respect the most insidious stereotypes of the Welfare Queen and the rapacious black male" (76) before concluding that the film is at once "a beautifully realized portrait of survival, and a nasty and pernicious piece of work" (81). Additionally, *Precious* falls within Keith Gandal's definition of a "class exploitation film," movies that "have traditionally contained a 'digestible' element of social outrage" but in which "the social critique component is swamped by a sensationalist rendition of the subject" (6). In particular, Gandal identifies a particular type of class exploitation film that suggests that "*The poor and lowlifes have it worse* because they repulsively prey on and humiliate each other" (emphasis original 7). In *Precious,* part of this predation includes the fact, gradually revealed, that Mary not only sexually abuses Precious herself, but allows Precious's father to rape Precious.

Mary thus embodies the "unfit" parent. She is fat, which itself is often deployed as a marker of bad character or laziness.[10] Further, for Mary, motherhood is a practice of exploitation: her actions reverse the "right" or natural order in which the parent provides, rather than demands care and in which the parent protects rather than preys upon the child. Mary's sexual abuse of Precious is not only a perversion of the mother-child relationship, but reveals a profound narcissism and selfishness. For example, Mary rationalizes her behavior, explaining that after her boyfriend left, she needed someone who would "love" and "take care of" her (*Precious*). She asks, "Who was gonna touch me and make me feel good late at night?" That Mary frames her abuse of Precious as rooted in her own physical and sexual comfort instrumentalizes her daughter, suggesting that her own child is but a means to her selfish end.

In "Pregnant Beauty: Maternal Femininities under Neoliberalism," Imogen Tyler follows Angela McRobbie, observing how responses to pregnant bodies are class-inflected and that the teenage mother in particular is "constituted as a site of failure.... It is the imagined economic redundancy and welfare dependence of this population which is repugnant" (22). Mary's nonproductivity and perversion of the maternal role renders her a "site of failure." Thus, part of what is so repulsive about Mary is her rejection of all that is held dear in late-capitalist society and she and Precious, as mothers, in particular, represent the non-compliant neoliberal subject. Mary seeks to literally capitalize on Precious by encouraging her to drop out of school and begin collecting welfare. The film's overarching question, then, is whether or not Precious will succumb to the environment Mary has created; in this way, Precious comes to represent the specter of multigenerational poverty and dysfunction.[11]

Precious and Mary exist as neoliberal boogeymen, an idea that Precious articulates when she describers her fear of being perceived as a "vampire" or a monster whose life-in-death is sustained through others' health and work. That Precious will follow in Mary's footsteps seems assured, in particular because not only is Mary's dominion over the apartment absolute, but even on the rare occasions that outsiders enter the apartment, they are depicted as weak and ineffective. In one scene, a social worker visits to check on Mary, Precious, and Precious' daughter.[12] Like the social workers' visit in *The Babadook*, this scene capitalizes on the audience's perception of the discrepancy between what outsiders or authorities perceive and where the true danger resides. Mary verbally abuses her family members (including Mary's own mother) in the moments immediately before and after the social worker's entrance, but effectively performs the role of the well-meaning but luckless caregiver when the social worker is present. The social worker apparently does not suspect abuse or neglect and, as a result, she fails to seriously investigate, instead focusing on whether or not Mary has purchased a "new microwave" (*Precious*). The social worker's interactions with Mary suggest that the welfare system itself functions as an elaborate game in which recipients of support try to trick authorities and authorities try to catch them. The dramatic irony is that Mary is in fact deceiving the social worker, just not in the way the social worker expects or is attuned to. The danger is not, of course, that Mary spends her money on luxury items or has another source of income. The danger, the viewer is acutely aware, is that Mary torments, tortures, and is slowly killing her daughter.

Part of *Precious*' larger project is to make visible those people and realities that many would choose to ignore or deny and, in one sense the notion that representatives of the state can and should enter private homes in order to determine which individuals will be allowed to parent and/or which individuals can and should receive public support is itself complex and problematic. However, in *Precious*, it is the insularity of Mary's world that must be disrupted in order for Precious to survive. Thus, early in the film, another institutional representative's visit to the home instantiates the plot's forward movement. Moments after Mary throws a heavy skillet at Precious' head, knocking her unconscious and dramatizing Precious' truly dire situation, the insistent buzzing of the intercom interrupts Mary's television watching. Mary's apartment is yellow-toned and the soft sound of the television plays in the background. The sound of the buzzer is an uncomfortable contrast and, after Precious answers the intercom, the scene plays out in alternating shots between Mary and Precious in the apartment (Mary sitting and smoking) and the principal, Ms. Lichenstein, in the dark street (also smoking). That both Mary and Ms. Lichentstein smoke cigarettes links the two in order to emphasize their disconnection, itself apparent in the contrast between the color tones in their separate shots as well as in the manner in which Precious serves as intermediary, communicating to her mother what Ms. Lichenstein says over the intercom.

In an earlier scene, Ms. Lichtenstein had expelled Precious for being pregnant. However, having discovered that Precious is doing well in her math class, Ms. Lichentstein has come to the apartment to invite Precious to enroll in an alternative school. When Mary asks who is buzzing, Precious answers, "White bitch from school." Ms. Lichenstein explains that she has come to speak to Precious and Mary about Precious' education, to which Precious responds, "Ms. Lichenstein, get out of here before I kick your ass." Mary warns Precious to "get that bitch away from here" and later accuses her: "Why did you bring that white bitch up in here? ... You gonna send a white bitch to my fucking buzzer?"

In this scene, Precious demonstrates an ability to navigate the world of Mary's apartment as well as the outside world; her threat of violence against Ms. Lichenstein is half-hearted and almost humorous, but does underscore that Ms. Lichtenstein is no longer in the school, the site of her authority. Rather, Ms. Lichtenstein's arrival can potentially imperil Precious and, in a later scene, Mary assaults Precious as a result of the visit. However, Mary's anxiety about the proximity of a school representative also indicates Mary's awareness of the tenuousness of her control. In fact, Mary's survival depends specifically on keeping the "white bitch" at bay; like the social worker who arrives later and like the government agents in *The Babadook*, Ms. Lichtenstein's arrival carries inherent danger of exposure.

Exposure is a threat because it is only in isolation that Mary's dysfunction can flourish. The incest perpetrated by both Mary and by Carl, Precious' father, is itself a symptom and a function of insularity. Mary appears outside of the apartment only twice in the film; both occur after Precious has left home and Mary is desperate to have her back (perhaps primarily to continue receiving welfare payments). However, in a scene in the welfare office, speaking to another social worker (Ms. Wiess, played by Mariah Carey), Mary at times performs again as the well-meaning, hapless mother. Even after this persona falls away, however, Mary remains clearly vulnerable in these exchanges, again revealing that, although she dominates the women in her family, as a single, black mother, living on welfare, she is incredibly powerless in the larger society.

Demonstrating an apparent ignorance of how intensely depraved her own behavior has been, Mary's conversation with Ms. Wiess lays bare Mary's profound psychological dysfunction. That is, in describing how she allowed Carl to abuse Precious, Mary doesn't appear to fully register how and why her actions might be perceived as immoral or contemptible. Instead, she accuses Precious of framing her to appear as "some kind of fucking monster" and retreats to blaming Precious, saying "I hated her.... She made him leave.... It's this bitch's fault." Although Mary cries and apologizes to Precious by the end of the scene, it is nevertheless clear that that she is deeply disconnected from functional, healthy, or "normal" conceptions of family, parenting, or community.

Mary is an uncomplicated villain in many respects. In *Mediated Maternity: Contemporary American Portrayals of Bad Mothers in Literature and Popular Culture,* Linda Seidel observes that the stereotype Mary embodies is "an ideologically-freighted cultural creation with a long history" (56), but that the character of Mary herself is unexplored: the "film gives us little sense of how Mary became Mary" (51).[13] However, the film does suggest that Mary's dysfunction is supported by a larger social system. Ms. Rain, Precious' teacher and the film's model of healthy, adjusted adult womanhood, discourages Precious from going on public assistance, asking her, "What has welfare done for your mother?" Ms. Rain, while not going so far as to claim that Mary's lack of employment or ambition is a result of public assistance, does gesture to the system's failure to effectively intervene in or improve Mary's life; if anything, it has encouraged her home-boundedness. For Precious to escape this fate—dependence and home-boundedness—she must develop literacy, but also have career aspirations. In fact, when Precious discovers Ms. Weiss's plan is for her to work as a home health-care aide, Precious rejects a life of "wiping white people's asses," work which would of course also keep Precious bound to the domestic: just as she had to take "care of mama" in Mary's house, Precious would again be taking care of another in a home that is not truly her own.

The film concludes with Precious carrying her two children as she strides down a city street, victorious in claiming her identity as a mother. As critics have pointed out (and as Sapphire's sequel to the novel *Push, The Kid,* indicates), Precious' journey will continue to be fraught with difficulties. However, this film, like *The Babadook,* concludes with the protagonist outside, rather than bound by the suffocating, dysfunctional home. While her choices are limited, Precious' narrative ends with increased autonomy and with an apparent awareness that she can, in fact, make choices at all.

Conclusion: "Bad" Moms

Jules in *What to Expect* exists on one end of the representational spectrum, while a character such as Mary in *Precious* exists on the other end. It is no accident, of course, that Jules is white and privileged, while Mary is black and poor. Both in film and in the "real world," a mother's fitness as a parent is often mediated by her class and race.

Another recent film, *Bad Moms* (2016), and its sequel, *A Bad Moms Christmas* (2017), bring into focus the notion that being a "bad" mom is acceptable, as long as the mother in question is white and, if not affluent, middle-class or middle-class adjacent. Suggesting that the institution of motherhood has become oppressive and even injurious to both children and women, Amy Mitchell (Mila Kunis), protagonist of *Bad Moms,* declares, "Being a mom today is impossible." And while she repeatedly asserts "I love being a mom," she also tells her friends, "We're killing ourselves trying to be perfect and it's making us insane" (*Bad Moms*). After Amy has a particularly terrible day, she and her friends resolve to be "bad moms," an identity which it is revealed includes activities such as drinking wine, smoking pot (but only when the kids are asleep), rejecting PTA responsibilities, and telling off people that they don't like. Despite the embrace of the label "bad mom," however, these behaviors serve to make them better parents: happier and more relaxed, these mothers allow their children greater independence and develop higher expectations for their partners. For the "bad moms," what may initially appear as selfishness is recast as self-care and, thus, a marker of maternal devotion.

However, when lower class, non-white women engage in problematic or taboo behaviors, they are stigmatized and scorned. This trend is of course reflected in public policy and law enforcement. According to Cris Beam, author of *To the End of June: The Intimate Life of American Foster Care*, "Doctors are more likely to report injuries in African American families as 'abuse' and in white families as 'accidents'" (62); thus, while African American children are 19 percent of the child population, they comprise 47 percent of those in foster-care (61). While this is not meant to suggest that Mary in *Precious* is not an abusive, dysfunctional parent, it is meant to highlight that, at the time of this writing, there are not films that depicts black mothers smoking pot as an activity that supports their parenting.[14]

As Vandenberg-Daves has pointed out, "As an institution, motherhood includes not only the laws that define and constrain a society's definition of legitimate forms of maternity and that control access to reproductive rights and to resources generally, but also the ideologies that define 'good' and 'bad' mothers in relation to cultural values" (Vandenberg-Daves 4). These cultural values are visible in particular in inequitable treatment in film: while again, the narratives discussed in this chapter are not all horror films, the repeated tropes of the home-bound mother who is increasingly dangerous, as well as the role of external authorities in monitoring and/or mediating the mother's control, suggests a trans-generic concern with the mother's authority as well as how, in mass media, the mother's fitness is related to the physical home and often to inherited stereotypes concerning how motherhood can and should revive traditional gender roles for women. That is, despite superficial gestures toward women's liberation, the process of maternity in the movies, it would seem, continues to return women to the home.

2
At Home in Patriarchy: Girly Moms and Worldly Girls in *Gilmore Girls, Parenthood* and *Teen Mom*

Discussing depictions of homeboundedness as a state that is at once inevitable and harmful for women, the previous chapter argues that narratives often betray anxiety over the unchecked power of the single mother. This chapter continues the investigation of fatherless (or father-free) families, turning to depictions of youthful single mothers in television series in order to suggest a return to the patriarch as a device that defuses the single mother's disruptive potential. The single mothers discussed in this chapter are potentially disruptive precisely because they are at once youthful and worldly, sexy, and independent. Thus, these narratives capitalize on the recent de-stigmatization of single-motherhood at the same time as they consistently depict young mothers as in need of patriarchal support and guidance.

The chapter begins by tracing overlaps between the characters Lorelai Gilmore on the series *Gilmore Girls* (2000–2007)[1] and Sarah Braverman on *Parenthood* (2010–2015), both played by Lauren Graham. Beyond the casting of Graham in both roles—itself significant in that Graham successfully conveys the qualities I will describe below—the characters' similarities reveal a fascination with what I term the "girly mom." The girly mom is a single mother who is goofy and often inept but also conventionally attractive (if not downright glamorous) and her popularity foregrounds a continued idealization of the girl (as opposed to the woman), consistent with the postfeminist valorization of the pursuit of youthfulness.

Following Diane Negra's contention that "postfeminism seems to be fundamentally uncomfortable with female adulthood itself, casting all women as girls to some extent" (14), I offer Lorelai and Sarah as distillations of the ideal postfeminist mother. First, as women who become mothers at relatively young ages (a plot move that contributes to the programs' verisimilitude, in contrast to the many other T.V. shows that cast youthful actors in the roles of mother[2]), Lorelai and Sarah's youthfulness becomes a defining characteristic for each. As a result, with the exception of those concerned with parenting, their plotlines are the kind usually associated with teenage or young adult characters, including stories about the pursuit of education, the development of career aspirations, and relationships with parents. Further, their statuses as single mothers allow multiple opportunities for romance plots.[3] Within these story arcs, Lorelai and Sarah emerge as clever but immature, sexy but emotionally arrested, highly motivated but nevertheless not living up to their potential and often, financially dependent on others.

The increasing prevalence of the "girly mom," I argue, takes place alongside an elevation of the sophisticated teenage girl. What I term the "worldly girl" figure is a daughter whose mature dependability is sharply contrasted with her mother's immature hijinks (which are themselves depicted as quirky, adorable, and desirable).[4] The worldly girl has migrated to MTV and is traceable in the depictions of teen mothers on various reality shows including *16 and Pregnant* (2009–present), *Teen Mom* (2009–2012), *Teen Mom 2* (2011–present) and *Teen Mom 3* (2013).[5] Considered alongside the girly mom, the depiction of the worldly girl reveals a troubling collapse between the identities of woman and girl, daughter and mother, adult and child. In this way, then, we see the emerging identity of the mother who is endlessly reinscribed as a daughter, in need of the patriarch's support, guidance, and approval, a woman who is at most at home in her father's house.

"You do not look old enough to have a daughter": The Girly Mom as a M.I.L.F.

While bad mothers are omnipresent in much literary and cultural representation,[6] until recently, the mother character on television had remained relatively unchanged and idealized: the anchor of the family, she retained her competence and maturity long after many television fathers were scrubbed of their gravitas to become buffoonish punch lines à la Homer Simpson.[7] In her discussion of the Showtime series *Weeds* (which also has a single mother as its protagonist) Panizza Allmark provides an overview of the shift away from the idealized mother of the "Golden Age" (1950s-1960s) of television and toward representations of mothers who are more complicated and flawed. Notably, this shift occurs during a time in which women begin to demand reproductive justice, access to educational and workplace opportunities and a greater presence and voice in the public sphere.

The ways in which mother-characters have changed as well as how they have stayed the same reveals much about the values of postfeminist media culture. While mother-characters (like most if not all characters on television) are generally conventionally physically appealing, for example, in recent years they have also increasingly become "hot,"[8] a form of physical attractiveness distinct from categories such as "beautiful" or even "glamorous" in its evocation of sexiness. In this way, Lorelai and Sarah's characters substantiate Rosalind Gills' contention that "instead of caring or nurturing or motherhood being regarded as central to femininity (all, of course, highly problematic and exclusionary), in today's media it is possession of a 'sexy body' that is presented as a woman's key (if not sole) source of identity" ("Culture and Subjectivity").[9] Further, as Jo Littler observes, the imperative to sexiness is a notable break with earlier representations of the mother's sexuality as at best, nonexistent and, at worst, in Adrienne Rich's words, "grotesque" (Rich 183); further, Littler argues, the "hot" or "yummy" mother figure is "not just allowed but *expected* to perform a specific kind of sexualization" (Littler 230).

On *Gilmore Girls* and *Parenthood*, Lorelai and Sarah exemplify the cultural figure of the M.I.L.F. (Mom I'd Like to Fuck)—a crude term never employed in either series, but an acronym which nevertheless evidences a cultural development in which mothers are now subject to a masculine appraising eye. Further, the identification of the woman as a "mom" not only reduces her to this one aspect of her identity, but suggests the position of the acronym's "I" as that of a young adult or teenage boy. That is, it is likely the woman's children's peers, rather than her own peers, that are observing her.

Both Lorelia and Sarah are presented as attractive to younger men and Lorelai's youthfulness in particular is a central conceit of *Gilmore Girls*; the opening scene of the pilot plays on Graham's looks for laughs. While she is sitting in Luke's diner, a young man hits on Lorelai and she rebuffs him, but when Rory enters, he uses his line on her. When Lorelai informs him that they are mother and daughter, the young man responds, "Wow. You do not look old enough to have a daughter. No, I mean it. And you do not look like a daughter" ("Pilot"). The series thus immediately introduces what will become a consistent punchline: the blurring of generational categories. Additionally, the interaction reveals that Lorelai's early maternity upsets expectations. The young man's attitude, reflecting widely held beliefs, is that mothers should be old, daughters, young, and both sexually unavailable/unappealing. However, perhaps also like the larger audience, the young man quickly overcomes his initial assumptions, following up with, "I have a friend," suggesting that they all might double date. The proposal is presented as absurd, but nevertheless immediately positions Lorelai and Rory as potential sexual peers and/or competitors, a tension which is discussed further below.

Thus, as demonstrated in the first moments of the pilot, much of the humor of *Gilmore Girls* is predicated on the ostensible incongruity of maternity and attractiveness. Lorelai's youth and sexiness is again highlighted in another episode in Season 1, when, because she has neglected to pick up her laundry from the dry cleaners, Lorelai is forced to wear cowboy boots and cutoff jeans to accompany Rory to her first day at a new school. By her own admission, Lorelai looks "like that chick from the *Dukes of Hazzard*," a well-known sex symbol ("The Lorelai's First Day at Chilton"). Lorelai is stopped and again hit on, this time by another parent. Rory wryly remarks, "You're feeling pretty good about yourself right now, aren't you?" ("The Loreleai's First Day at Chilton").

Both of these scenes thus rely on the discrepancy between how a mother is supposed to look and act and how Lorelai looks and acts, as well as the

Figure 4. Rory and Lorelai's characters blur generational boundaries. Rory Gilmore (Alexis Bledel, left) and Lorelai Gilmore (Lauren Graham) (*Gilmore Girls,* WB, season 3, November 5, 2003).

ways in which teenage girls are supposed to look and act and the ways in which Rory, the "sensible one," looks and acts ("Pilot"). Crucially, the apparent inappropriateness of Lorelai's dress can be humorous because the audience is already aware that Lorelai is a "good" and caring mother, or in other words, a mother who makes sacrifices for her daughter. That is, like the "Bad Moms" in the eponymous film (discussed in the previous chapter), Lorelai's eccentricities are tolerable (and even charming) because Lorelai is white, able-bodied, thin, not obviously poor, and conventionally attractive.[10] If Lorelai was a person of color, "low class," fat, or physically impaired, her revealing outfit might be read as evidence of maternal unfitness.

Similarly, Lorelai's love of junk food and "bad" movies and her self-righteous irresponsibility regarding all things domestic are characteristics framed as charming rather than dysfunctional or neglectful. The show's creator, Amy Sherman-Palladino, makes clear her intention to collapse the distinctions between Rory and Lorelai, explaining in an interview that she had to battle with studio executives over her depiction of Lorelai:

> I got a lot of notes early on about motherness. "A mother wouldn't do this." And I said: "This mother would. Because the relationship I'm doing here is not mother and daughter, it's best friends." They're used to mothers saying, "That's right and that's wrong," and Lorelai doesn't do that, because she's still trying to figure out what's right and what's wrong herself. That was one thing that was constant [qtd. in Heffernan, 2005].

As an individual still "trying to figure out what's right and what's wrong," Lorelai thus emerges as someone still in the process of growing up. In contrast, Rory is often depicted as affectionately scolding and correcting her mother, as when she tells Lorelai, "you're impossible" ("Teach Me Tonight") or when she more directly infantilizes her mother, announcing, "my mother is two." Rory's character, in many respects, is a precursor to the "worldly girl" but remains, at least while she is still in high school, relatively earnest and unsophisticated.

Nevertheless, as indicated in the opening scene of the pilot, the series relies on the sexual desirability of both mother and daughter for laughs as well as tension. Thus, a repetition of a crucial plotline in both this series and *Parenthood* betrays a preoccupation with the daughter and mother characters sharing a love interest. On *Gilmore Girls,* Lorelai dates Max Medina, Rory's sophomore year English teacher. Mr. Medina is presented as attractive to his students: one of Rory's classmates announces that she "could listen to him talk about passion all day" and asks, "Do you think he's dating anyone?" ("Paris Is Burning"). Several episodes explore the difficulties faced by Lorelai and Max and the awkwardness of the situation for Rory.

Similarly, on *Parenthood,* Sarah dates her daughter Amber's sophomore-year English teach, Mark Cyr. Notably, Mark is also ten years younger than

Sarah, putting him pretty solidly in the middle of the age gap between mother and daughter. In this way, he is a potential romantic partner for either. Sarah's brother Adam advises against the relationship:

> ADAM: Amber has a major crush on the guy.
>
> SARAH: She doesn't have a crush on him.
>
> ADAM: Just like you didn't have a crush on Mr. Levitsky your Junior year. How would you feel if Mom slept with Mr. Levitsky?
>
> SARAH: Ew. That's gross.
>
> ADAM: Exactly.
>
> SARAH: And it's different. Mom was married. And … Mom.
>
> ADAM: I just don't want to see you fall into another…
>
> SARAH: Another what?
>
> ADAM: Nothing.
>
> SARAH: Another bad relationship? Make another mistake? What? Say it, Adam.
>
> ADAM: Sarah, I see Amber looking happier. I see her engaged. And I wouldn't want to see her shut right back down. That's all ["What's Goin' on Down There?"]

In this exchange, Sarah is forced to confront a number of uncomfortable realities, including that her daughter is a sexual being for whom Mr. Cyr is a potential romantic interest. In reminding Sarah of her own youthful crush on a teacher, Adam not only allows Sarah to see what she has in common with Amber, but also the ways in which Sarah has failed to differentiate herself as appropriately maternal; that is, Sarah cannot imagine her own mother as a sexual competitor.

Further, the end of the above exchange reminds Sarah of her unfortunate choices, as well as her duty as a mother to make sacrifices for her children. Adam's comments indicate that only a selfish mother would jeopardize her daughter's academic success by putting her own romantic interests first. Adam thus suggests that by engaging in—and winning—a sexual competition with her daughter, Sarah might be precipitating Amber's slide back into reclusiveness and delinquency. Sarah's choice to end the relationship with Mark Cyr is presented as the right one: when she initially tells Amber that she might date Mr. Cyr, Amber pretends to take the news in stride, but Sarah overhears her crying in her room, verifying Adam's suspicion.

Parenthood, more so than *Gilmore Girls*, capitalizes on the tension inherent in the recognition of the mother's sexuality. In *Parenthood*'s pilot, Sarah's son Drew inadvertently walks in on her and a man in his underpants searching for wine in the kitchen in the middle of the night; when Drew leaves the room, Sarah announces that she is "so dead." Sarah's remark, of course, is an echo of teenage hyperbole, highlighting the reversal of parent-child roles. Thus Sarah inhabits the role of the teenage child at the same time that her daughter Amber, who is independent, wry, and world-weary, lays increasing claim to the role of the adult woman. In the series pilot, Amber attempts to move in with her boyfriend; by Season 3, when Amber is 19, she is working and living on her own (unlike her own mother, who still lives with her parents). Like Lorelai, then, Sarah's immaturity is often brought into focus when contrasted with her daughter's maturity and worldliness.[11]

"With no help from anyone": Postfeminists and Patriarchs

In addition to being sexy, the ideal postfeminist mother is also proudly independent and ambitious. In "Postfeminist Inflections in Television Studies," Karen Orr Vered and Sal Humphreys write that postfeminism "describes the political moment in which the material and ideological gains of second-wave feminism have been accepted and incorporated into our mainstream values and common ambitions at the same time as neoliberal economics and its associated social practices—including a reduction in social welfare support—have become entrenched." The postfeminist single mother, then, represents a unique indicator of postfeminist values. Long ignored in popular culture, according to Angharad Valdivia, "on the rare occasion when a single mother is presented in contemporary popular culture, she tends to conform to negative discourses that suggest that she is failing her children and falling short of parenting ideals" (qtd. in Feasey, "From Soap Opera" 38). This vilification of single mothers conforms to a long-standing tradition of blaming "divorce and unwed motherhood" for "poverty and other social ills ... even though poverty and material hardship were more widespread in the marriage-centric 1950s than they are today" (Coontz, *The Way We Never Were* xvii).

If she is a good parent, the young/single mother is a potential threat to the patriarchal order precisely because her existence suggests the irrelevance of the old order and the possibility of health and happiness beyond the traditional nuclear family unit. As a result, the teen and single mother are often cast as social problems (Vinson xiv) and identified as a cause of social disorder.[12] In my analysis of Lorelai and Sarah, however, I suggest that these characterizations try to have it both ways. That is, they depict single mothers who are sexy, smart and (sometimes) successful, but assuage fears about the dissolution of the traditional family by consistently depicting the patriarchal home as the scaffolding which supports these single mothers. That is, the existential challenge presented by the self-sufficient single woman is absorbed when she is re-rendered as daughter.

Many of the postfeminist girly mom's plotlines emphasize her need to be independent, which in true neoliberal/postfeminist style, means that she does not feel entitled to assistance from male partners or governmental institutions. Thus, both *Gilmore Girls* and *Parenthood* emphasize the single mother's self-sufficiency at the same time that they derive drama from her occasional inability to provide what her children need. Neither Sarah nor Lorelai is depicted as seeking child support from her child(ren)'s fathers and there are no references to any governmental programs or assistance, such as welfare or access to low-income housing. While in part reflecting the realities of many single mothers' experiences, these omissions nevertheless reify the notion that children are ultimately and appropriately a mother's responsibility, not a father's or a larger community's.[13]

The invisibility of social services is particularly significant in *Gilmore Girls*, as Lorelai's experiences as a single teenage parent who avoids homelessness through an individual's private charity is a central overarching plot point.[14] In "Hip Mamas: *Gilmore Girls* and Ariel Gore," Robin Silbergleid quotes Lorelai, who declares of her job at an inn: "I worked my way up. I run the place now. I built a life of my own with no help from anyone" (98) in order to suggest that "Lorelai's story is unlikely, even fantastical and utopic" (98), ultimately concluding that the show's "characterization of Lorelai is not in itself a marker of significant social change and respect for single mothers and teen pregnancy. Ironically, its very representation has the potential to obfuscate the real conditions of single/teen mothers in the political sphere" (107).

Yet despite her assertion that she managed "with no help from anyone," *Gilmore Girls* begins with the premise that Lorelai is unable to fully provide what her precocious daughter most needs: she cannot afford to send Rory to Chilton, an expensive private school. Lorelai's parents, Richard (Edward Hermann) and Emily (Kelly Bishop), agree to pay Rory's tuition in exchange for increased participation in their daughter and granddaughter's lives. This situation humbles Lorelai, who initially tells a friend that she'd rather reenact "several chapters from a Stephen King novel" than ask her parents for assistance ("Pilot"). That Lorelai must ask for money despite her desire for self-sufficiency demonstrates that she is not as independent as she might seem but also that she is nevertheless a "good" mother who sacrifices her pride in order to further her daughter's best interests.

Notably, on *Parenthood* Graham again portrays a single mother who turns to her parents for financial assistance in order to best provide for her children. A bartender who also briefly works as an "intern" at a shoe company (a position that Sarah is well aware is generally occupied by college students or other young people seeking work experience), Sarah's situation is more infantilizing than Lorelai's. In one episode, her parents offer to buy her a car. Sarah's objection foregrounds her dependency, as well as attempts to establish autonomy: "Mom, isn't it bad enough? I'm living at home, you're feeding me, you're feeding my kids. You may not buy me a car" ("The Deep End"). Her dictum, "you may not buy me a car," is perhaps a last-ditch effort to preserve some sense of control, but not long after, Sarah relents and accepts a car, in part, in order to provide for her children (the situation particularly annoys and embarrasses her son).

Crucially, while both Lorelai and Sarah's own mothers are presented as competent individuals, neither is depicted as gainfully employed and it is Richard Gilmore and Zeke Braverman, Lorelai and Sarah's fathers, who ultimately financially prop up their daughters.[15] The message seems to be that regardless of their apparent competence in other areas of their lives, these single mothers are not capable of fully providing for their children without the assistance of a father-figure.[16] As a result, Lorelai and Sarah can safely behave like their children's peers, because their own parents exist as the normative heterosexual model, as the true authority figures on these programs.[17] In this way, the single/young mother on these programs is at once deployed as a potentially disruptive force only to be contained and resituated in the traditional patriarchal family, as otherwise intelligent, capable adult women become, at least in part, vulnerable, dependent, and grateful.[18]

In "Wrecked: Programming Celesbian Reality," Dana Heller argues that postfeminist television relies on "the pathologization of women—single women especially—through a disciplinary gaze that revels in their moral failings, vulnerabilities, and excesses" (133). While both *Gilmore Girls* and *Parenthood* feature other female characters who are mature and who have complex storylines, the characters of Lorelai and Sarah reveal that mother's roles and stories come more and more to resemble the roles and stories typically associated with teenagers. As the girly mom and the worldly girl continue to migrate closer to each other, the characteristics of the adult woman and the teenage girl begin to overlap, finally lining up completely in the character of the "teen mom": the young woman who is simultaneously and literally both child and mother.

"Once I mature more, I'll grow up": The Rehabilitation of the Teen Mom on MTV

Unlike Rory and Amber, who are depicted as smart young women, intellectually and possibly emotionally precocious, the "worldly girl" who appears on several MTV reality shows[19] is often fascinating in the manner of the child who dresses up in adult clothing: at once adorable, attractive, and ridiculous, she reveals adulthood as, in part, communicated symbolically through adornments, postures, and attitudes. These programs typically use adult situations in order to highlight the contrast between the physical and/or sexual maturity of *les enfants terribles* and their emotional and/or intellectual immaturity. That is, the worldly girl employs vocabularies that she doesn't fully understand, reminding us not only of her innocence, but also of her looming and irresistible entry into the world of knowledge and maturity. At times, the worldly girl is not adorable, but infuriating in her assumption of adult prerogatives and responsibilities. Her struggles, failures, and humiliations are the price she must pay before ultimately conforming to conventional adult behaviors, including appropriate compliance to a patriarch, an adult male who will guide and instruct her.

One injurious incarnation of the worldly girl appears on MTV's *My Super Sweet 16* (2005–2008, 2017–present), a program that documents the preparation for and celebration of a teenager's birthday party. The typical protagonist is usually female and is a self-identified "diva" who imperiously demands goods and services that are expensive and often reserved for (wealthy) adults: cars, extravagant entertainment and food, expensive gowns and jewelry. In addition, she has accommodating—if not downright fawning and oppressed—parents. In one infamous example, birthday girl Audrey Reyes screams at her mother, "you ruined my life…. I fucking hate you" because her mother has made the mistake of giving her a new Lexus *before* rather than *after* Audrey's party ("Audrey").

My Super Sweet 16 thus ironizes the purported sweetness of sixteen-year-old girls, instead depicting the teenage girl as a monstrous child-in-adult's-clothing, demanding ever more excessive luxuries from her cowed parents.[20] Given the success of this program, it is unsurprising that MTV subsequently unveiled another show focused on girls at this transitional age undergoing a rite of passage: *16 and Pregnant*. Like *My Super Sweet 16*, *16 and Pregnant* often features teenage girls behaving badly; unlike *My Super Sweet 16*, the protagonists of *16 and Pregnant* and its spinoff, *Teen Mom*, are often working-class or poor young women who, although they might make immature choices initially, generally develop into increasingly responsible, heteronormative, appropriately maternal figures.[21] This development is guided and overseen by MTV's resident patriarch Drew Pinsky, who, through his series' finale specials titled "Life After Labor" and "Check Up with Dr. Drew," serves to frame the girls' experiences as cautionary tales, rendering otherwise difficult, complex lives as intelligible coming-of-age narratives.[22]

Like its predecessor *My Super Sweet 16*, *16 and Pregnant* is formulaic and relies heavily on the discrepancy between the protagonist's age and her situation/behavior. Thus, each episode of *16 and Pregnant* opens with a teenage girl who, in a rather strangely affectless voice-over, describes her engagement in "typical" teenage activities, such as cheerleading or going to the beach, before announcing that she will have to abandon those pursuits "because … I'm pregnant."[23] Teen mom Chelsea DeBoer (née Houska), for example, announces that her "life is all about having fun" before concluding her opening segment with the claim that her difficult boyfriend is "in my life for good now because ... I'm pregnant" ("Chelsea"). Over and over again, the recitation of this phrase is accompanied by a final shot revealing the young woman's swollen abdomen. Thus, the teen mom's lifestyle and her third-trimester pregnant body are presented as incongruous: her emotional and intellectual maturity has not kept pace with her physical and sexual development.

After the introduction, *16 and Pregnant* follows each girl through the final weeks of pregnancy and the first weeks of maternity, weeks that usually coincide with the dissolution of her romantic relationship. Most episodes conclude with the protagonist remarking that she loves her child, but wishing vaguely that she had "waited." In this way, each episode tracks the protagonist's evolution from an irresponsible teen into a self-sacrificing and self-critical, and thus more appropriate, parent. The thus aptly titled *Teen Mom*[24] series then capitalizes on the synthesis of the two figures, following four young women, each initially featured on *16 and Pregnant*, through her first several years of motherhood.

Considered alongside the depictions of Lorelai and Sarah, the presentation of young mothers on *16 and Pregnant* and *Teen Mom* suggests that the contradictory imperatives to sexiness and naiveté, youthfulness and sophistication, and self-sufficiency and dependency have migrated in both directions and now apply to both older and younger females. That is, the positive figures on these MTV shows are at once sexually knowing but not promiscuous, as well as economically and emotionally dependent on male figures despite their strenuous insistence on their independence and ambition. In addition, they are often simultaneously immature in their speech and interests and parodically glamorous in appearance.

Chelsea DeBoer and Leah Messer are presented as "good" moms who ably balance these contradictions and emerge as worldly girls who, not unlike Lorelai and Sarah, are ideal postfeminist mothers. Chelsea and Leah show deference to males, sacrifice for their children, insist on their independence, and yet exhibit profound immaturity, often, it would seem, strategically. For example, while several of the "moms" retreat to childlike behavior, Chelsea and Leah in particular fall into immature posturing when seeking support from parents and boyfriends (perhaps as authentic responses to difficult situations, but perhaps also because they not inaccurately imagine female deference and dependence is often appealing to others, including viewers). Chelsea, a self-described "daddy's girl," often uses baby-talk in conversation with her daughter as well as her father and her boyfriends.[25] Jennifer A. Fallas forwards a similar observation in "Othering the Mothering: Postfeminist Constructs in *Teen Mom*": "*Good* mothers ... are made accessible and agreeable through qualities such as submissiveness and acquiescence and through their generally quiet affects toward most people (but especially male partners) ... [their] subjectivities are also based on the girls' altruistic natures and their sole focus on the children. These figures usually stipulate that all their efforts (employment, schooling, maintaining relationships) are for their children's benefit" (ital. orig. 53–54).

Additionally, both Chelsea and Leah embrace an aesthetic of female beauty dependent on exaggerated symbols of femininity: long and often brightly colored hair extensions, elaborate nails, and dramatic and obvious facial makeup. At times, these trappings of adulthood seem at odds with other aspects of the moms' presentations; in Season 4, driving to their wedding, Leah's fiancé remarks on her orthodontia: "in my wedding picture it's gonna look like I married a teenager with them braces on" ("For Better or for Worse"). Similarly, several cast members have had breast enlargement surgeries, a physical alteration that again emphasizes a particularly female sexual characteristic and which is especially prominent on many of the young women because they are also extremely slender. MTV has reportedly charged the casts to forgo plastic surgeries, suggesting the network's discomfort not only with explicit displays of wealth, but also, perhaps, with these young women embracing their status as sexualized celebrities (Fuller).

Thus, while "good moms" such as Chelsea experience setbacks, they nevertheless adequately perform a hyperfemininity which is valued in contemporary patriarchy: they are playful, dependent, accommodating or forgiving of the men in their lives, and often tearful. In contrast, although many of the "bad moms" also embrace a highly performative and constructed version of female beauty, these mothers appear more aggressive, promiscuous, and selfish. Jenelle Evans and Amber Portwood, for example, are unapologetically un-childlike—perhaps to their peril—and each young woman's story arc exemplifies and departs from the typical protagonist's narrative trajectory. Jenelle in particular, is depicted as both immature and impossibly arrogant (a winning formula that clearly works for MTV, as evidenced by the success of *My Super Sweet Sixteen*).

Jenelle's *16 and Pregnant* episode is rich with dramatic irony as Jenelle reveals herself to be laughably unprepared for parenthood. She tells a friend she imagines motherhood will be "like dressing up a doll. You ever do that when you were little?" ("Jenelle") and later, when confronted with her irresponsible behavior, earnestly asserts, "Once I mature more, I'll grow up." At another point she remarks that, "I thought being a mother would be, you know, fairly easy." These kinds of statements are MTV gold, as even a casual viewer of the program knows Jenelle is in for a rude awakening.

Unlike many of the young mothers who discover the unrelenting difficulties of caring for an infant, however, Jenelle persists in hard-partying ways after her son Jace is born. She allows her mother Barbara to "take the lead" in Jace's care, insisting she has a right to focus on her "social life" (which she unironically declares she will do once she returns to school) and she reiterates to friends and in voice-overs that it is important that she "make time" for herself, coopting the language of women's magazines and television which encourages busy mothers and working women to spend money on products and experiences to relieve the pressure of their over-booked lives ("Jenelle"). The entertainment value of Jenelle's claim to self-care, of course, resides in audience's awareness that it is Barbara who works full time and cares for Jace.

Near the end of her episode, Jenelle appears to begin to conform to the *16 and Pregnant* model, acknowledging that "it started to become clear how big this responsibility is" and saying, "I never thought motherhood was going to be this hard and I never knew how much I was going to miss just being a regular teen." In another scene, she frankly tells a friend, "Imagine being in prison. That's what it's like. Being in prison." She ultimately declares, "I just wish I would've waited" ("Jenelle").

Each teen mom's grudging admission that parenthood is hard thus supports the overarching message that the challenges of maternity are an appropriate punishment for a young woman's active sexuality, self-centeredness and irresponsibility, echoing conservative and anti-choice rhetoric insisting that young women should suffer the "consequences" of premarital sex. May Friedman, in "'100% Preventable': Teen Motherhood, Morality, and the Myth of Choice," expertly unpacks how the series and the larger culture "begin from the same fundamental oversimplification: that the specific challenges faced by young women who choose to parent are individual difficulties, evidence of bad choices or bad value or both" (67) and that, as a result, the teen mom's suffering is presented as necessary and appropriate punishment. Friedman points out, for example, that the show disproportionately represents intimate partner violence as occurring against men and perpetrated by women and uses extra-narrative devices to remind audiences of the seriousness of such abuse. At the same time, however, "the emotional abuse inflicted by young men toward young women on virtually every episode is seen as par for the course, a necessary by-product of young women making poor choices and allowing themselves to get 'caught'" (70).

The teen moms are expected to perform remorse and, at the conclusion of her dedicated *16 and Pregnant* episode, Jenelle appears appropriately penitent, ready to assume the yoke of parenthood and to endure the suffering Friedman describes. However, Jenelle's dedicated episode provides only a glimpse of her controversial—and often disastrous—choices depicted in the *Teen Mom 2* series[26] and, in failing to conform to the model of the reformed party girl turned self-sacrificing mother, Jenelle comes to represent the threat of the worldly girl/girly mom, a manifestation of the "social problem" that is the teenage mother (Gregson 5).

Juxtaposed with the other moms, Jenelle clearly emerges as a "bad" mother, an isolated and excluded individual who fails to engage in happy, fulfilling parenthood. While episodes often conclude with montages of the teen moms engaged in positive interactions with their children, suggesting that even if other areas of their lives are challenging, motherhood remains rewarding, many episodes conclude with images of Jenelle's mother caring for Jace before cutting away to images of Jenelle alone or with a boyfriend. For example, the episode "Keeping Hope Alive" concludes by showing Jace and Barbara in a playground while Jenelle cries in her car.[27]

However, Jenelle is not vilified simply because she fails to behave in an appropriately maternal fashion. Rather, Jenelle comes to represent an almost caricaturish vision of what third-wave feminism has wrought: a sexually liberated young woman who uses the rhetoric of personal choice to defend a variety of selfish decisions, but who also retreats quickly to the position of "victim" when it is useful to her. Self-righteous and self-pitying, Jenelle is dependent, but not on her own father or her child's father. Rather, Jenelle is often dependent on her mother, with whom she has a turbulent and inconsistent relationship, but who has legal custody of Jace.

Further, Jenelle is depicted, in an episode titled "Too Much Too Fast," as actively seeking government assistance, a rare occurrence in the *Teen Mom* franchises. The framing of her attempt to secure financial aid for college, rather than suggest that she is a noble young mother committed to improving her life, instead serves to depict Jenelle as a contemptible freeloader. The episode follows Jenelle as she visits a college financial aid office with the expectation that she will "get her life on track" by going to school. In a dead-pan voice-over, Jenelle explains to the audience that "getting financial aid shouldn't be a problem because I'm a single mom." Jenelle, however, is disappointed to discover that her decision to let her mother have legal custody of Jace may "ruin [her] chances" of getting government assistance.

Here, Jenelle embodies the worst stereotypes of the entitled "welfare mom," assuming that she is owed an education or at least a handout simply by virtue of being a single mother. However, Jenelle's decision to relinquish custody of her son—possibly a very mature and responsible decision—is the very act that might undermine her eligibility for that assistance. Viewers of the show might recognize Jenelle as precisely the type of young woman who could benefit from a college education as, although she is troubled, immature, and impulsive, Jenelle is also seemingly bright and confident. Education is a key tool for overcoming poverty, as without college or high school degrees, young mothers tend to remain uncompetitive in the work force ("Teen Pregnancy").

But the scene is structured to yet again highlight Jenelle's arrogance and ignorance; her voice-over in which she claims that "it shouldn't be a problem" to get financial aid was surely recorded after the scene was shot, suggesting that the show's creators intentionally feature Jenelle ventriloquizing the attitude of the single mother who manipulates the system. Jenelle not only confidently uses language she doesn't understand and enters situations she is unprepared for, but she is depicted as making claims to that which she doesn't deserve and hasn't earned.

That Jenelle's attempt to secure financial aid is presented as both grasping and futile is consistent with other depictions of governmental assistance on *Teen Mom*. More insidiously than *Gilmore Girls* and *Parenthood*, *Teen Mom* generally elides discussions of governmental programs that might prove useful to economically struggling families. In "Teen Momism on MTV: Postfeminist Subjectivities in *16 and Pregnant*," Caryn Murphy draws on Gill's understanding of the relationship between postfeminist and neoliberal ideology in arguing that *16 and Pregnant* over-emphasizes the importance of self-discipline and self-reliance, downplaying the effects of larger social and economic forces on the protagonist's lives and decisions, suggesting the irrelevance of social support systems, such as welfare, health insurance, or subsidized day care.[28] Further, Melanie Ann Stewart argues that not only are discussions of governmental financial assistance absent, so are discussions of familial support; that is, the shows "dangerously misrepresent the financial burden of child rearing" (104). In short, these programs present the young mothers as grappling with financial difficulties at the same time as they erase discussions of welfare and social support or the salaries that the cast members are earning for appearing on MTV. In a notable exception, teen mom Kailyn Lowry receives support from a non-profit that assists teen mothers ("Curveball"); she has since also come forward to say that she spent time in a homeless shelter (an event she concealed from MTV producers) (Bacchiocchi). However, in general, when welfare or assistance is referenced, as demonstrated during Jenelle's visit to the financial aid office, it is depicted both as a last resort and one which, as a result of bureaucratic red tape, may not be all that helpful after all.

While critics have warned that *16 and Pregnant* and *Teen Mom* "glamorize" teen pregnancy, "bad" moms such as Jenelle are excoriated on the show and on the Internet.[29] In its valorization of young women who are "hot," dependent on males, hard-working, and self-sacrificing and vilification of young women who are independent, lazy, and selfish (and yet, still, "hot"), MTV is simply rehashing the same formula that has been so successful on countless other reality television programs. However, these programs capitalize on an enduring anxiety concerning the status of the young mother in society, suggesting that there are only two possible outcomes for the "teen mom": the achievement of a nuclear family and middle-class lifestyle through hard work and self-sacrifice, or social failure, as represented by institutionalization in the form of a drug rehabilitation facility or and prison, widespread scorn and social isolation.

Conclusion: "Horrible, horrible choices"

In 2013, MTV's resident patriarch, Dr. Drew Pinsky, commented on Jenelle's downward trajectory, remarking that she needs "long term treatment" and suggesting that her MTV celebrity did not contribute to her poor choices (qtd. in Takeda). More recently—and more troublingly—Pinksy has endorsed the behavior of Jenelle's volatile and potentially dangerous husband, David Eason, suggesting that Jenelle needed to be taken firmly in hand. During the "Season 8 Teen Mom Reunion," when Jenelle's mother voiced her concern that David was "controlling," Pinsky responded, "To be fair to David, Jenelle, like, needs containment. Right? That's been one of her problems. She couldn't be contained." Pinsky earlier conceded that Jenelle is often "attracted to aggressive men" and Jenelle has disclosed being in violent relationships in the past. That Pinsky would suggest that David, who has been portrayed on the show as angry, unpredictable, and verbally abusive, is somehow a positive influence on Jenelle operates according to the logic that first, women who are abused are somehow at fault and perhaps provoke abuse and second, that perhaps Jenelle deserves such treatment, thus reinforcing the thinking described above, that the teen mom's suffering on the series is framed as appropriate. Most important for the purposes of this chapter, Pinksy's remark brings into focus the valorization of deference to and dependence on a patriarch.

Affable and unflappable, Pinsky himself functions as the voice of the mature, mainstream patriarch, appearing on reunion specials and "Check Up" programs to publicly chide, congratulate or advise the "moms," thus framing audience understandings of the young women's decisions both on and beyond the show. For example, in the interview referenced above, Pinsky criticized former teen mom Farrah Abraham's participation in a pornographic film, *Farrah Superstar: Backdoor Teen Mom* (2013), saying that Abraham, who appeared on the *Teen Mom* series, "is making horrible, horrible choices" (qtd. in Takeda).

Pinsky's condemnation of Farrah's "sex tape," however, is ironic considering that he has otherwise made a career out of exploiting others' most private moments: their drug relapses and sexual mistakes, their break ups and break downs. In particular, the climax of each episode of *16 and Pregnant* is the birth of the child and, often, the MTV cameras are in the delivery room, capturing this moment in order to broadcast it to the viewers. Pinsky's critique that Farrah is making "horrible choices" is hypocritical—if unsurprising—given that he has financially benefited from the popularity of a program in which she is filmed giving birth. That is, he tacitly approves of Farrah's willingness to commercialize one physically and emotionally intimate and dramatic event (birth) and not another (intercourse). As Brenda R. Weber and

Jennifer Lynn Jones write, in "Sperm Receptacles, Money-Hungry Monsters and Fame Whores: Reality Celebrity Motherhood and the Transmediated Grotesque," although Abraham's move into pornography may be "unsettling" (331) in part because of her appearance on *Teen Mom,* she nevertheless is following the "rules" of postfeminist neoliberal celebrity, "using medical technology to alter her body in ways that reinforce normative, even excessive codes of white female beauty, and then parlaying this body-as-commodity into a free market of celebrity that requires one earn attention through any means possible" (239–330).

Pinsky's objection is perhaps consistent with the reason for others' prurient interest in Farrah: her status as a sexualized "teen mom." That is, her performance in pornography again capitalizes on the supposed discrepancy between the identities of the mother and the sexual woman (as though other actors in the adult film industry are not parents or mothers). Further, interest in teen moms is itself potentially pornographic; the taboo surrounding teenage sexuality underlies the MTV show's success and is clearly part of the appeal of Farrah's video, which capitalizes on her fame as a "teen mom."

Thus, Farrah has violated several of the rules to being a good postfeminist girly mom/worldly girl. First, by participating in a pornographic film, Farrah defies the expectation that she remain deferential, as Pinsky complains, "If she had called me for advice, I would have told her not to do this" (qtd. in Takeda). Second, Farrah is financially liberated from MTV-as-benefactor. Pinsky suggests that Farrah's financial gain from the film is somehow invalid: "Let's say she takes that $2 million and opens a restaurant, which has always been her dream, how are you going to talk a 21, 22-year-old out of that? I just don't know" (qtd. in Takeda). While Pinsky's comments are somewhat unclear, he seems to suggest that the ends do not justify the means. According to Pinsky's logic, earning over $200,000 a year for allowing MTV camera crews seemingly unlimited access to one's private life is preferable to earning $2 million for pornography.[30] Thus, Farrah is unapologetically sexual, in charge of that sexuality, financially independent, and unconcerned with the patriarch's perspectives on her choices.

Regardless of whether or not these choices are "horrible" or liberating (Farrah has explained that she wanted to "celebrate [her] awesome body and get [her] own sexy shots" [Bonner]), the controversy surrounding her sex tape suggests yet again the perilousness of the position of the young mother. Ultimately, the patterns emerging across current network and cable programming suggest that the ideal female is always physically and emotionally on the cusp of maturity and that even mother-figures can be measured against this ideal. The ascent of the girly mom/worldly girl demonstrates that we want our female characters and mothers sexy, but if they are too sexy, or insist on the terms of that sexuality, they run the risk of being labeled sluts, of making "horrible choices." Television mothers must love fun and concern themselves with the superficial, the trivial, the juvenile, but they must always remember that their first priority is their children and be willing to sacrifice all for those children. Thus what appears as a move away from the sentimentalization of maternity and motherhood reveals itself as simply a re-entrenchment. A mother may love junk food or alcohol or sex; she might struggle with the responsibilities of parenthood or her relationship with her own parents, but in the end these are simply idiosyncrasies, not fundamental challenges to the cultural expectations surrounding femininity and motherhood.

As discussed throughout this chapter, a key element of postfeminist femininity is woman's consistent return to the patriarch. "Girly moms" appeal to their fathers for help, while "worldly girls" (at least those who are rewarded with positive depictions), meet the approval of fathers, male romantic partners, or father-figures. My investigation of how challenges to the status quo are absorbed through a reassertion of patriarchal power in some form or other is taken up again in the next chapter, which discusses how maternal legacies are cast aside and replaced with paternal inheritance in popular young adult novels, as well as in the discussion of representations of domestic violence in Chapter 5. Overall, in much of postfeminist media culture women are again and again represented as most at home in a patriarchy.

3
"Some kind of monster": Fraught Motherhood in *Twilight* and *The Hunger Games*

The protagonist's love interest in Suzanne Collins' *The Hunger Games* trilogy, Peeta (Josh Hutcherson), suggests that individuals can be transformed by the state, declaring in the first novel, "I don't want them to change me.... Turn me into some kind of monster I'm not" (Collins 141).[1] In a significant correspondence, in the first film of the *Twilight* series, romantic figure Edward (Robert Pattinson) explains to Bella (Kristen Stewart) that despite his status as a vampire, "I don't want to be a monster" (*Twilight*). What's striking about these overlapping announcements is that these male characters articulate what will gradually become each heroine's ultimate goal: to become a killer of sorts without truly sacrificing her humanity and becoming "some kind of monster."

Neither male character is truly in danger of becoming a "monster" because, as each series makes clear, Peeta and Edward have already made commitments to behave according to a code of conduct within the constraints of their difficult situations; thus, they have already arrived at their ethical positions. However, the task of negotiating her identity is rendered ever more complex for Katniss (Jennifer Lawrence) and Bella in that each protagonist experiences her transformation with very little guidance or support from mothers or other adult women. In these series, young women take the cue from men in order to survive in a violent patriarchy. Importantly, in addition to resisting obvious monstrosity, the protagonist is also on a much more banal mission: she is trying to avoid turning into her mother.

The previous chapter investigates how the mother-figure has become ever more youthful and girlish in contemporary television and that positive mother-characters are endlessly reinscribed as daughters, deferential to and dependent on a patriarch. In this chapter, I argue that young adult franchises go even farther in divesting mothers of power and relevance and that the ostensible insignificance of the mother-figure in the popular *The Hunger Games* and *Twilight* franchises is directly related to the larger devaluation of mothers in our culture.[2] Thus, this chapter considers the ineffective mother beyond her status as plot device, arguing that "bad" mothers serve as foils to the protagonists, providing them with types to define themselves against.

Of course, narratives often rely on absent or dysfunctional parents; dead mothers populate fairy tales, and much canonical literature—for example Austen and Dickens' work—includes absent or ineffective mothers, as do beloved novels for young people such as *The Little Princess, Sarah, Plain and Tall*, and the *Nancy Drew* series, and television shows that target young adult audiences such as *Buffy the Vampire Slayer* and *Riverdale*.[3] Kathleen Rowe Karlyn contends that the mother-daughter relationship in particular is often "unexplored" in popular media; when mothers do appear, Karlyn states, contemporary films "dispatch mothers with a vengeance, relegating them to sentimentality (*Stepmom*), hysteria (*American Beauty*), monstrosity (*Titanic*), or mere invisibility (*Rushmore*)" (8).

In *Twilight* and *The Hunger Games* franchises, the female protagonist's rejection of the mother is presented as necessary for a successful transition to adulthood.[4] Such a rejection evokes the concept of "matrophobia" as described in Adrienne Rich's *Of Woman Born: Motherhood as Experience and Institution*. Drawing on poet Lynn Sukenick's use of the term, Rich says matrophobia is "fear of ... becoming one's mother" (ital. orig. 235) and she explains that "Thousands of daughters see their mothers as having taught a compromise and self-hatred they are struggling to win free of, the one through whom the restrictions and degradations of a female existence were perforce transmitted. Easier by far to hate and reject the mother outright than to see beyond her to the forces acting upon her" (235). Rich thus suggests that matrophobia is often predicated on an inability or refusal to acknowledge how the larger culture devalues women because such an acknowledgment would force the daughter to recognize her own oppression. Instead, the daughter must perceive herself as different from the mother in order to escape the mother's fate. Although first published in 1976 (and republished in 1986 and again in 1995, around the time that many members of the *Twilight* and *The Hunger Games* series' target audiences were born), Rich's observations resonate today. Crucially, while the *Twilight Saga* and *The Hunger Games* series feature selected successful and accomplished women as well as active and competent heroines, both heroine's mothers are depicted as useless; in general, older women are depicted as at best irrelevant and at worst injurious to the protagonist's growth and development. Such a dismissal of older female figures is symptomatic of a larger cultural amnesia, a "postfeminist" failure to recognize how many current freedoms are predicated on the demands our foremothers made.

At the same time that these narratives devalue mothers and older women, they nevertheless shore up the "motherhood mandate"—a term that Nancy Felipe Russo used in 1976 to describe how motherhood is constructed as an inevitable and most desirable culmination of a young woman's strivings. Donna Musialowski Ashcraft argues that in the Twilight series, for example, Bella's embrace of motherhood suggests "that women have an all-consuming drive to have children and those who want to remain childless just do not know any better" (57). Crucially, in both *Twilight* and *The Hunger Games*, the protagonist ultimately refutes an earlier declaration that she will remain childfree.

In their apparent rejections of feminism, these franchises support the postfeminist principle that feminism is no longer necessary precisely because of the gains of the feminist movement. The success of *Twilight* in particular may be representative of an attitude identified by Angela McRobbie, discussing the 2001 film *Bridget Jones' Diary*: "It is as though this is the vengeance of the younger generation who had to put up with being chided by feminist teachers and academics at university for wanting the wrong things" (Aftermath 21). Both the *Twilight* and *The Hunger Games* series conclude with the vision of a postfeminist utopia, a utopia which is predicated on divisions between women, a disavowal of the political, and the repositioning of the heroine squarely in the domestic.

Thus, the contradictions abound: in narratives that ostensibly celebrate strong females, girls are diminished, in worlds in which women have access to diverse life paths, protagonists steadfastly cling to conventional lifestyles, and in stories populated by sociopaths and vampires, the adult female is in fact the most despised figure of all.

"I got my father's blood": Renouncing the Mother in The Hunger Games

As many critics have noted, there are some obvious overlaps between *Twilight* and *The Hunger Games*: both series present a misfit young woman (who is nevertheless white,[5] thin, able-bodied, and conventionally attractive) who embarks on adventures, all the while negotiating the advances of two adoring males, each of whom represents a different flavor of popular masculinity. In addition, both series rely on anxiety about older women, a lack of positive peer support, and, ultimately, a perversion of feminism which suggests that girls and women no longer need a political or gender consciousness and that feminism in fact impinges on their rights. These series' representations depend heavily on constructing a maternal inheritance as useless if not harmful, thus presenting the heroine's task as a rejection of older women and a construction of an adult identity that is successful within and despite the patriarchy.

In *The Hunger Games* series, Katniss is failed by her mother (Paula Malcomson), who needs, rather than provides care. The premise of *The Hunger Games* is that a tyrannical government located in "the Capitol" and led by President Snow (Donald Sutherland) forces citizens to offer up two children from each "district" to participate in an annual fight to the death. Katniss volunteers as a "tribute" in order to save her sister Prim who has been selected to represent their district in the games. After winning the games with her partner and romantic interest Peeta, Katniss becomes the face of a revolution led by Alma Coin (Julianne Moore), the next would-be president of the districts.

The society Katniss inhabits is violent and cruel. Her family's survival is itself tenuous, and Katniss hunts in order to provide food for herself, her mother, and her sister. And, like the daughter described by Adrienne Rich at the beginning of this chapter, rather than directing her anger at the state which caused her father's death or which would have allowed her family to starve while her mother mourned, Katniss directs her fury at her mother. In the first film, when leaving for the games, Katniss warns her mother, "You can't tune out again … not like when dad died. No matter what you *feel*, you have to be there for her" (*The Hunger Games*). Katniss emphasizes the word "feel," suggesting contempt for the weakness her mother betrays in succumbing to emotion. While Katniss does develop a grudging acceptance of her mother over the course of the series, she never truly sympathizes or reconciles with her. Instead, when Katniss returns to her home district after the rebellion, clearly emotionally traumatized, Katniss' mother chooses to remain in the Capitol.[6] In this way, *The Hunger Games* series discards the mother-daughter relationship as perhaps irreparable and, ultimately, inconsequential.

Katniss' mother's helplessness is a symptom of dysfunction in the family as well as the larger society; in her inability to protect her children, Katniss' mother is thus a stand-in for all the district parents, as well as the other adults who perpetuate or who fail to stand up against the state—itself metaphorically the punishing, murderous parent. Yet it is worth repeating that Katniss's contempt does not extend to her father and that Katniss generally embraces the masculine. For example, although Katniss admits to admiring her mother's talents as a herbalist and healer, she makes clear that she has no interest in inheriting those gifts. Katniss positions herself as her father's daughter and, in *The Hunger Games* novel, Peeta repeatedly suggests that Katniss is "good with this healing stuff," once telling her, "It's in your blood." Katniss responds, "No.... I got my father's blood" and thinks to herself, "The kind that quickens during a hunt, not an epidemic" (Collins, *The Hunger Games*, 322). Here, Katniss insists on aligning herself with the masculine and imaging herself as a life-taker rather than a life-saver. Her refusal of her maternal inheritance demonstrates a disdain not only for her individual mother, but for the traditionally feminine healing arts.

Katniss' competence as a hunter, determination to protect more vulnerable girls, her stoicism/emotional frigidity and her independence thus align her more with heroes of the old west more than any female literary predecessors. This depiction suggests that in order to be a hero, to be admired, one must reject the traits girls are usually encouraged to cultivate: pleasantness, attractiveness, a willingness to work with others. In this way, *The Hunger Games* embraces a version of feminism that suggests that in order to succeed in a man's world, a woman has to be more like a man. As Nodelman notes: "much popular literature [...] attempts to make what was once a traditional image of masculinity desirable for all of us, regardless of sex. Nowadays, it seems, we are all supposed to be just one of the boys" (Nodelman 11).

Thus while Collins' novels and the films based on them do complicate gender roles (it is worth noting that Peeta is a baker and a painter and that he is depicted as more overtly emotional than Katniss), overall, the women in *The Hunger Games* are often negative characters: they are foolish, like Effie, or cruel, like Peeta's mother, or even monstrous, like Coin.[7] There are exceptions, but overwhelmingly, Katniss is identified with males: Gale, Peeta, Cinna, Finnick, Boggs, and Haymitch, and as mentioned above, her deceased father.

While her characterization is taken to an extreme, Effie in particular is thus emblematic of the useless, silly females populating *The Hunger Games* series. Although positioned as Haymitch's counterpart, Effie, unlike Haymitch, has never participated (or triumphed) in the games. In part, her role is to advise Katniss on self-presentation and etiquette. Effie's characterization is not unlike those of many of the characters from the Capitol—characters of questionable morality because they apparently fail to recognize the tributes as human beings. Strikingly, the majority of these characters (such as the team who give Katniss a makeover) are female. The only member of the team who seems to understand the gravity of Katniss' situation is Cinna, who is a male.[8] Thus, Katniss is surrounded by decent, strong, supportive men throughout the films. The only females who seem to truly "get it" are either often children (like Prim or Rue) or themselves masculinized (like Johanna in *Catching Fire*).

Particularly in contrast to Effie, Katniss emerges as defying many traditionally feminine behaviors that oppress young women, including the imperative to care about one's appearance, to act nice, and to put others at ease.[9] Advising Katniss before a public appearance, Effie says, "be your usual self ... actually, be your happy self" (*Catching Fire*); elsewhere, Katniss makes clear that she is "not very good at making friends" (*The Hunger Games*), that she isn't aware of her beauty and isn't capable of trying to appeal to others. Dubrofsky and Ryalls astutely note that, "Katniss's performance of not-performing is what situates her as authentic and true (not willful or guileful) and, therefore, heroic. The value of not-performing and behaving in a natural-seeming manner is transposed onto the body in the film: altered bodies—bodies marked as surgically transformed or adorned with makeup and ornate clothing—are constructed as deviant, in opposition to Katniss's natural, unaltered white femininity, dangerously entrenching notions of naturalized embodied feminine whiteness" (396).

However, if Effie is unnatural and ridiculous, Katniss' other potential female mentor, Alma Coin, is unnatural and monstrous as, after defeating the Capitol, Coin proposes a reintroduction of the Hunger Games, enlisting children of the Capitol as the tributes. Neither figure functions as a role model for Katniss.[10] Instead, it is male adults and other young people—Peeta, Gale, Finnick, Haymitch, and even Plutarch Heavensbee—who act as midwives (or midhusbands?) to the young woman's maturity and coming-of-age. The self she develops into, for Katniss, is a coming to fruition of the ethical position she has been developing all along. Peeta, of course, is the primary instrument that facilitates this development. That is, her final selection of Peeta as her romantic partner rather than Gale represents her embrace of Peeta's philosophy over Gale's. Brian McDonald argues that Peeta's position is instrumental in Katniss's philosophical and moral development so that she can embark on "a life truly worth living" (McDonald 83).

"Make it personal": Ambivalent Motherhood in The Hunger Games

Over and over again, Katniss insists that her actions are not designed to make political points but only to serve personal interests: she volunteers to fight in the Hunger Games in order to save her sister Prim, she fights to survive the Hunger Games in order to return to her family, whom she provides for, and she fights to protect Peeta and to avenge the harm done to him and to her sister. For example, in *Mockingjay Part I*, when Katniss argues that she must rescue the captive Peeta, Coin attempts to convince her that the "revolution is about everyone. It's about all of us." In other scenes, Coin and her advisors demonstrate an awareness that the promise of overthrowing tyranny and promoting the common good does not motivate Katniss. Thus, when Plutarch wants an effective "propo," or propaganda short featuring Katniss, he allows Katniss to visit her destroyed home, stating, "We need to make it personal." Additionally, in *Mockingjay Part 1,* the conspirators who rescue Katniss from the games conceal their larger plot from her, accurately predicting that the larger goal of overthrowing tyranny will not move Katniss to action; she cares only about saving Peeta.

In short, making the world a better place is of secondary concern to Katniss, whose foremost interest is her immediate family and community. Katniss can be a hero in part because she doesn't want to be a hero. Perhaps this is how we like our female leaders best: reluctant and unambitious and uninterested in politics generally. For example, as discussed in the following chapter, mothers often justify activism or political leadership by claiming they are primarily motivated by protecting their own families' best interests. Of Katniss specifically, critic Laura Miller observes that the series presents "profound ambivalence about desire and power" and states that "If Katniss sought to be the center of attention … if she dreamed of leading the revolution, if she longed to compete and to win—if she had any ambition at all—she would be a bad girl."

Katniss' retreat to private life at the series' end, although problematic, is nonetheless consistent with her avowed disinterest in politics throughout the series. In the final novel, Katniss renounces public life, declaring, "I no longer feel any allegiance to these monsters called human beings, despite being one myself" (Collins, *Mockingjay* 377). The monster, at the end of the Hunger Games, is not necessarily the state or the warrior, but the ordinary human individual. And yet Katniss, who tells Gale in the first film that she will "never have kids" (*The Hunger Games*) apparently chooses to create ever more monsters. Of course, before Snow's overthrow, choice is illusory, as the patriarch has robbed the mother of the right to protect her child. However, Katniss' position at the end remains cynical and her announcement that she has no "allegiance" to others is false; she is clearly still connected to and committed to Peeta, her children, and perhaps Haymitch. Thus, what Katniss means is that she will no longer ally herself with humans *other than* her immediate family.

Further, Katniss is apparently completely domesticated: the final scene of the series shows her, wearing a dress, her hair down, holding an infant as Peeta plays with another child nearby. It is a significant reversal that Katniss is not only not hunting, but is totally immobile, and the scene hews closely to the traditional ideal of nuclear family life. In "The Masks of Femininty: Perception of the Feminine in *The Hunger Games* and *Podkayne of Mars*," Rodney M. DeaVault bemoans this conclusion: "Given her violent bid for autonomy and independence throughout the trilogy, relegating Katniss to the domestic sphere seems to do her a grave disservice by destroying the power of her 'other-ness'" (197). Similarly, in "'The Dandelion in Spring': Utopia as Romance in Suzanne Collins's *The Hunger Games* Trilogy," Katherine R. Broad critiques the series' end, contending that though the series ostensibly promotes "gender equality ... Katniss is hardly a feminist figurehead" and arguing that depicting "an epic heroine defaulting to a safe, stable, highly insular heterosexual reproductive union—a union so much like the social and sexual status quo of our own world—raises questions about just what has been transformed by Katniss' harrowing fight" (125).

Both critics' assessments suggest a capitulation to the motherhood mandate; this conclusion implies that a teleology of motherhood has underpinned the entire series. However, there is an eerie quality to the sepia-toned final scene of *The Hunger Games* series. The figure of Katniss, who, in the establishing shot is shown from behind, evokes the central figure in Andrew Wyeth's painting *Christina's World*: both women are placed in yellow grasses and gaze toward a symbol of the domestic. For Christina, this is the house in the distance; for Katniss this is Peeta and the child. Like the painting, the image of Katniss suggests a boundedness or the female desire for that which seems if not impossible, perhaps painfully distant. After this shot, camera angles provide the child's view of the vaguely smiling Katniss as, with an almost Stepford wife-esque complacency, Katniss tells the infant that she still has "nightmares" and that although making lists of kindnesses she's seen performed gets a little "tedious," that "there are worse games to play" (*Mockingjay, Part II*).

Despite its reassertion of the motherhood mandate, this final scene nev-

Figure 5. Katniss (Jennifer Lawrence), shown from behind, gazes at Peeta (Josh Hutcherson) and child in the distance (*The Hunger Games: Mockingjay Part II*, Lionsgate Films, 2015, directed by Francis Lawrence).

ertheless gestures to the ways in which the safety of the heteronormative, nuclear family may be predicated on repressions of past injustice, violence, and trauma. Katniss' demeanor and immobility are suggestive of an individual who is calm through force of will, of someone, perhaps, who clutches her child to keep her hands from shaking. In the novel, Katniss describes her feelings during her pregnancy with her daughter: "When I first felt her stirring inside of me, I was consumed with a terror that felt as old as life itself" (Collins, *Mockingjay*, 389). Here, Katniss articulates fear at participating in creating and protecting—rather than destroying—life. Despite her rejection of her own mother, then, this quote begins to indicate a connection to context, to the "ancient" and to a maternal inheritance. Further, parenthood is often an act of optimism, a belief in the viability of a future, and in Katniss' final speech to the infant she promises, "Someday I'll explain it to you," suggesting that as a mother, the literal and metaphorical steward of the next generation, she will account for who she is and what she has done. In this way, then, perhaps this conclusion suggests that parenthood is itself a process of grappling with the consequences of our choices, with coming to terms with the self we have been and the self we will be.

"Loving, erratic, hare-brained": The Useless Mother in Twilight

Like Katniss, *Twilight*'s Bella must ascend to adulthood without her mother's guidance and, later in the series, Bella moves from a position of indifference to parenting to an embrace of transformative maternity. Also like Katniss, Bella exists in a perilous world. In *Twilight*, Bella falls in love with vampire Edward Cullen, who is part of a vampire "family" that chooses to live on animal rather than human blood.[11] Throughout the series, Edward and Bella face attacks from evil vampires and suffer through Bella's physically and emotionally traumatic pregnancy. During all this, Bella's mother Renée (Sarah Clark) is only intermittently present. Yet, for all of her absence, Renée is a crucial figure in the series: the first words of the first *Twilight* book are "My mother" and it is Renée's new marriage that catalyzes the novel's action.

Renée is depicted as a free spirit who puts her own needs and desires above those of her husband and children. Bella characterizes her as well-meaning, but frustratingly irresponsible; she calls Renée her "loving, erratic, hare-brained mother" (*Twilight*). Like Lorelai and Rory in the *Gilmore Girls*, Renée and Bella are a girly mom and worldly girl pairing, with Renée acting "very young for her age" while Bella, according to her mother, "was born thirty-five years old" (Meyer, *Twilight*, 106).

In several respects, Renée embodies the backlash stereotypes of what feminism has wrought: self-absorbed, spoiled, immature adult women. While her character is presented as good-natured and generally harmless, Renée's abandonments of Charlie and, later, of Bella are inarguably selfish. In the first pages of the first novel, as Renée and Bella separate so that Renée can travel with her baseball-player husband, Renée assures Bella that "'I'll come right back as soon as you need me.' But [Bella] could see the sacrifice in her eyes behind the promise" (Meyer, *Twilight*, 4). The irony is that Bella will go on to find herself in incredibly desperate, life-threatening situations, not to mention a debilitating depression when Edward breaks up with her in *New Moon*. But Renée apparently does not anticipate and cannot comprehend the ways in which her daughter might need her. Further, her inability to conceal that staying with her daughter would be a "sacrifice" further signals her failure to conform to idealized maternity. In fact, it is Bella, rather than Renée, who makes sacrifices: Bella lives in a town she hates with a father she doesn't know very well. Bella's sacrifices for her mother are crystallized in the climax of the first episode of *Twilight* as Bella risks her own life in an attempt to protect her mother's (a reversal of a more traditional narrative of maternal self-sacrifice). In this way, the series constructs a conservative argument against a larger culture that permits this kind of long-distance mothering and me-first mentality for women. Renée is not a bad mother, necessarily, but she is certainly not a good one, nor is she a role model, at least for Bella.[12]

Like Katniss, Bella aligns herself with her father, announcing in the first film that she is a "loner" and explaining, "I guess I'm kind of like my dad in that way" (*Twilight*). Bella does, however, find female friendship and a surrogate-mother in the Cullen household. However, that her only female friends are vampires suggests again that Bella, like Katniss, is somehow cooler—smarter and more worldly—than her peers. Early in the novel *Twilight*, Bella announces that "It wasn't just physically that I'd never fit in.... I didn't relate well to people my age. Maybe the truth was that I didn't relate well to people period" (Meyer, *Twilight*, 10). Despite this assertion, Bella's interests and behaviors, and most importantly, how others treat her, suggests that she is not truly a misfit (she is by no means ostracized or bullied), but rather that she is simply more sophisticated than other students.

Significantly and not unlike *The Hunger Games* series, while girls and young women are an important demographic for the *Twilight* franchise and some readers might identify with the protagonist, overall, the series depicts girls as frivolous and irrelevant.[13] Jessica, for example, one of Bella's few friends in Forks, is a stereotypical girl, interested primarily in shopping, boys, and competing with other girls. In her toast at Bella and Edward's wedding, Jessica not-so-subtly suggests that she herself, as "captain of the volleyball team" and "president of the student council," would have been more deserving of Edward's romantic attentions (*Breaking Dawn, Part I*). Casey Ryan Kelly forwards a compelling argument that Jessica is "the film's postfeminist foil…. She represents the supposedly naïve optimism of contemporary mainstream feminism" (42).

On the one hand, then, Bella is set apart from other girls; on the other, she embraces many of the traditional choices available to young women. These choices replicate and reverse her mother's choices. Like Renée, Bella marries and has a child at a relatively young age. Renée, however, also divorces young. Bella rehearses her parents' split in an attempt to run away (and thus protect) her father in the first film. She tells her father, "If I don't get out now I'm just gonna be stuck here like mom" and then explains to Edward, "I told him the same thing my mom told him when she was leaving him" (*Twilight*). This brief scene suggests that the breakup of Renée and Charlie's marriage is clearly painful to Charlie, but only a youthful misstep to Renée. It is not a dramatic event or passionate feeling that catalyzes the end of their marriage. Rather, Renée doesn't want to be "stuck."

Bella too winds up dumping Charlie, although in true patriarchal style, her abandonment of her father functions to more fully position her as part of her romantic partner's family. Further, as a reenactment of Renée's history, this scene brings into focus Bella's conviction that her choices are and will remain different from her mother's. That is, unlike Renée, Bella's very first romantic relationship is presented as unquestionably monogamous and permanent. Where Renée saw young marriage and motherhood as a trap and a mistake, Bella willingly embraces them—as well as the geographical limitations that will come with being a Cullen. The series suggests that Bella and Edward will also remain physically and emotionally unchanging and that they are confident they will never grow to feel "stuck" with each other. For Bella, then, a side effect of becoming a monster is that she will also remain a young adult, never developing into a mature, middle aged, or old woman, an idea that is dramatized in the dream sequence that opens *Breaking Dawn*. Bella sees her grandmother, only to realize, to her horror, that she is looking at herself in a mirror. By becoming a vampire, Bella literally forestalls the old anxiety about "turning into" one's mother (or grandmother) once and for all.

We Should All Be Vampires: Transformative Maternity

Bella initially declares disinterest in motherhood: "I'd never imagined myself as a mother, never wanted that…. Maybe I just had a really bad imagination" (Meyer, *Breaking Dawn*, 132). However, when she becomes pregnant, Bella immediately embraces her potential maternity, rejecting Edward and Carlyle's suggestions that she have an abortion. The familial conflict over whether or not Bella should carry the fetus to term thus obliquely engages contemporary debates over abortion, particularly in cases when a woman's life or health may be compromised by pregnancy. Bella's unwavering determination to have the child positions her as the ideal self-sacrificing mother and the rather gruesome scenes of her emaciated body and pregnant abdomen evoke protagonists of another popular young adult genre, what Julie Passanante Elman calls "teen sick-lit."

Bella's transitions into motherhood and vampirehood occur almost simultaneously: because the labor and delivery of her daughter kills her, Bella is bitten, healed, and turned into a vampire moments after giving birth. Although Bella remains essentially herself—Jacob remarks, "I didn't expect you to seem so ... you"—she is now super-Bella (*Breaking Dawn, Part 2*). This entire episode can function allegorically to suggest the perils and promise of maternity. Bella is "born again": after a physically torturous ordeal, she is more beautiful, capable, and sensitive than before. Thus, just as some women experience motherhood as revealing competencies or strengths they were previously unaware of, Bella is an improved version of herself, her strengths amplified and supplemented.[14] Further, that Bella's vampire gifts include the ability to act as a "shield," or to spread her consciousness in order to protect those she cares about, is also suggestive of many mother's heightened ability to care deeply about and for others.

Bella's transformation represents a final rejection of Renée as Edward, in turning Bella into a vampire, takes his place as her parent or creator—new vampires are called "newborns"—and is permanently installed as the all-loving and adored figure in Bella's life. Bella is thus reconceived by the male and indoctrinated in a more explicitly patriarchal, perfectly postfeminist system.[15] For example, abortion exists as an option, but an option that no good mother, no matter how ill, would choose; non-monogamy exists as an option as well, but again, is not an option that any virtuous vampire would select.[16] Further, early marriage is prioritized over higher education. In the era of "choice feminism," Bella's choices remain radically conventional.

Significantly, the postfeminist vampire world Bella inhabits in many ways resembles a world many second-wave feminists would have embraced. In 1970, Shulamith Firestone, for example, argued that "Nature produced the fundamental inequality—half the human race must bear and rear the children of all of them—which was later consolidated, institutionalized, in the interests of men" and called for "freeing women from the tyranny of their reproductive biology by every means available" (qtd. in Vandenberg-Daves 227). After her transformation, Bella is in fact liberated from the physical and cultural limitations that accompany femaleness in a patriarchy. No longer able to conceive, she cannot be saddled with another pregnancy or child. Additionally, her parenting responsibilities are negligible as her husband and in-laws provide round-the-clock childcare. The child herself grows at an accelerated rate, skipping over some of the more challenging infant and toddler years. And finally, as a being that doesn't need any sleep—and because of the Cullens' wealth doesn't need to work—Bella is freed from the "time scarcity" that affects so many mothers. When not preparing for big battles, Bella is generally free to cavort, have sex with Edward, and pursue her own interests.[17] Who needs feminism when not only are all one's needs met by a community of attractive, tireless, and helpful family members, but one lives isolated from the larger, patriarchal world in which systemic sexism persists?

Further, Bella the newborn-vampire is physically superior to Edward. Significantly, much of the tension that drives the first three installments of the *Twilight* series arises from the fact that Edward and Bella's relationship is *not* the ideal. Bella articulates a desire for equity with Edward, telling him, "I can't always be Lois Lane.... I want to be Superman too" and explaining to him (and perhaps to many young readers) that in a healthy relationship, the partners "have to save each other *equally*" (ital. orig. Meyer, *Twilight*, 474). In *Eclipse*, she reiterates this desire, imagining, "we would be partners.... I would do my part" (Meyer 435). In this way, Bella's personal goal evokes a central tenet of pretty much all feminist movements: the desire not only for equality, but for the ability to contribute to her family and community in a meaningful way of her own choosing. And, of course, Bella here forecasts a happily-ever-after conclusion: even though Bella and Edward's relationship is extremely problematic for most of the series, that relationship is untenable. It is only the relationship between equals that is cast as literally and metaphorically perfect and eternal.

While Bella is thus placed in a vampire-vacuum, her maternity nevertheless allows her to act as a force literally and metaphorically promoting a larger unity and peace. First, she effects a change in the coven, as even the coldest vampires gather to nurture and protect her daughter.[18] Further, the birth creates an occasion for a reconciliation between apparently incompatible species and sworn enemies, improving human-vampire and vampire-werewolf relations. Finally, when the daughter is imperiled, the Cullens call together vampires who don't share their beliefs but who will stand by and "witness" Bella's daughter as a miracle (rather than an abomination), dramatizing the formation of community in a group of beings who are otherwise un-communal. Crucially, then, Bella doesn't just change what it means to be a vampire or how the Cullens conduct themselves, but her existence as mother-and-vampire demonstrates the viability of qualities such as empathy, compassion, and connection. Through maternity, then, Bella thus manages to become a literal monster without sacrificing her humanity.[19]

Thus, the endings of both *The Hunger Games* and *Twilight* begin to indicate a potentially transformative maternity, or a maternity that promotes a positive change in the protagonist as well as in her community. To their credit,

Twilight and *The Hunger Games* present motherhood as an experience that can force a recalibration or even expansion of the individual's identity and broadening of the self. However, both series also present motherhood occurring without the presence or input of the new mother's own mother, or in fact, without much help from other mothers. While the "return" home is often a part of hero myths, these series deploy maternity as a conclusion which apparently forces the heroine's retirement; this elevation of maternity to a vocation thus problematically suggests that the female will most appropriately focus her energies in the home. As Kelly writes, "The construction of Bella's ... powers confirms the ideological narrative emerging from postfeminist discourses that for women 'real' strength and empowerment come from motherhood, domesticity, and traditional family life" (45).

Further, the homes they inhabit are visions of postfeminist utopias, untroubled by gender disparities in either the public or private spheres. Motherhood apparently relieves these protagonists of the pressure to engage with the larger world: Katniss can renounce humanity and spend her time picnicking with Peeta rather than rebuilding society; Bella can devote herself to Edward and her daughter Renesmee, never worrying over global maternal mortality or the "motherhood penalty" and lack of adequate childcare for working U.S. mothers. Katniss and Bella, then, opt-out of heroism.

Conclusion: The Most Important Job in the World

In May 2017, Americans spent more money on Mother's Day gifts than ever before (Thau). Perhaps lavishing mothers with gifts was an unconscious attempt to assuage American guilt over the election of President Donald Trump the previous November, a candidate notorious for his disparagement of women generally and not above articulating contempt for the mothers of his own children.[20] This apparent incongruity—the widespread spending of money to celebrate individual women at the same time that elected government representatives vow to dismantle social welfare programs and safety nets (such as the Planned Parenthood organization) that are crucial for women and mothers' well-being, is typical of the neoliberal, postfeminist understandings so prevalent at the turn of the 21st century.

Because despite all the lip service, having children remains an incredibly costly social and economic enterprise for women. As Jodi Vandenberg-Daves states in her overview of the history of modern motherhood: "We are continually told that no job is more important than motherhood and that all women are essentially maternal. Yet there seem to be a million ways to fail at this crucial job and an abundance of complex claims on women's time" (3). Women are still held primarily accountable for their children's physical and emotional health[21]; psychologist Paula Caplan writes that upon doing research into the treatment of mothers in psychological literature, she and her colleague found that "mothers were blamed for virtually every kind of emotional or psychological problem that ever brought any patient to see a therapist" (100). Discussing approaches to mother-daughter relationships, Caplan concludes, "anything associated with mothers becomes devalued and pathologized" (101).

In *Of Woman Born,* Rich contends that it is the mother "finally, who is held accountable for her children's health, the clothes they wear, their behavior at school, their intelligence and general development" (53). This imbalance persists today.[22] Beyond being held primarily, if not solely, accountable for their children's comportment and appearance, women also bear a disproportionate economic burden as parents. Women and children make up the majority of those living in poverty in the United States. In "Evaluating the Poverty Status of Single Parent Families: Evidence of the Feminization of Poverty," Ashley Provencher and Audrey Sabatini review Pearce's 1978 concept of the "femininization of poverty" in order to study the current situation of both male and female single-parent households, concluding that "Despite the growing number of single fathers, single mothers may continue to be at greater risk of falling into poverty than their male counterparts" (Provencher and Sabatini 159).

The unpleasant realities that many mothers experience do not end there. A 2017 NPR investigation found that "more American women are dying of pregnancy-related complications than any other developed country. Only in the U.S. has the rate of women who die been rising" (Martin). Meanwhile, excellent, accessible and affordable childcare remains illusive for many families (Glynn). Finally, if families manage to secure good childcare, a woman is nevertheless subject to a potential "motherhood wage gap": "One of the worst career moves a woman can make is to have children. Mothers are less likely to be hired for jobs, to be perceived as competent at work or to be paid as much as their male colleagues with the same qualifications" (C. Miller).

Given this grim picture of motherhood, Rich's notion of "matrophobia" continues to resonate, as there may be many young women who perceive the ways in which adult women and mothers in particular are devalued in our culture and who might, as a result, seek to distance themselves or even reject their mothers' fates. And, in fact, there is a decreasing stigma surrounding childlessness; in *Mediated Maternity: Contemporary American Portrayals of Bad Mothers in Literature and Popular Culture,* Linda Seidel observes that more women are opting out of motherhood. Nevertheless, this ostensible liberation comes with a cost. Drawing on Jane Juffer's work, Seidel argues that "Now ... we can pretend that motherhood is simply each individual woman's 'choice' and that this choice weaves no thread through the larger social fabric" (xiii). According to a neoliberal logic, then, all of the injustices and indignities described above—a parent's time scarcity, lack of familial or communal support, the wage gap—are the results of individual choices, rather than the systemic devaluation of caregiving and motherhood.

Further, as suggested above, very few media depictions ever suggest that a woman might not want to become a mother. Over and over again, motherhood is presented as the end point of a woman's narrative trajectory. Countless movies and television series end with maternity: recently, for example, the generically different HBO programs, *Girls* (2012–2017) and *True Detective, Season 2* (2015) concluded with a "strong" female character whose life is apparently rounded out through maternity. The message that repeatedly surfaces is that, regardless of a woman's goals or accomplishments, she must become a mother in order to be truly fulfilled.

Similarly, in their depictions of intergenerational female relationships, *Twilight* and *The Hunger Games* suggest that, despite larger problems in the worlds the female protagonists inhabit, their rightful place is in the home. The films naturalize the thinking that regardless of any other ethical, political, or romantic commitments, a woman's first priority is to her children (even if they are as-yet unborn).[23] Thus, despite each protagonist's alienation from her own mother, as well as early announcements that she does not want to become a mother, the *Twilight Saga* and *The Hunger Games* conclude with the protagonist's parenthood, shoring up the "motherhood mandate," at the same time that these texts render invisible any objections to motherhood that a young woman might have.

4

The Real Housewives of Post-Industrial USA: Hysteria and Toxic Discourse

Despite recent reality-show suggestions that a "housewife" might be an upper-class woman of leisure, housewives are more often women who perform low-status, unpaid domestic labor. According to Stephanie Coontz, for example, the majority of "stay-at-home moms" are women "married to men in the *bottom* 25 percent of wage earners, not the top 25 percent" (ital. orig., *The Way We Never Were* xxix). These are women who may not have academic credentials or claims to scientific expertise. These are women who often spend much of their time touching and inhaling petroleum-based chemicals in the metaphoric "battle" against germs and dirt on the home front. And ultimately, as a result, these are women who may disproportionately suffer the negative effects of toxic exposure (Scott, Rakowski, Harris 3).[1] Thus, while many articles in popular magazines and advertising for cleaning products exploit fears of hidden dangers of germs in the home (see fig. 6), ironically, the true hidden dangers may arrive in the cleaning products themselves.[2]

Housewives are, in the words of a character in *The Incredible Shrinking Woman* (1981), on the "frontlines of chemical warfare." It is incredibly apt, then, that many individuals who identify as environmentally ill have taken up a metaphor rich in literary and historical significance: the canary in the coal mine ("The Canary Report"). The caged canary is often associated with domesticity's injuriousness generally; see, for example, the symbol of the canary in Susan Glaspell's feminist play "Trifles" (1916). In addition, to "sing like a canary" is to snitch or to implicate oneself as well as others in a crime. Finally, the literal "canary in the coal mine" was a creature deemed disposable, sacrificed in order to alert others—others who mattered—that the environment had become toxic (Eschner).

Figure 6. The tagline in this Clorox ad, "For a Healthier House and a Happier Home," naturalizes the thinking that health—and happiness—is obtained through the use of powerful chemical cleaners (Clorox, 2014).

In this chapter, I turn to fictional housewives across the decades who raise the alarm regarding toxicity in the home. In films such as the 1981 Lily Tomlin vehicle *The Incredible Shrinking Woman* and Todd Haynes' 1995 cult classic *Safe*, the toxic housewife's physical reactions are warnings of a poisonous environment, of a world which, as the result of human activities (including their own), is becoming inhospitable to human life. Additionally, Darren Wein's 2015 indie film *Consumed* presents a working mother who connects her child's physical suffering to the genetically modified organisms in his food. As the canaries in the coal mines, these wives and mothers implicate a larger toxic culture. Bullied, cajoled, and discredited, the protagonists are doubly injured: first by toxicity and second by unaccommodating and disbelieving communities. Like Lois Gibbs, whose activist work at Love Canal in Niagara Falls, New York, resulted in the creation of the Superfund, the postindustrial housewife in each film is labeled alarmist, irrational, and hysterical. Yet these protagonists are, in fact, astute cultural readers: they are aware that others are aggressively uninterested in the information they possess.

The Incredible Shrinking Woman, Safe and *Consumed* reveal how metaphorization is itself an instrument of silencing. Metaphor, of course, is the act "of conceiving of one thing in terms of another" (Lakoff and Johnson 37); often, a more obscure or complex concept is understood through an ostensibly more comprehensible or familiar concept. Following disability studies scholars who have identified a tradition in literature and film in which disabled bodies are "always an interpretive occasion" (Garland-Thomson 1), I suggest that the label "hysterical" and the charge of "hysteria" function as metaphors by removing attention from the original complaint and focusing that attention on another, possibly unrelated issue. In these films, understanding an illness as a symptom of a personal and/or psychological problem empties the illness of its environmental relevance (and, potentially, of its legitimacy). In *The Incredible Shrinking Woman, Safe,* and *Consumed,* experts and doctors construe illness as metaphor, thus ignoring the sick body's indictment of American practices of production and consumption. Importantly, while *Safe* in particular also depicts the housewife-figure's struggle against the attempts to explain away her mysterious illness as psychological, attempts to read the protagonist's illness as metaphor occur beyond the film itself, as *Safe*'s critics neglect the film's depictions of toxicity, instead focusing on the film's allegorical dimension. While I am not writing to defend the existence of environmental illnesses specifically, I do want to foreground the necessity of disabusing ourselves of a mindset that insists on metaphorizing, euphemizing, and otherwise avoiding commentary on physical and environmental corruption.

Toxic Discourse and TILT: The Postmodern Condition

In her landmark text *Silent Spring* (1962), Rachel Carson details the injurious effects of chemicals like DDT on plant, animal, and human life. Initially met with virulent opposition from the chemical industry as well as those within the mainstream of the scientific establishment, Carson was attacked as an "emotional" ("Pesticides") and "hysterical" woman (Hazlett 710); in *Time* magazine, her work was characterized as giving expression to "high-pitched sequences of anxieties" ("Pesticides"). In "'Silence, Miss Carson!': Science, Gender, and the Reception of *Silent Spring,*" Michael B. Smith argues that part of the reaction against Carson was fueled by the fact that a woman dared challenge the male-dominated scientific establishment. Smith suggests that for many of Carson's adversaries, women and nature existed as analogous: both were destined for male domination and exploitation.

Laurence Buell's positions Rachel Carson's *Silent Spring* as the fundamental text of contemporary "toxic discourse," a tradition in which narratives often include a hero's "shock of awakened perception" (43) to toxicity, the development of a "totalizing image of a world without refuge from toxic penetration" (35), and a "moral" (38) conflict reminiscent of "a David versus Goliath scenario" (40). Several late 20th century narratives exist within the toxic discourse tradition, including Lois Gibbs' memoir *Love Canal: My Story* (1982) and the films *Silkwood* (1983) and *Erin Brockovich* (2000). Each of these focuses on an unlikely heroine who seeks truth and justice, despite the emotional, economic, or social hardship her investigation incurs. In these texts, the heroine attempts to understand and publish the contamination of her own or others' bodies and ultimately effects a positive change in her own life and/or in an imperiled community.

In many toxic discourse narratives, it is the protagonist's identity as a mother which allows her to challenge the status quo. Discussing conceptions of motherhood in 18th and 19th centuries, Rebecca Jo Plant writes that the "angel of the house" ideal "provided middle-class women with a convincing rationale for engaging in a host of reform activities: in the name of protecting the home, they increasingly ventured beyond it" (2). Similarly, in late 20th and early 21st century texts, many women continue to center concern for their children, or children generally, in order to justify their environmental activism. The protagonists of the films under review in this chapter, however, depart from or revise the toxic discourse tradition in important ways. In *The Incredible Shrinking Woman* and *Safe,* the poisoned homemaker is unable to reach a broader audience with her urgent message. The protagonist of each is thus a postmodern Cassandra: a woman whose body testifies to the untenability of America's 20th-century trajectory but whose message remains unarticulated and unheeded. The protagonist of *Consumed* is more effective, but she too is unsuccessful in her campaign to raise broad awareness or to challenge a powerful multinational corporate force.

Each film presents the housewife/mother as discredited in part because she lacks scientific credentials; in addition, toxic contamination is, as Carson wrote, "admittedly difficult ... to 'prove.'" (192): "Like the constant dripping of water that in turn wears away the hardest stone, this birth-to-death contact with dangerous chemicals may in the end prove disastrous. Each of these recurrent exposures, no matter how slight, contributes to the progressive buildup of chemicals in our bodies and so to cumulative poisoning" (173).

Although Carson's primary concern in *Silent Spring* is with pesticides and herbicides, more recent research has revealed the accuracy of Carson's contention, as for example, with regard to cancer. Epidemiologist Devra Davis writes, "the total of a person's exposure to all the little amounts of cancerous agents in the environment may be just as harmful as big doses of a few well-known carcinogens."[3] Since the release of *Safe* in 2005, the scientific community has begun to accept the legitimacy of illnesses activated by environmental toxicants. First called multiple chemical sensitivity (MCS)[4] or environmental illness, the condition is now called toxicant induced loss of tolerance (TILT). While the later film, *Safe*, more directly responds to the MCS/TILT debate, it would be anachronistic to claim that *The Incredible Shrinking Woman* comments on MCS. Both films nevertheless engage the discourse of illnesses caused by the by-products of technology and industry and in doing so reveal a profound anxiety regarding the integrity of our homes and bodies, as well as a distrust of the solutions offered by scientific and technological advances.

TILT, a term introduced by physician Cynthia Miller (Neimark), is a condition that arises when, after significant exposure to a toxicant, "individuals become sensitive to low levels of diverse and unrelated triggers in their environment such as commonly encountered chemical, inhalant or food antigens"; the reactions "may involve various organ systems and evoke wide-ranging physical or neuropsychological manifestations" (Genius 6047). In "Sensitivity-Related Illness: The Escalating Pandemic of Allergy, Food Intolerance and Chemical Sensitivity," Stephen J. Genius acknowledges continued skepticism regarding TILT (just as there was of MCS in the 1980s and '90s), writing, "Other various common disorders have also met cynicism, disbelief and resistance in the past, particularly those diseases that affect women. Menopause, premenstrual syndrome, and chronic fatigue syndrome were initially dismissed as non-entities.... Despite resistance from the prevailing medical community each time, however, these health problems have subsequently been confirmed to be credible physiologically-based disorders rather than psychologically-based confabulations" (Genius 6057). As Genius suggests, the historical skepticism concerning women's complaints (traceable in nineteenth century understandings of hysteria), coupled with the impossibility of identifying a specific cause of MCS/TILT, contributes to the obstacles sufferers face in dealing with family, friends, employers, and doctors.[5] Furthermore, without official recognition, sufferers may be denied accommodation and government benefits.

Further, disbelief may be a response to illnesses activated by environmental degradation because these conditions challenge medical-scientific hegemony. Foregrounding the often unpredictable results of scientific and technological advancements (the contradiction between the promise of the eradication of suffering, disease, and disability and the unintentional production of suffering, disease, and disability as a result of the processes of remediation), environmental illnesses complicate the notion of scientific "progress," as well as reveal medicine's incomplete understanding of the relationship between the environment and the body.[6] It is this uncertainty, according to philosopher Susan Wendell, that renders MCS/TILT so problematic to the Western medical science institution. Wendell argues that conditions such as MCS are often diagnosed as psychosomatic not because of evidence that a psychological problem exists, but because doctors find the evidence that does exist—the physical symptoms—unintelligible. According to Wendell, this diagnosis is consistent with the "myth of control"—the myth that our bodies can be understood and managed with certainty—promulgated by the medical science establishment. Wendell concludes:

> the diagnosis of psychosomatic illness props up the myth of control in two ways. First, it contributes to the illusion that scientific medicine knows everything it needs to know to cure us (provided we cooperate fully), because there is no physical problem for which it cannot provide a diagnosis. Second, it transfers responsibility for controlling their bodies to the minds of those patients who cannot be cured; the problem is not that medicine cannot control their bodies, it is that their minds are working against them [100].

As a result, according to Wendell, "by creating a culture of individual responsibility for illness and accident, the myths of individual control and medical control through cure discourage any search for possible social and environmental causes of disease and disabilities, thus inhibiting efforts to prevent them" (106). Rather than deal with an incomprehensible body or confront the ramifications of a poisonous environment, doctors' identification of the condition as self-created defuses its potential. The condition has no relevance beyond the individual's experience.

The sufferers in *The Incredible Shrinking Woman, Safe* and *Consumed* may be interpreted as hysterics, as individuals whose emotional discontent is expressed through physical ailments. While this reading is certainly arguable, it allows us to circumvent discussion of each film's representation of toxic environments. In addition, attempts to "solve" MCS/TILT through the discovery of its allegorical/hysterical function or through disproving or proving its existence, while often illuminating, should not forestall further investigation of a condition which is definitively variable, amorphous, and uncertain.

"You don't need me to tell you what's wrong with the world": Silencing the "Incredible" Body

The Incredible Shrinking Woman appeared the same year—1981—that the federal government finally agreed to relocate families living in the Love Canal housing development in Niagara Falls, New York.[7] Lois Gibbs had campaigned tirelessly for government acknowledgment of and assistance at Love Canal, a community constructed atop a toxic waste site. In her autobiographical narrative *Love Canal: The Story Continues* (1998), Gibbs describes the official response to parents' complaints about the health of those who lived in the area: "they were often described as 'hysterical women' or 'housewives' in an attempt to belittle the women who drew the links between exposure to chemicals and adverse health effects" (5). Gibbs persisted; she was primarily motivated not only by concern over her own health, but by concern for her children's well-being. Gibbs asserts that the Love Canal story functions as "a warning of what could happen in any American community," and assures readers that we "take control of our own lives by insisting that we be heard" (19).

The Incredible Shrinking Woman exists, in some ways, as the obverse of Gibbs' narrative. While Gibbs feels committed to protecting her children and others' children, Pat, the protagonist of *The Incredible Shrinking Woman*, seems to perceive herself as the only casualty of a toxic environment. In addition, whereas Gibbs emphasizes the importance of being "heard," even when one is "not that type of person" (Gibbs 61), Pat consistently refuses to speak out when she is given the opportunity to share her knowledge. The film suggests that, unlike those at Love Canal, Pat's community would rather not know about the dangers upon which their lifestyles are predicated. Within this context, Pat's reluctance to act as an ecological alarmist may be understood as an awareness of how women who speak out are dismissed and discredited. If Pat's body indicts her society, no one in her society seems to care. In fact, when Pat refuses to go along with one of her husband's schemes to capitalize on her condition by allowing a toy company to make a doll based on her, he abandons her. Pat's husband's behavior sends the message that intransigent women—or worse, women who need care—will not be tolerated.

Although *The Incredible Shrinking Woman* makes little pretense of serious social commentary, the film nevertheless suggests the staggering impact of technological development on everyday life as well as the limitations of our scientific understanding. In the film, Lily Tomlin's character, Pat Kramer, shrinks as a result of exposure to the combinations of chemicals in household and cosmetic products. Near the film's end, she is apparently killed when she becomes invisible and is blown away in a gust of wind. Later, Pat returns. This time she is uncontrollably growing.

Despite the apparent absurdity of the film's premise, its diagnosis approaches the accurate: given the multiplicities of toxic exposures the average American encounters, it is not inconceivable that an individual might have an extreme adverse reaction. Pat's doctors don't tell her that it's "all in her head"; instead, the doctor treating Pat tells her:

> You are shrinking from a combination of the tap water, the flu shot, the perfume, the glue, the solvent, your bubble bath, talcum powder, shampoo, hair conditioner, scenting lotion, hand lotion, mouthwash, hair spray, breath spray, feminine hygiene spray, deodorant, toothpaste, detergent, eye drops, nose drops, hair coloring, diet soda, birth control pills and smog, set off by an imbalance already present in your system [*The Incredible Shrinking Woman*].

Although exaggerated, the litany of elements contributing to Pat's condition emphasizes the amounts of chemicals each individual is exposed to in daily life, thus functioning as an acknowledgment of the impossibility of isolating or even truly parsing out the contaminants that negatively affect the human body. In fact, recent estimates suggest that the "average American adult is exposed to more than one hundred distinct chemicals from personal-care products every day" (Schapiro 22).

Following her doctor's imperative that Pat resume her everyday life and thus resume, at least partially, her self-contamination, Pat and her husband Vance focus their attention on the promise of a cure, rather than on untangling and remedying the cause, allowing them to bypass an indictment of those who profit from the mass consumption of harmful substances. Vance, in particular, has a stake in ignoring the causes of Pat's condition: as an advertising executive whose clients produce many of the products that result in Pat's shrinking, Vance is pressured—and, in turn, pressures Pat—to remain silent regarding the products' possible side effects. Pat and Vance's feigned ignorance is an attempt to preserve the status quo of uncritical production and consumption.

Thus, crucially, although Pat knows her condition isn't hysterical, her silence, coupled with the hyper-visibility of her body, invites others to interpret it as such. Further, that Pat allows males in particular to manipulate her speech and meaning is depicted as consistent with Pat's "every day" experience of the world. Male control of female speech is foregrounded immediately, as the film opens with the sound of a conversation over a dark screen; women are being solicited to try a cheese product for a commercial. The male voice insists on positive responses. He prompts, "is that good or is that good?" and tells the female shoppers that they "have to look like" they're "enjoying it" (*The Incredible Shrinking Woman*). The man's directions foreground a lack of alternatives: a woman can choose between "good" and "good." Further, he makes clear the narrowness of the options available for demonstrating pleasure—at least if a woman wants the male adjudicator's official recognition. One of the last women tells the man that the product tastes like "shit." The audience knows that because this woman's speech doesn't conform to the unofficial script, this comment will not make it into the advertisement. In this way, the opening sequence draws attention to how media images are crafted: unwanted speech will be elided and women's images will be manipulated in the service of sales, regardless of how the women "truly" feel. One female acknowledges this, asking, "If I don't love it, I don't get in the commercial, right?" The male voice answers: "That's right."

This scene thus establishes the dynamic of male-female relations which will persist throughout the film. Although women consistently frustrate men by saying things that men find inappropriate, men retain the symbol and tool of public speech as embodied in the microphone and ultimately decide what speech is valid or acceptable. Midway through the film, Pat is invited to be a guest on *The Mike Douglas Show*. Although Pat initially plans to "go on national TV and tell all" and she "feels the public should be warned," when Douglas asks her why she is shrinking, Pat lies: "It hasn't been determined yet, Mike." Vance nods his approval from the wings. Douglas then asks Pat if there have been any positive developments as the result of her condition. Pat begins: "Nobody cared what I had to say when I was my normal height. For instance, I—" but Douglas interrupts Pat to go to commercial. The joke is, of course, that nobody really cares what Pat has to say either before or after she started shrinking. In a manner similar to the opening scene, the humor of this scene is predicated on knowledge of the inauthenticity of mass media personas and performances. More importantly, despite Douglas' ostensible concern for Pat, he is uninterested in her as anything other than a spectacle. Without context or history, Pat is safely categorized as a curiosity and an exception.

Relying on the well-worn notion of female hysteria as an event in which the body speaks because the individual cannot, Pat's community attempts to explain her body as communicating a larger social message.[8] A male newscaster, for example, suggests that Pat is a metaphor for the "modern woman," claiming that "it's no secret that the role of the modern housewife has become increasingly less significant." Later, a female newscaster asks: "Did she begin to shrink because her role as homemaker was belittling when she looked at herself through society's eyes?" Because they are ignorant of Pat's specific bodily history and context, both newscasters misapprehend the meaning of Pat's body. Pat's condition is, in fact, a response to a social development, just not the one the newscasters choose to focus on. As a result, if the public believes that Pat's shrinking is psychosomatic—a manifestation of Pat's feelings of "insignificance"—then Pat is primarily responsible for her condition. Further, Pat's refusal to disclose the true cause reifies the metaphorization of disability because if Pat exists primarily as a metaphor, then nothing need be done to accommodate her or to prevent others from experiencing the same or similar conditions.

As her knowledge is a direct threat to the practices of production and consumption that, the film suggests, are definitive of 20th-century American life, Pat's reticence is a form of collusion. In a scene near the end of the film Pat not only has an opportunity to address others, but is motivated to warn the public. A tiny Pat, standing on a table in front of a microphone, begins to speak, but then inexplicably stops, saying, "you don't need me to tell you what's wrong with the world." Whatever the reason for Pat's withdrawal, her ostensible rationale—that the community doesn't "need" to hear her testimony—is ironic: she is speaking to a crowd of consumers in a shopping center. But Pat's neighbors do already know "what's wrong with the world"; they seem to have agreed simply not to discuss it. This climactic moment thus echoes the film's explicit connection of the suburban with consumption and consumption with contamination. While the implicit message is that these products hurt people and more specifically, that they hurt women, the explicit message is that the community is willing to make these sacrifices in order to maintain the status quo.

Pat's silence and her community's tacit endorsement of that silence are satirized upon Pat's apparent death when a newscaster issues the platitude that "even the smallest of us can make a difference." In light of what she knows—and what her "incredible" body evidences—Pat has categorically failed to "make a difference." The specter of an uncontrollably growing Pat at the film's conclusion is thus both humorous and chilling: Pat's family rejoices at her return, but these are the same individuals who failed to accommodate and ultimately abandoned her when she was no longer effective as a mother and wife. More importantly, that the film ends with Pat's return to the home suggests that Pat's experience remains a private affair; Pat is not yet capable of confronting her condition as evidence of systemic injustice or corruption. She will not voice the message that, it seems, no one really wants to hear.

As an artifact, the film suggests that willful ignorance is part of the joke. Audiences can laugh at Pat and her neighbors (and, in the process, alleviate some of their own toxic anxiety), because they perhaps recognize the caricatures of their own communities and aspirations. Underlying the humor, however, is an indictment of the cosmetic and consumer practices that both conceal and contribute to toxicity, as well as of a nation which represses and silences those who threaten to expose the hidden price of the suburban dream.

"Reading labels and going into buildings": Interpreting the Environment in Safe

Set in the same era, *Safe* appears almost fifteen years after *The Incredible Shrinking Woman* and takes a more serious tone in its depiction of a potentially poisonous environment. Like Pat, Carol (the protagonist of *Safe*, played by Julianne Moore), is a suburban Californian homemaker; also like Pat, Carol is assisted by a Latina domestic worker. That both protagonists employ a woman of color who presumably has even more direct contact with household chemicals than her white employer immediately throws into question the authenticity of each protagonist's illness: wouldn't the domestic worker also suffer from some sort of sensitivity? In fact, toxicity disproportionately affects populations of color in the United States.[9] Thus, the inclusion of a "cleaning lady" in both *The Incredible Shrinking Woman* and *Safe* not only further complicates our understandings of each protagonist's condition, but it also begins to suggest each protagonist's inability to make connections between her illness and systemic racism, classism, sexism, and economic and environmental exploitation.

This failure is particularly pronounced in *Safe*. Carol White, as her surname suggests, exists in some ways as a representative of white upper-class America. Fair-skinned and often dressed in white, Carol is ensconced in the ostensible safety of white suburbia.[10] Additionally, if Pat in *The Incredible Shrinking Woman* may be read as an obverse of Lois Gibbs, Carol may also exist as the obverse of some "real world" counterparts: most notably, Charlotte Bullock and Robin Cannon of the Concerned Citizens of South Central Los Angeles, a group that, in 1985, began protesting the construction of an incinerator in their predominantly African American community (Di Chiro). As women challenging corporate and governmental agencies, Bullock and Cannon describe obstacles similar to those faced by both Carson and Gibbs. Bullock, a "concerned mother," recounts some males' dismissive attitudes: "I noticed when we first started fighting the issue how the men would laugh at the women ... they would say, 'Don't pay no attention to them, that's only one or two women ... they won't make a difference'" (Hamilton 216, 215). Additionally, Cannon remarks on her increased consciousness of the interconnectedness of issues as a result of her involvement with the activist group: "Things are intertwined in ways I hadn't realized.... All these social issues as well as political and economic issues are really intertwined" (221).

In *Safe,* Carol fails to recognize how "things are intertwined." Like Pat, Carol understands her illness as private; she remains unable to imagine or articulate how her personal experience may be related to larger issues such as corporate greed, class and race privilege, or systemic sexism. Set geographically as well as temporally close to the Concerned Citizens of Los Angeles protests—in the San Fernando Valley in 1987—*Safe*'s plot focuses on Carol's apparent development of a disabling illness as a result of chemical exposure and her subsequent attempts to get well. About halfway through the film, Carol discovers the environmental illness community and their ideas begin to inform her understanding of the world and her health. Rather than affiliate with an activist group, however, Carol absconds to Wrenwood, an apparently expensive compound in New Mexico that caters to the needs of the environmentally ill. The strategies Wrenwood's director advocates for healing, including self-scrutinization, prove ineffectual, as Carol becomes increasingly ill. Sequestered in her ceramic igloo in the final scene, a gaunt and bruised Carol looks into a mirror and tells herself: "I love you" (*Safe*). This scene, like the entire film, refuses certainty. *Safe* does not assume the validity of MCS as an illness; the introduction of Carol's condition is a mystery which is never completely resolved. Neither does Carol's journey to self-knowledge reach a recognizable narrative fruition. Carol's declaration of self-love exists in a literal and metaphoric vacuum.

Haynes' choice to withhold evidence for or against a physiological basis for Carol's illness is consistent with his larger project of deferring traditional narrative expectations and generally resisting closure.[11] Although, as many critics have noted, some of Haynes' cinematic techniques tend to distance the viewer and make it difficult to identify with Carol, I argue that Haynes' depiction invites the audience to share Carol's perspective. As the film progresses, Carol increasingly understands the world around her as saturated with invisible dangers. Just as Carol learns to be vigilant with regard to "reading labels and going into buildings," as she says at the film's end, the audience too becomes aware of the potential and invisible dangers lurking in otherwise innocuous locales.

Unlike Pat, who is visibly different and may thus refuse to name her condition, Carol is forced to articulate and interpret her invisible condition for an incredulous audience, including her husband and her physician, both of whom suggest that Carol's illness is hysterical. At least initially, Carol is forced to rely upon language to signify her distress. (Later in the film, her physical reactions and appearance, as well as the oxygen tank she wheels behind her, signal illness). Carol's difficulty using language effectively is important because as Carol becomes increasingly disabled by her reactions to invisible fumes and toxins, she is also dis-abled by the attitudes of an unsympathetic community.

But privy to scenes which begin to authenticate her illness, the audience is invited to imagine a legitimate cause-and-effect relationship between environmental toxins and Carol's condition. Carol's reactions are thus potentially explicable, including, for example, her first attack of coughing and wheezing when she is driving behind smoke-spewing trucks. As a result, just as Carol begins to identify problematic places and substances, so too does the viewer become alert to the elements that may set off Carol's reactions. In this way, Haynes produces a heightened awareness of the toxic in his audience; whereas establishing shots seem innocuous in other films, shots of cars or industry, suburban streets and hair salons takes on an insidious cast in *Safe*. Haynes' film thus enacts what it describes: the familiar built environment contains clues that both Carol and the audience must learn to identify and interpret.

In particular, Haynes foregrounds the chemicals saturating sites traditionally associated with the feminine and generally considered harmless: the kitchen, the beauty parlor, the dry cleaner's. For example, one of the more horrifying episodes takes place in a salon, when Carol makes the spontaneous decision to get a permanent. A familiar convention in narratives about women's empowerment, the "make-over" sequence in television and film is a montage which contains the promise of hope and redemption. In other films, these "makeover" shots are often accompanied by upbeat music which cues the audience to anticipate a positive outcome.[12] However, those elements that signal the positive or hopeful in other films become portentous or malignant in *Safe*. Just as the stylist swivels Carol's chair for the triumphant moment when Carol can recognize herself transformed in the beauty parlor mirror, Carol's nose begins to bleed. Carol cries out, clearly unnerved. Both Carol and the viewer presumably make the connection between the chemicals in the perming solution, hair spray, and nail polish that Carol has been inhaling and Carol's reaction; in fact, the viewer has been primed to expect a negative outcome. The film's focus on toxicity thus trains the audience to see differently: a close up of a hand applying perming solution to a scalp no longer contains a benevolent promise, but instead is an ominous image that reminds us that we unthinkingly put ourselves in close contact with dangerous chemicals everyday. Carol's illness may be invisible, but so too are the fumes and chemicals that have permeated our lives in the past fifty years. In making visible the previously invisible—the potentially harmful but quotidian substances—Haynes thus also makes visible Carol's illness (at least to the film's audience).

Further, the audience may also begin to more critically interpret Carol's social environment. Although Carol cannot yet acknowledge how class and race privilege, sexism, and ableism might affect her condition and experiences, Haynes' film allows these (also often invisible) forces to emerge. For example, when Carol's husband Greg incredulously asks his hospitalized wife, "You think you're sick … because of bug spray?," Greg's question not only reflects a persistent skepticism of environmentally activated illnesses—despite increased acknowledgment of the danger of pesticides in a post–*Silent Spring* world—but more importantly, his disbelief performs what philosopher Miranda Fricker has termed an act of "epistemological injustice" based on "identity prejudice": in large part because she is female and his wife, Greg denies Carol credibility as a "knower" of her own experience, as well as of the world around her (1). In this way, Haynes' film brings into focus the largely invisible sexism that colors Carol's interactions with the men in her life.

Although Carol leaves her husband to live at Wrenwood, there is little else to suggest that Carol is developing any sort of feminist consciousness. Carol does, however, gain confidence as an interpreter of her environment; further, Carol's self-identification as a person with environmental illness provides her with a cause, a vocabulary, and a community. Carol's determination to discover the reasons for her illness despite the discouragement she receives from her husband and doctors is thus apparently Carol's first truly autonomous act. Her decision to admit herself at Wrenwood—however problematic—is a turning point for Carol's character. That Carol becomes increasingly ill while she is at Wrenwood has multiple implications. Not only is the program at Wrenwood revealed to be counter-productive, but Haynes' choice to locate Wrenwood in New Mexico—the site of the original Trinity tests of atomic bombs—suggests that the compound itself is located in a toxic area.

In "'There's Nothing More Debilitating than Travel': Locating U.S. Empire in Todd Haynes' *Safe*," Danielle Bouchard and Jigna Desai identify the most insidious aspect of Wrenwood's agenda: the community's endorsement of self-scrutinization as the answer to sickness. Peter, Wrenwood's leader, encourages his clients to blame themselves for harboring ideas and emotions that result in their illnesses, thus construing illness as a metaphor for emotional distress.[13] During a lecture, Peter tells the community: "I've stopped reading the papers. I don't need it" (*Safe*). He announces that negative media representations are potentially damaging to his health: "I'm afraid my immune system will start believing it.... And I can't afford to take that risk. Neither can you." Peter's advocacy of tending to the self, even at the expense of the rest of the world, underpins the logic of the last scene in which Carol looks into a mirror and says, "I love you." Gaye Naismith writes, "Without a free flow of 'contaminating' information into Wrenwood, its inhabitants cannot place their illness within a social context, they thus have no basis from which to engage politically with the environmentally based issues that have directly affected them" (Naismith 377). Peter's solution is to escape, rather than to attempt to better understand, or change, the world.

Like *The Incredible Shrinking Woman*, *Safe* nears its conclusion with the protagonist attempting to make a speech. Carol's receptive audience at Wrenwood listens, nodding with encouragement as she awkwardly tries to articulate her new relationship to her environment:

> I've never made a speech in my life. Oh, god umm.... I don't know what I'm saying ... (laughs) it's just that I really hated myself before I came here and, um, so I'm trying to see myself hopefully more as I am, more positive, like seeing the pluses, like, I think it's really opening up now people's minds ... cause of educating and ... and AIDS and ... um, and other types of diseases, cause ... cause and, it is a disease, because it's out there and we just have to be more aware of it ... um ... make people more aware of it, even ourselves going, reading labels and going into buildings... [*Safe*].

Despite the shortcomings of her speech, unlike Pat, Carol publicly shares her experiences. However, neither Pat nor Carol makes a substantial change, even in her immediate community. Carol's behavior, in particular, may be read as perhaps typical of mainstream American passivity with regard to environmental corruption at the turn of the 21st century. Carol only confronts environmental degradation because it impacts her personally and dramatically. Further, even as she begins to alter her habits in order to limit her exposure to "toxins," she is never depicted as second-guessing those activities (like driving a car or having her clothes dry-cleaned) that contribute to environmental toxicity. Thus, although heightened awareness and deliberate interpretation are important first steps, Carol persists in failing to recognize how her own lifestyle—both in the suburbs and at Wrenwood—are implicated in her illness. While Carol's declaration of self-love, like her speech in the dining hall, suggests that she is allowing an identity to emerge, Carol's behavior is inadequate. To love and value oneself is important; however, in order to effect change, one must recognize oneself as a part of, rather than apart from, the natural world.

"Join the movement": Consumed *(2015)*

The Incredible Shrinking Woman and *Safe* suggest how metaphor might fail us by concealing, rather than revealing; in both films, metaphor is deployed to shift attention away from the toxic chemicals and consumer practices that might result in illness. The failures of metaphor are particularly pronounced in and regarding *Safe,* as several characters as well as several of the film's critics assume that Carol's illness is psychosomatic. Reading Carol as a hysteric, of course, suggests that her symptoms are manifestations of psychological distress rather than reactions to a polluted environment. The failure to acknowledge Carol's illness is itself symptomatic (to use a medical metaphor) of a larger denial of the potential of human industry to have unintended effects on human life.

Pat and Carol, like many American women, seemed to believe the role of housewife was one of dignity, value, and safety. Also like many American women in the late 20th century, however, both Pat and Carol find themselves victims of unintended side effects, casualties to a corporate culture that conceals and dissembles. And again, like many late 20th century American women, Pat and Carol discover that being a housewife is not, in fact, valued or honored. Rather, they find that to their husbands and perhaps to the larger society, they too, like so much of consumer culture, are disposable.

In many respects, *The Incredible Shrinking Woman* and *Safe* reflect a neoliberal dismissal of the medical challenges facing individual women, as they conclude with each protagonist apparently resigned to continued solitary suffering and, in Carol's case, to a dramatic turn inward. The 2015 film *Consumed,* about a mother's struggle to link her son's illness to the existence of genetically modified organisms (GMOs) in foods, follows in the tradition of these films, but departs in its embrace of a turn outward and a call to public action. A Karen Silkwood–type figure, protagonist Sophie (Zoe Lister-Jones), is a working-class single mother who waits tables and goes to college at night.

Sophie becomes alarmed when her son begins developing mysterious allergic reactions, resulting in her visits to doctors, research scientists and finally, the head of "Clonestra," a Monsanto-type corporation. The film's title, "Consumed," thus has multiple implications; it most obviously refers to the foods we ingest or consume. However, the title may also suggest that Sophie has become consumed with her quest for answers. Finally, this quest is doomed to failure, as Americans have been consumed or taken over by a corporate culture that rather than acknowledge harmful or untenable practices, levels the charge of hysteria in order to isolate—and silence—those whose bodies exist of evidence of a problem.

Dramatizing many of the issues surrounding GMO use, *Consumed* is an overtly political film. Filmmaker Daryl Wein[14] is straightforward regarding his attempt deliver a political message: "We wanted to make an entertaining movie while weaving in some of the socio-political issues and we thought the best way to do that was to root it in the average mom who typically goes out to buy the groceries for her family.... We wanted to hit it on several fronts while synthesizing the information so that it was easily digestible—no pun intended!" (D. Miller). Perhaps as a result, *Consumed* participates in the toxic discourse tradition, following many of the same narrative beats described above. In addition to dramatizing "testimonial injustice," or the undermining of an individual's credibility as a "knower" (Fricker 1), the film traces Sophie's "shock of awakened perception" (Buell 43) once she begins to realize that mundane objects may contain hidden dangers. Thus, a scene in a supermarket shows Sophie behaving in the manner Carol attempts to describe during her speech in *Safe*: Sophie is clearly "more aware" and is depicted carefully "reading labels" (*Safe*). Sophie becomes increasingly panicked in the supermarket and flees without buying anything. Another shopper seems to register Sophie as crazy or eccentric; the irony, is of course, that Sophie is not the danger, the otherwise innocuous food is. Finally, *Consumed* includes the dismissal of the alarmed woman as hysterical: Sophie is patronizingly told by a scientist that she is not an "expert" on food science or medicine, a medical doctor says her son's illness is "hysteria," and a corporate representative describes Sophie as a "hysterical mother with a sick son" (*Consumed*).

Although *Consumed* addresses different anxieties and suggests different outcomes than *The Incredible Shrinking Woman* or *Safe*, all three films overlap in important ways. First, Sophie is not strictly a housewife, but her identity as a mother (rather than her identities as employee or student) is clearly primary in the film. Crucially, Sophie's activism originates in a desire to protect her child, a move that re-renders a potentially threatening empowered woman as a self-sacrificing mother. In her review "GMOs are Haunting in the new Thriller *Consumed*," Jaqueline Raposo underlines how the film generates sympathy for Sophie: "Lister-Jones's Sophie is raw and vulnerable, easy to relate to.... She's on a mission not to change the world, but, in an Erin Brockovich–like parallel, simply to fix one flaw in a huge system that will snowball if left in the shadows."

In addition, in *The Incredible Shrinking Woman*, *Safe*, and *Consumed*, the home is contaminated by the introduction of the consumer products that have become so prevalent as to be generally invisible. In *Consumed*, Sophie empties the fridge in frustration, tossing out foods that may potentially contain GMOs, drawing attention to Western consumer ignorance surrounding many foods—where they are from, what's in them, and how they've been modified—an ignorance that is maintained through policies lobbied for by various food industry interests.

On the one hand, *Consumed* suggests that the challenges facing Sophie are insurmountable; on the other, the film seems designed to inspire others to take up Sophie's cause. Despite the disbelieving doctors and Clonestra's menacing agents, Sophie persists, breaking into a lab and, ultimately, obtaining files that prove that the Clonestra is aware of potentially harmful aspects of GMO consumption. Like Pat and Carol, Sophie, armed with damning information, makes a speech near the film's end. Also like the earlier protagonists, Sophie's speech initially seems ineffectual; however, Sophie ultimately reaches a broad audience as her surreptitious recording of a confrontation with the Clonestra CEO goes viral, indicating the increased possibilities of citizen-activism as a result of the Internet. It is noteworthy that of the three films discussed in this chapter, *Consumed* is the only one to appear in a significantly online world. The Internet as an information-sharing vehicle that may empower those who lack traditional power in the form of money or a public platform, of course, is often hailed as one of the most liberating aspects of the web.

Nevertheless, the film's ending indicates that entrenched practices will not be so easy to overturn. Sophie, her boyfriend and their children sit at a football game and the final image is of Sophie's shocked and horrified face as she observes individuals around her eating junk food such as hot dogs and popcorn. This moment reveals that Sophie's victory has not resulted in others' altered eating habits or even increased awareness. Further, her shocked face and still body suggest that she is so overwhelmed as to be unable to act. In one respect, then, this ending suggests a neoliberal return to the private. Individuals, the film suggests, can self-educate and embrace the tenets of personal responsibility, carefully monitoring their own consumption, but a crusade for broad change remains quixotic.

However, the credits are interspersed with information about genetically modified foods as well as clips from news programs. At the very conclusion, the words "Join the movement" and a web address appears on the screen. In this way, then, *Consumed* makes connections beyond itself, suggesting that the film is a starting point for viewers' continued education and potential activism. That the viewer can "join the movement" is an invitation to community and collective action, the like of which appear unavailable to Sophie.

Conclusion: "I'm just a mom": Activism and the Flint Water Crisis

Although not centrally focused on environmental toxins, *Consumed* taps into concerns about the integrity of our homes and kitchens, suggesting a generalized distrust of corporate food as well as the government agencies charged with safeguarding consumer products. In addition, like the *Incredible Shrinking Woman* and *Safe*, the protagonist of *Consumed* may be paired with a real-world counterpart: Lee Ann Walters. Walters, a housewife, mother, and resident of Flint, Michigan, reports that representatives of government and government agencies suggested that she was a "liar" and was "stupid" when she insisted that her children's rashes and hair loss were related to compromised water (Jacobo). For months, state officials were unconcerned with the reported problems in the majority-black city of Flint; a memo from Michigan Governor Rick Snyder's office called the high levels of lead in the water "not a top priority" (Eligon).

Like Carson, Gibbs, and others, Walters was ultimately vindicated, but also like those other women, her victory was bittersweet in that it served to confirm that she and her family would have to deal with the long-term health effects and trauma of being poisoned by their own government. Also like many of the women described in this chapter, Walters centers her maternal identity as well as the home as a sacred site in her appeal for justice. Testifying before the Congressional House Oversight and Government Reform Committee, Walters, who described herself as "Just a mom," enumerated multiple injuries perpetrated against herself and her family, including the ways in which the contamination of the water compromised the integrity of her home: "My home used to be a place of comfort and safety for my family. It used be what a home should be, a place of peace and protection from the outside world. That was taken from us, and not just from my family, but from every home, and every citizen in Flint. Now my home is known as Ground Zero" (Akin). Although Walters' statement takes for granted the idea that a home "should" be distinct from the "outside world," her complaint brings into focus anxieties surrounding the permeability of both the home and the body. In addition, in defining her home as "Ground Zero" Walters evokes the 2001 terrorist bombing of the World Trade Center in New York City. While the term "ground zero" initially referred to the site under or above which an atomic bomb was detonated (Kaplan 83), it became synonymous with the site of the 9/11 attacks. Here, Walters connects the injustice perpetrated against herself and her family with the infamous attacks, implicitly framing the U.S. government, as well as the local Michigan and Flint governments, as terrorists from whom the home is not safe.

Ultimately, each of these narratives reasserts the inextricability of the domestic from the public. Here, as elsewhere, the violation of the private impels the mother to herself participate in the public sphere, forcing her to confront the fiction that the home exists in a vacuum. Rather, the home is and always has been a part of, rather than apart from, the larger culture and, in some ways, replicates and even amplifies the injustices of the larger culture. And within the larger culture, some populations—women, low income people, and people of color—continue to be deemed less valuable than others; some people continue to serve as the canaries in a chemically toxic 21st century. And the canary, of course, might alert others to danger, but will probably perish in the process.

5
"When did he stop treating you like a princess?" Domestic Violence in *Enough* and *Waitress*

The previous chapter discusses threats to the domestic that emerge from outside the home, arguing that despite the myth of a separation between public and private, domestic dynamics often reflect larger cultural values. This chapter investigates a threat that emerges from within the home itself: intimate partner violence. While marriage to an affluent man is often depicted as the ultimate prize for a woman in heteropatriachal society, contemporary media has been forced to reckon with the reality that the marital home may be the most dangerous place for a woman (Finley xx and Garcia-Moreno). In a post–*Feminine Mystique* (1963) world, we are no longer presented with the image of "the housewife as the happiest person on the planet" (Coontz, *Strange Stirring*, 22); perhaps this is in part due to the reality that, in the United States, one in four woman will be victims of their partners' "severe physical violence" ("National Statistics"); between 2001 and 2012 11,766 women were murdered by current or former male partners (Vagianos). Yet while several mainstream and independent films of the late 20th and early 21st centuries, including *The Burning Bed* (1984), *Sleeping with the Enemy* (1991), *Enough* (2002), *Personal Velocity* (2002), *Waitress* (2007), *Precious* (2009), and *Yelling to the Sky* (2011),[1] begin to grapple with violence in the home, too many depictions often recirculate antifeminist agendas, suggesting that victims who avail themselves of legal channels, social safety nets or even the label "victim" are weak, corrupt, or in part to blame for their own victimization.[2]

In this chapter and the next, I review several depictions of domestic violence in order to identify how they engage in larger public discourse about domestic violence.[3] After discussing the continued power of the "fairy tale" of heterosexual romance, I turn to Michael Apted's *Enough*, a film that is in some ways emblematic of Hollywood's treatment of women's issues generally. I argue that despite the overt attempt to render *Enough* a "message" movie or a film that contributes meaningfully to a larger public conversation about domestic violence, *Enough* at once functions as a perversion of the feminist ideas of empowerment, a renunciation of feminism itself, and a reassertion of the naturalness of the patriarchy. Following a discussion of how *Enough* participates in neoliberal postfeminist discourse around domestic violence, I turn to the independent film *Waitress* (2007). Although in some respects departing from well-worn scripts concerning domestic violence, *Waitress* nevertheless reaffirms domestic violence as a personal rather than a political issue and follows *Enough* in the suggestion that protecting her daughter is a woman's most compelling reason to leave an abusive situation (rather than her self-preservation). Finally, both films feature financial rescue by a benevolent patriarch, a move that deflects attention from a lack of effective social or governmental resources available to the protagonist.

Still Going Strong: Troubling the Fairy Tale

In 2016, artist Saint Hoax developed the "Happily Never After" campaign, a series of images each featuring a recognizable Disney heroine (Ariel, Cinderella, Jasmine and Sleeping Beauty) with a battered face, including a black eye or bloody lip, and the caption "When did he stop treating you like a princess?" (Figure 7).[4] Provocative and powerful, Saint Hoax's work links the fairy tale narrative that naturalizes notions of heterosexual marriage as the ultimate goal for women, and injurious patriarchal understandings of romance and womanhood. As Saint Hoax's work suggests and several feminist scholars have noted, patriarchy creates the conditions for a woman's abuse. That is, understandings of women as in need of men's protection and guidance exist on a continuum with understandings of women as childlike, as a man or husband's property, and as appropriately subject to a male's power. In the 2002 film *Enough,* character Ginny puts it this way: "The problem is ... you want a man man. Meaning his veins run thick with testosterone. Which is good ... but then he can just turn around and without any warning he can just hit you." While Ginny seems to suggest that violence is arbitrary ("He can just turn around and ... hit you") she is also indicating that not all men are capable of such violence; it is the "man man" or the hyper-masculine man that women desire who is potentially so volatile.

Ginny's diagnosis may not be inaccurate; while there are several factors

Figure 7. Saint Hoax's "When did he stop treating you like a princess?" part of the *Happily Never After* campaign, SaintHoax.com (courtesy Saint Hoax).

that can lead to violence between individuals in an intimate relationship, men who adhere strictly to conventional gender norms may be at increased risk of behaving violently toward their partners.[5] Additionally, women who have been victims of violence often describe troubling behaviors that, during the initial stages of a romantic relationships, may be interpreted as positive caring. For example, in 1987, Angela Brown interviewed women who had killed their husbands or attempted to; of the study, Meloy and Miller write, "The women ... related that during courtship and early marriage, a husband's jealousy, possessiveness, and control intermingled with and became confused with signs of romantic love. Physical violence usually started after marriage" (60). That control can be "confused" with love begins to indicate the entrenched understandings of traditional masculine and feminine gender roles in many heterosexual relationships.

Thus the question in Saint Hoax's work, "When did he stop treating you like a princess?," suggests a specific trajectory from traditional romance to abuse. And lest one assume that contemporary consumers are immune to the allure of the fairy tale, one need only consider that the images Saint Hoax uses—the Disney princesses—are so powerful precisely because they remain so popular. The fairy tale romance persists.

In particular, the "Cinderella" story, or the story of the virtuous but oppressed young woman who is identified as desirable and swept off her feet by a "prince," continues to inspire remakes, including *Pretty Woman* (1990), *Ever After* (1998), *Cinderella* (2015), and most notably for my purposes, Wayne Wang's *Maid in Manhattan* (2002). In Wang's film, Jennifer Lopez plays Marisa, a Latina hotel maid who is mistaken for an upper-class society woman by a wealthy white politician. He apparently falls in love at (second) sight (he had earlier encountered Marisa when she was cleaning his bathroom, but hadn't noticed her). An uncritical "Cinderella" reboot, *Maid in Manhattan* includes the upper-class male's pursuit of the mystery woman, her appearance, again arrayed as his class-peer,[6] the revelation of her "true" identity, private and public consummation of their love and a suggestion of "happily ever after" through a montage of magazine and tabloid covers, one of which announces that the couple is "still going strong" after a year together[7] (*Maid*).

However, as mentioned above, another Lopez vehicle was released in 2002: Michael Apted's *Enough*. Although generically disparate, *Enough* and *Maid in Manhattan* follow many of the same narrative beats. *Enough* also begins with a Latina in the service industry who is swept off of her feet by a wealthy white male. But while *Maid in Manhattan* culminates with a "fairy tale" ending, *Enough* suggests the perils of "too good to be true": after several years together, protagonist Slim is emotionally and physically abused, menaced, and stalked by her husband, Mitch. *Enough* concludes with Slim battling Mitch and ultimately killing him. Looking at these films together, one can't help but notice the similarities between Marisa and Charles' relationship in *Maid in Manhattan* and Slim and Mitch's: in each, the male's disproportionate social and economic power in the form of racial privilege, prestige, and wealth is at once attractive and dangerous. Will Charles and Marisa's relationship also result in humiliation and abuse?

This comparison raises the question of whether it is simply luck—good or bad—that determines a woman's fate. How can a woman tell the difference between the man who will be a "prince" and the one who will turn out to be an ogre, especially when the two are superficially so similar?

"You're one of the lucky ones": The Fine Line Between the Fairy Tale and the Nightmare

It is noteworthy that "domestic violence" as a concept didn't really exist until second wave feminists campaigned to publicize and criminalize wife battering.[8] In fact, a man's physical violence toward a woman was often played for laughs in popular culture: the opening scene of 1940's *The Philadelphia Story* features Cary Grant shoving his soon-to-be-ex-wife so hard in the face that she falls backwards (she later reconciles with him and they remarry); a 1952 ad for Chase and Sanborn coffee playfully depicts a husband's physical chastisement of his wife (Figure 8).[9] In the 1950s Al Kramden's threats to send his wife "to the moon" with a punch were still considered comedic.

Films begin to deal with male violence with more nuance in the 1970s. In the film *Alice Doesn't Live Here Anymore* (1974), one man's abuse of his wife is depicted as dangerous, scary, and inappropriate; however, later in the film, a different male love interest hits the protagonist's son. While she initially condemns his behavior and the two split up, the movie resolves with their reconciliation, suggesting that patriarchal violence is, to some extent, acceptable. *Raging Bull* (1980) depicts Jake LaMotta's abuse of his wife as contemptible (although LaMotta remains, of course, in some respects celebrated by the film).[10] By 1984, the television film *The Burning Bed* sympathetically portrayed Francine Hughes, a woman who murdered her husband after suffering his abuse for over a decade; the 1980s and 1990s saw an explosion of television movies using domestic violence as a narrative trope.[11]

In 1997, the protagonist of *Good Will Hunting* screams in his girlfriend's face before rearing back and punching the wall next to her head. While this behavior is represented as inappropriate, the scene contextualizes Will's violence, suggesting that he is not a "bad" person, but that the abuse he suffered as a child has led to his inability to engage healthily in a romantic relationship. Perhaps problematically, the film concludes with the promise of the couple's reconciliation. In 2012's *Silver Linings Playbook,* protagonist Pat is released from a psychiatric hospital after brutally beating a man who was having an affair with Pat's wife. Pat's wife has a restraining order against him, yet the film presents Pat not as a potentially dangerous ex-partner, but as a lovable, if disturbed, nice guy.

As this overview suggests, in popular cultural, wife-battering becomes increasingly taboo and depictions often more complex in the second half of the 20th century. By the turn of the 21st century, only a villain would be depicted as unremorsefully violent toward his wife or girlfriend. While this is certainly progress, many critics have noted that the common representation of the wife-batterer as a one-dimensional character or murderous psychopath is not only inaccurate, but suggests that wife-abuse is rare and not part of a

5. "When did he stop treating you like a princess?" 95

Figure 8. This ad positions a wife as, like a child, subject to whatever punishment the patriarch sees fit (Chase & Sanborn coffee advertisement, 1952).

larger epidemic: "A focus on a perpetrator as a social 'outsider' creates the impression that violence against women is a rare action by a deviant individual, rather than the widespread social problem as measured by global crime victim surveys" (Devries, Mak, Garcia-Moreno, et al. qtd. in Easteal, Holland, and Keziah).

In *Enough*, Mitch is an irredeemable monster; Slim simply has the bad luck to have crossed his path. After beating and threatening Slim, Mitch stalks her, cuts off her access to money, and plots to take their daughter, Gracie. In some respects, *Enough* participates in the "rape-and-revenge" genre, a staple of horror films, which trace a woman's victimization followed by her systematic retributive violence.[12] (Strictly speaking, however, there is no depiction of rape in *Enough*, although of course the threat exists.) Instead, *Enough* is superficially a feminist film about female empowerment, illustrating a trend that Kim A. Loudermilk has observed in much contemporary literature and film directed at women which "contains and recuperates feminist politics" (13). *Enough* demonstrates mainstream engagement with some fundamental feminist concepts, such as the abuse of women in the home and the inadequacy of social services to support battered women, at the same time that these critiques serve to shore up the overarching message of the film that if you can't beat 'em, join 'em. That is, patriarchy is inescapable and a woman's most effective strategy is to embrace the (toxic) masculine ideals of the larger culture.

Enough presents domestic violence as a private issue, de-politicizing Slim's narrative and reaffirming the thinking that a man's violence against his wife or girlfriend is not part of a larger public health epidemic or even, at the very least, a women's issue which should be addressed through governmental means. Indeed, even the title "Enough" suggests that Slim's ability to leave her marriage is not contingent on a web of support and resources, but most immediately on her decision that she has had "enough" of the abuse and will no longer tolerate it.

Throughout, *Enough* wavers—at times gesturing to a larger political context but always returning the central conflict to the private sphere. For example, the film initially suggests that all women may be vulnerable to the "fairy tale" mystique or to men's deceit. By opening with the words "how they met," the film cues the audience to expect the unfolding of a romance narrative. A white male, played by Noah Wyle, sits holding a rose in a booth at the diner where Slim works, leading the viewer to initially believe that he and Slim will comprise the "they" of the first title. But Wyle's character, Robbie, is actually involved in an elaborate scheme with Mitch, whom Slim has not yet met. The plot involves Mitch pretending to expose Robbie as having made a crude bet that he could seduce Slim, a trick from which Mitch emerges looking like a decent guy. The scheme has the desired effect and Slim pursues Mitch. Even before the audience (and Slim) learns that Mitch was in on the scheme all along, the opening immediately suggests that both Slim and the viewer are vulnerable to mistaken first impressions and to the allure of old-fashioned romance (as represented by Robbie). Further, that Mitch emerges as the love interest underscores Slim (and perhaps the viewer's) susceptibility to narratives dependent on heroine's rescue by the "knight in shining armor" or the brave and pure-hearted hero (as represented by Mitch).

In this way, the first scene of *Enough* begins to engage in a critique of heteronormative romance. In addition, the film foregrounds how those characteristics of Mitch's that make him "successful" and attractive, including his intelligence, his tenacity, and his strength, are also the characteristics which will make him such an effective batterer. For example, immediately after their wedding, a scene depicts Mitch and Slim visiting a suburban home. Mitch offers to buy the house from the surprised and unwilling homeowner. The homeowner remarks, "You're crazy," and Mitch responds, "Think how miserable one determined, crazy person can make you." While Mitch successfully secures the home—making Slim very happy—his words, of course, eerily foreshadow his later persecution of Slim. "Determined" and "crazy" are possibly positive qualities if someone is working in your interest, but undeniably frightening if the individual wants to harm you.

The largest deception is perhaps the "lie" of equality that Slim—and many contemporary women, it would seem—have bought into. First, in moving quickly through Slim and Mitch's first years of marriage and the arrival of their daughter Gracie, *Enough* gestures to Mitch's marital deceptions. Close-ups of Slim after the birth of her child or during a family trip to the beach often include a passing look of concern before Slim is shown smiling again, suggesting that Slim may have suspicions that all is not as perfect as it seems. However, Slim's predicament is fully revealed when the sanctity of the home itself is jeopardized and Slim is forced to confront the reality that her ostensibly perfect life is predicated on her ignorance of this inequality. Foregrounded by the positioning of Slim in the family kitchen when she first discovers Mitch's infidelity and, in a later scene, when Mitch first strikes her, Slim apparently learns that what she thought was a choice—being an agreeable and accommodating housewife—is in fact compulsory; Mitch will not countenance a challenge to his authority. She is literally kept in her place—the kitchen—both times she attempts to object to Mitch's behavior. On the first occasion, Mitch's beeper is shown as insistently buzzing on the kitchen counter. Slim looks guilty as she picks it up, but proceeds to dial the number on Mitch's cell phone. The scene suggests that Mitch's deceit is impossible to ignore when it inserts itself into Slim's space.

The second time Slim confronts Mitch and the first time he hits her also take place in the kitchen. After accusing Mitch of continuing his infidelity, Slim retreats to the stove and stirs something in a pot. She claims, "you can't do this to me" before coming out from behind the counter. Mitch strikes Slim and asks, "I can't hit you?" She defiantly responds, "No, you can't" and he strikes her even harder. He goes on to coldly explain, "I make the rules" and tells Slim that abuse and domination "is the price you pay for having such a good life."

This scene reveals that while Slim believed that her relationship was predicated on mutual respect and equality, Mitch instead sees their marriage as an exchange. The placement of these scenes in the home's kitchen suggest that even that which Slim assumes "belongs" to her, including the home, her child, and her own body, are in fact, in Mitch's understanding, his property to do with as he wishes. In response to Mitch's demand that Slim remain in *his* home, Slim runs away. Much of the remainder of the film is concerned with Slim trying to survive while she is literally and existentially homeless.

Thus, violence against wives and mothers is also presented as resulting in a displacement and self-alienation and in this way, Slim is not only forced to flee her home, but to grapple with a threat to her identity. Slim tells Ginny that she is "not a person whose husband beats her up."[13] While perhaps reflective of the feelings of many victims who find that trauma affects their sense of self, Slim's remark nevertheless casts domestic violence victims as "others." Thus, when Ginny suggests that Slim go to a domestic violence shelter, Slim rejects the proposal, saying that she cannot bring her daughter Gracie, as Gracie has not been "tainted." While many shelters could certainly be improved with regard to providing a safe, supportive environment for victims and their children, the notion that going to a shelter will somehow contaminate a child, rendering her less-pure, not only forwards classist assumptions about the "type" of people who might need to be in a shelter, but sends the overarching message that those who would bring their children to shelters are themselves poor parents who corrupt their children by exposing them to the pain of others or who fail to suffer out of their children's sight.

In addition to depicting Slim's rejection of the shelter as a reasonable parenting choice, *Enough* suggests that Slim is different or unlike other victims. At the film's conclusion, after Slim has killed Mitch, a police officer wryly remarks, "you're one of the lucky ones." That being one of the "lucky ones" entails surviving (but only after being beaten and stalked and having to kill the father of your children) is perhaps not inaccurate, but outrageous nevertheless. While the officer's remark connects Slim's abuse to a larger epidemic of violence against women, it does so only barely as no other vicitimized women besides Slim appear in *Enough*. Further, Slim is only "lucky" in that she is able to personally overcome her abuser's attempts at control and domination. As a result, while *Enough* is ostensibly meant to reveal the brutal realities of domestic violence, the film too often places Slim's story in a political vacuum; race and class privilege are rarely acknowledged and police or governmental agencies designed to support victims of intimate partner violence are either not presented or dismissed as ineffectual. Speaking to a police officer early in the film, Slim asks if a woman should "throw the order of protection" at her abuser if he were to violate it. While Slim's observation that police often inadequately protect endangered women is important, this is the only attempt in the whole film to engage law enforcement. In order to establish the necessity of Slim's violence, the film thus invalidates those systems that do exist.

"You've really screwed yourself": Neoliberalism in Enough

While perhaps Slim is lucky to have survived, the overall point of the film is that after having had "enough," after being beaten, economically disenfranchised, and stalked, in addition to seeing her friends harassed and abused, Slim chooses to empower herself. Her female body is what has rendered her vulnerable, and the reshaping of her body will be her primary tool for and most visible evidence of her subsequent empowerment. This is a dangerous message, of course, in its implication that first, women who remain in abusive relationships have simply not yet had "enough" and second, that women should take matters into their own hands and get revenge against their batterers. *Enough* resolves its narrative crisis through the cooption and reinterpretation of second-wave radical feminists' vision of domestic equality watered down into a liberal/postfeminist understanding of female empowerment as predicated on self-defense and retributive violence. In this thinking, we don't need increased education about domestic violence, or increased commitment to social safety nets for victims; we need more women to take martial arts classes.

A turning point of the film occurs when Slim, desperate after Mitch finds her in hiding and assaults her, goes to see a lawyer. After Slim explains her situation, the lawyer rather smugly responds, "I hope you derived pleasure, because you've really screwed yourself." While delivered by a minor character in a scene that seems to exist primarily to justify Slim's violent actions, this bizarrely inappropriate metaphor is nevertheless outrageously offensive: it includes a sexual pun, the implication that Slim's lack of action in the face of abuse was somehow masturbatory or pleasurable, and concludes that Slim is ultimately without legal or social recourse. These remarks, which basically blame the victim, are presented as neutral observations about reality.

And while the lawyer is depicted as a relatively kind character, his ultimate indifference to Slim is consistent with the world of *Enough,* which is populated by cruel, cold, violent men. While there are a handful of positive male characters—including Slim's old-boyfriend/romantic interest, Joe, and her surrogate father, Phil—Mitch, Robbie, Jupiter, and Mitch's fearsome henchmen suggest the inescapability of patriarchy. In fact, it is only through her embrace of patriarchy and the apparent masculinization of her body and mind that Slim can survive.

Slim's biological father, Jupiter—whose name of course calls to mind the Roman god—abandoned Slim and her mother when she was a child (we learn that he has several children that he has not cared for). A desperate Slim approaches Jupiter to ask him for money, itself a symbolic capitulation to the patriarchy in that earlier Slim had denounced Jupiter. A playboy millionaire, he is initially unmoved by Slim's plea. However, after he is threatened by some of Mitch's men, Jupiter has his "interest" piqued. In this way, again, *Enough* draws upon the fairy tale tradition, in which the unfairly oppressed young woman is assisted by a magical elder. Like a fairy godmother, Jupiter tracks Slim down and sends her money, suggesting that there is now an endless reserve of cash at Slim's disposal. Notably, it is a threat from another man, or a challenge to Jupiter's power and masculinity that motivates his action. In addition, later, Jupiter's resources enable Slim to pull off what appears to be magic, securing a last-minute Slim look-alike decoy to trick Mitch.

In addition to availing herself of the resources Jupiter provides, Slim uses gender stereotypes in order to outsmart Mitch. Just as Slim believes that Robbie is a "bad" guy and Mitch a good one in the opening scenes, Slim tricks Mitch into believing she is naïve and helpless. He doesn't believe that she is capable of manipulation, plotting, and physical violence and yet it is through using each of these tactics that she is able to ultimately defeat him. Thus, Slim plays stupid and calls Mitch's mother from a phone, pretending she is unaware that Mitch will be able to track her. In addition, her strategy for a final confrontation with Mitch in his home is based on the assumption that Mitch will underestimate her.

Slim's victory is a reclamation of the home. Although Mitch is living in a new house—one perhaps meant to reflect a masculine taste in its use of concrete and metal design—Slim breaks in and turns the domestic against Mitch, hiding his guns, manipulating the electrical panel, and blocking the phone lines. She plants letters that he will touch when looking for his guns in order to make it seem as though the two of them had planned a meeting so that her presence in the house will be later justified.

In addition to penetrating the home and re-engineering it for her own ends, Slim has also transformed herself in preparation for the confrontation. Without any explanatory context, the film shows Slim training with a large, African American, hyper-masculine Krav Maga instructor, yet another almost-magical figure who will indoctrinate Slim into the world of male power. Throughout the training montage, the instructor provides Slim with inspiration and advice. His final lesson, which of course becomes relevant at the end of the film, is that Slim must realize that if she is on the floor and apparently beaten, "As sure as he is a coward, [Mitch] will try to kick you." Thus, as a result of the instructor's insights, Slim is ultimately able to anticipate Mitch's action, something she was clearly not able to do from the very first scene in the film. When Mitch rears back to kick her, Slim uses his own momentum and violence against him, literally and metaphorically pulling his legs out from under him.

One of the pleasures of *Enough* is watching the hubristic villain realize he has been outwitted and about to perish; further, the notion that one might take back what is hers or resist domestic violence by reclaiming and reshaping one's own body as an instrument against oppression is potentially feminist, particularly in its rejection of oppression as the price of the "fairytale" of suburban affluence. However, the solution the film offers to a real-life problem is unsustainable and borderline offensive, particularly as the vast majority of women do not have the resources, such as Jupiter's money and the Krav Maga's instructor's expertise, that Slim has access to. As Cristina Lucia Stasia points out in "Wham! Bam! Thank You Ma'am: The New Public/Private Female Action Hero," at the end of *Enough*, Slim "is repositioned firmly within the private sphere—and in her 'proper' place as wife and mother ... the reincorporation of the female action hero within traditional familial and domestic paradigms functions to mitigate the threat of her action" (180). Stasia continues, "self-defense does nothing to affect the institutional structures that maintain violence against women" (181).

Depicting physically abusive relationships as the outcome of bad luck, suggesting that women have little to no legal or social recourses when they are being abused, and celebrating the female victim's embrace of manipulation and violence as empowering, the film suggests that the patriarchy itself is inescapable. That Slim can only survive if she beats Mitch—literally and metaphorically—at his own game reaffirms the notion that equality for women is only truly achievable through an embrace of conventional masculinity. A similar concept emerges in the 2005 film *Mr. and Mrs. Smith*, which features married assassins engaged in a fight-to-the death. Depicting stars Angelina Jolie and Brad Pitt as the titular couple, the film revels in the ostensible equality of males and females as neither participant pulls any punches: scenes depict John choking and kicking Jane and Jane punching John in the face and breaking bottles against his head. Equality, then, is presented as women's rights to be just as vile and violent as men have often been. Unfortunately, this fantasy of equality participates in the misperception of gender parity in domestic violence, the popular but incorrect notion that women abuse men just as much as men abuse women.[14]

Dangerously perverting feminist ideals, films such as *Enough* and *Mr. and Mrs. Smith* propose violent masculinity as a means to equality for women. Notably, violent women and women who kill their husbands and partners often serve longer prison terms than men who kill women.[15] Embracing violent masculinity, one might conclude, is only a solution in the movies.

"Dear baby": Motivating Motherhood

Enough suggests that motherhood and the desire to protect one's children function to motivate women to leave abusive relationships. The notion that a woman is most valuable as a mother is apparent in Slim's attempts to protect Gracie not only from Mitch but also from the corrupting influence of the domestic violence shelter. Adrienne Shelley's 2007 film *Waitress*, like *Enough*, suggests that domestic violence is a private problem. Rather than through the embrace of masculinity, however, *Waitress* suggests that violence in the home is most appropriately overcome by a (re)commitment to maternal identity and responsibility. In addition, like *Enough*, *Waitress*'s conclusion relies on the intervention of benevolent patriarch who will enable the protagonist to overcome seemingly insurmountable obstacles.

Waitress is heir to *Alice Doesn't Live Here Anymore* (and its spin-off television program, *Alice*, which ran from 1976–1985): the protagonist is a working-class woman whose true passions lie elsewhere; her friends are the other waitresses, including a wisecracking blonde and her more mousey counterpart; their boss is unpleasant, but not unkind. Also like the earlier film, *Waitress* explores the heroine's attempt to succeed in an inhospitable world. While Alice's husband dies early in the film and in the television series (forcing her to "make it on her own" as the television show's theme song puts it), Jenna (Kerri Russell) in *Waitress* is trapped in an emotionally and physically abusive marriage to her husband Earl. Despite its inclusion of Earl's violence and intimidation, the film attempts to remain somewhat lighthearted. As a result, Jenna's decision to stay or to leave an abusive relationship is rendered as just another lifestyle choice. That is, Jenna is clearly in crisis, but a crisis more akin to a young person's ennui and metaphorical paralysis than the life-threatening situations depicted in *Enough*.

In keeping with the overall quirky tone of the film, Earl's treatment of his wife is upsetting but not monstrous. He hits and shoves Jenna, threatens her and demeans her, but his physical abuse always stops short of injury. In addition, although Jenna claims her pregnancy occurs as a result of "Earl getting me drunk that night," his coercive sex is never presented as rape. Finally, Earl's emotional abuse manifests as almost-comic insensitivity: he often tells the pregnant Jenna she is "fat" and seems oblivious to the disgust and disappointment almost constantly registering on Jenna's face.

Some of Earl's most extreme behavior is his control of the finances. In one of the more dramatic scenes, Earl finds money Jenna has hidden. In a rage, he corners Jenna against a kitchen counter and demands, "Tell me you were gonna buy me a present." This is the clearest expression of the form of Earl's abuse: he tells Jenna who to be, how to be, and what to think. Here, his control manifests as literally telling her what to say. That this scene takes place in the kitchen again suggests the vulnerability of the wife in a space that is supposedly her seat of power. Like Mitch in *Enough*, Earl reminds Jenna that he is the primary provider; Earl also demands that Jenna surrender the money she earns at the restaurant. It is as a result of Jenna's economic instability that she feels she cannot leave Earl. Thus, upon discovering that she is pregnant, Jenna declares, "I ain't never gonna get away from Earl now."

While much of the setting and background apparatus of *Waitress* make clear that this is a contemporary film (Earl buys a video camera in preparation for the baby's birth; Jenna has a sonogram), the film nevertheless conjures a nostalgic fantasy of a pre-women's movement world and depends heavily on classist stereotypes about Southerners. Thus, although Jenna insists she does not want to become a parent, refuses to be congratulated upon her pregnancy, calls herself the "anti-mother" and at one point floats the idea of selling the child once it is born, abortion is never presented as an option. Similarly, Jenna never considers seeking legal or governmental help. Even her obstetrician, Dr. Pomatter, with whom Jenna is having an affair, fails to counsel her to leave her abusive relationship. Instead, the only viable escape for Jenna is presented as winning the prize money in a pie-baking contest, suggesting that it through her superiority at a traditionally feminine activity that Jenna might be able to overcome her circumstances.

Throughout the film, although Jenna thinks about, discusses, and makes plans to leave (particularly as these plans relate to the contest), she seems constantly thwarted by events, including her pregnancy and Earl's discovery of the money she has been hiding in the house. Her daughter's birth, however, has an almost mystical effect on Jenna, as upon having the child placed in her arms, Jenna has an apparent epiphany. Immediately after Jenna is handed the baby, a shot of Dr. Pomatter and Earl from Jenna's perspective shows them falling out of focus. The angle changes and the figures of Dr. Pomatter and Earl stand, blurred, in the foreground, framing a sharp image of Jenna and the infant in the middle of the screen. The males have become irrelevant. Emboldened, Jenna rejects Earl, telling him that she wants a divorce and threatening to "flatten" his "sorry ass" if he comes near her again. Earl is depicted as objecting and as being forcibly removed from the room; his voice, however, has now been silenced and he is drowned out by the musical soundtrack.

The film clearly suggests that Jenna's focus and priorities have fundamentally shifted. She calls her daughter Lulu the "love of my life," suggesting a replacement of romantic love with maternal love. This is underscored a few scenes later when Jenna breaks off her relationship with Dr. Pomatter. In addition, Jenna's ability to create a female-only family is facilitated by a check from the restaurant owner (and Jenna's customer), Joe, who dies and leaves her a large sum of money with a note reads which reads, "To my only friend. Start fresh."

Waitress concludes with the image of Jenna and her daughter, Lulu, walking down a country road together, holding hands, waving back at Jenna's waitressing friends. This ending suggests the importance of sustaining female community and celebrates the survivor. It is worth noting that Jenna does not run off with Dr. Pomatter and that the film does not rely upon the promise of future romance to suggest that Jenna is happy.

That she is now a successful business owner and happy single mother is certainly a hopeful message, but this ending is problematic in several ways. First, that Earl simply disappears after Jenna tells him off is a pleasant fantasy, but is a fantasy nevertheless, as statistically, the most dangerous time for a woman in an abusive relationship is when she is trying to leave ("What Happens When the Abusive Relationship Ends?"). It seems unlikely that Earl would not seek to reassert his dominance, to punish Jenna directly, or to punish her indirectly through asserting a claim to their child. In addition to a controlling and abusive husband who apparently walks away from his wife and daughter without much fuss, the film depicts Jenna as able to escape suffering any post-traumatic stress. Finally, the money Joe bequeaths to Jenna apparently enables her to enter and win the pie competition, and this in turn financially enables her to get divorced, establish a new home for herself and her daughter, and open her own business. This seems like a fairy tale indeed.

Joe's bestowal of money to Jenna again functions as a contemporary *deus ex machina*, an improbable stroke of good luck. That Jenna has always been kind to Joe suggests a sort of karmic reward; however, more important is that she had confided in Joe that Earl was a "bad husband" and here, Joe's action suggests an intervention which is also a form of competition. Jenna's autonomy thus must be granted to her by a man; her freedom is predicated on another man recognizing her need for it and making it possible. The recurrence of this narrative trope suggests that while the figure of knight-in-shining armor who rescues the damsel in distress has become passé, in contemporary film, he has perhaps been replaced by the benevolent patriarch who economically "rescues" the heroine.

Crucially, the central predicament for the protagonist in each of the films discussed here is in fact her economic instability. In both, the heroine is working class and/or financially dependent on her husband; in both, her ability to leave her husband is compromised because she lacks resources. As a result, she is forced to leave the home and is thus displaced. While economic exploitation is a reality in many abusive relationships, the introduction of the male benefactor allows these films to sidestep this important issue. Additionally, the repeated depiction of poor women as those who cannot immediately leave abusive relationships buttresses the myths that affluent women can easily leave abusive relationships and/or that affluent women are not abused.

Perhaps the character of Joe functions allegorically as a representative of the role many believe the government plays: old, white, male and out-of-touch, ostensibly uncaring, but in fact deeply compassionate. In this interpretation, both Joe in *Waitress* and Jupiter in *Enough* suggest that women aren't or don't actually have to do it on their own, that the neoliberal imperative to "personal responsibility" is of course flawed, at least when a woman is oppressed and abused by her husband. The recurrence of this character, however, may also simply suggest that even in films that purport to describe women becoming empowered, that empowerment is predicated on the kindness of a patriarch. A woman can leave her husband as long as, at least symbolically, she returns to the father.

Conclusion: More Than Enough

The feminist movements of the 1970s through the '90s make it possible for *Enough* and *Waitress*, films that highlights male violence against women and gesture to the failures of institutional resources, to exist. Further, the films advocate for, in Ginny's words, a "divine animal right to protect your own life and the life of your offspring." However, *Enough*'s ostensibly empowering message of individual retribution undermines core feminist values. As Rebecca Stringer notes in "From Victim to Vigilante: Gender, Violence, and Revenge in *The Brave One* (2007) and *Hard Candy* (2005)," "Lone vigilantism is the very opposite of the actual strategies advocated in feminist anti-violence efforts, which have primarily assumed the form of collective political struggle and non-violent direct action, in the making of campaigns for public visibility, law reform, and resources for challenging a spectrum of forms of gendered violence, including rape, child sexual abuse, and spousal violence" (280).

Similarly, *Waitress*' endorsement of a good-natured wait-and-see approach to an intolerable marriage begins to suggest that domestic violence in and of itself really isn't all that bad. That is, Jenna tolerates Earl's abuse and boorishness and only leaves when she feels a calling to protect her daughter. Both of these films, of course, indicate that the only real reason for a woman to leave is the protection of her child. It is notable, too, that in both of these films, the child is a daughter; one wonders if a mother taking a son and leaving her husband would be so uncritically accepted, as many voices often call for the importance of the father-son relationship.

These films exist in a media environment already rife with misconceptions about violence in the home. In "Enduring Themes and Silences in Media Portrayals of Violence Against Women," Patricia Easteal, Kate Holland and

Judd Keziah argue that "news media and popular culture may provide (or not) members of the public with knowledge to understand (however poorly) violence against women and the correlating complex social, legal and political issues." Elsewhere, Easteal and Carline observe that "safety campaigns and messages directed at informing women about strategies to avoid being a victim of male violence can inadvertently work to obscure the reality that 'the vast amount of abuse women suffer takes place within the home.' They can also construct avoidance of violence as the responsibility of women, as opposed to perpetrators, and unwittingly perpetuate victim-blaming attitudes" (258). In the suggestion that it is the battered woman—not her husband or society—that needs to change, these films enact "avoidance of violence" as the victim's responsibility.

The next chapter discusses films that resist many of the offensive and damaging concepts re-circulated in *Enough* and *Waitress,* but the legacy of these films remains. *Enough* may recede into irrelevance despite Lopez's celebrity; in "The Representation of Domestic Violence in Popular English-Language Cinema," Duncan Wheeler maintains that *Enough* "has the dubious honour of being, perhaps, the least accomplished and most ridiculous film ever released on the subject of domestic violence" (170). *Waitress,* however, has been adapted into a popular Broadway musical. In addition, these films that reinforce the postfeminist neoliberal valorization of independence and resistance to governmental intervention precede a decade in which we can anticipate further slashes to services designed to educate and prevent violence in the home as well as to support survivors ("NCDVA Denounces President Trump's FY'19 Budget Request"). The fairy tale of the benevolent patriarch remains just that: a fairy tale.

PART II: HOPE

6
"Little boys don't get to go around anymore hurting little girls": Evolving Depictions of Domestic Violence

The previous chapter discusses two early 21st century films that incorporate feminist thinking about intimate partner violence—most notably that it is intolerable and unacceptable—at the same time as these films propose unsustainable and even offensive responses to this pressing problem, including that women should become more like men (*Enough*) or they should persevere until a workable solution presents itself (*Waitress*). These films reflect a growing awareness of the problem of violence in the home and a desire for "happy endings" in which the protagonist is able to escape and/or overcome her violent husband. Both films' endings, however, rely on a benevolent patriarch's financial rescue of the abused woman.

Enough and *Waitress* thus reflect a neoliberal postfeminist ideology that emphasizes the importance of personal responsibility and action over social safety nets and systemic analysis. However, these depictions may also indicate the problematic nature of many of the social and legal services that do exist ostensibly to assist and support women in abusive relationships.[1] That is, although second-wave feminists succeeded in not only raising awareness of the problem of domestic violence but also in using grassroots networks to establish shelters for battered women, the feminist anti-violence movement was radically altered as it became "part of the apparatus of the regulatory state" (Bumiller 5). As Kristin Bumiller observes in *In an Abusive State: How Neoliberalism Appropriated the Feminist Movement Against Sexual Violence* (2008), these practices thus "promote *problematic* state control over the disrupted lives of victims" and "strategies employed to help victims of sexual violence are narrowly focused on individualistic forms of solving problems rather than seeking a more comprehensive understanding of this phenomenon or counteracting other forms of domination in women's private and public lives" (ital. orig. xiv). In fact, as a result of their experiences with criminal and social justice bureaucracies, many abused women report feeling victimized not only by their abusers, but also by the state (97, 120, 123). Further, Bumiller contends, the feminist anti-sexual violence campaign's inadequate understandings of the "racialization of rape" or the way the threat of a rape-accusation has been used to control black men has contributed to a racist criminal justice system (10) which disproportionately incarcerates men of color.

Thus, depictions of therapeutic solutions to domestic violence in the media are lacking, but perhaps that lack is indicative of women's not-unfounded wariness of some of these institutions and systems. In this chapter, I continue a discussion of domestic violence in popular culture, turning toward nuanced and complex depictions, including those found in the films *Personal Velocity* (2002), *Madea's Family Reunion* (2006) and the first season of the HBO mini-series *Big Little Lies* (2017). Each of these narratives grapples with the obstacles that face women in abusive relationships as well as the difficulties many women may have leaving and constructing lives free of violence. Each reflects and contributes to the continuing cultural conversation about violence in the home as well as imaginable responses to such violence. The identification of repeated tropes—including the lack of viable social systems to assist abused women—allows us to gauge cultural attitudes about domestic violence—its victims and its perpetrators—as well as areas in which writers, directors, and producers are incorporating complexity, sensitivity, and political consciousness. While discussions are not meant to serve as an ideological litmus test, the texts under consideration in this chapter move beyond some of the more facile treatments identified in the previous chapter, instead demonstrating a more full engagement with public discourse around violence in the home. Just as domestic violence does not occur in a vacuum, neither do representations of domestic violence.

"Let me explain": Personal Velocity *as a Genealogy of Violence*

Rebecca Miller's independent film *Personal Velocity: Three Portraits*[2] was released in 2002, the same year as Michael Apted's *Enough,* a film which depicts a battered woman who plots and trains in order to overcome—and ultimately murder—her abuser. The first of the three vignettes in *Personal Velocity*, "Delia" tells the story of a woman, Delia (Kyra Sedgwick), also trying to escape a physically abusive relationship. Although, like *Enough*, "Delia" constructs domestic violence as an issue that the victim must deal with privately, the narrative also explores the complexities of women's physical autonomy. If Slim in *Enough* has to transform herself, or become a physical aggressor, in order to overcome abuse, Delia must reclaim her body and reconcile the division between her body and self that has arisen from living as a female in patriarchy. Rather than suggesting that perpetrators of domestic violence are rare psychopaths best overcome through retributive violence, *Personal Velocity* explores the larger systems that may facilitate domestic violence, including the exploitation of girls and women more generally, as well as more viable—and more feminist—responses to battering.

Delia, like Slim, is initially presented as not the kind of "person whose husband beats her up" (*Enough*) as the film opens with a male narrator's voice-over explaining that Delia is a "tough" woman: "She beat up a guy in a bar once for grabbing her ass. He hit her back and she broke a chair over his head" (*Personal Velocity*). Delia is thus initially presented as a woman who will brook no male disrespect and who, in fact, is the physical equal to a man in a fight. Further, Delia is also clearly positioned as in-control in her domestic space. She is shown in the kitchen, standing at the sink and looking out the window at her husband and son playing catch in the yard. She authoritatively hollers, "Supper. Now." With this introduction, it is thus shocking when, a few moments later, after Delia looks at her husband with slight disapproval, he grabs her by the back of her hair. There is a freeze frame before the husband, Kurt, slams Delia's head into the table and the narrator interjects, "Wait. Let me explain. Delia's father, Pete Shunt, was the first hippie in Catskill, New York." The seemingly unrelated description of Delia's father as a "hippie" allows the narrator to sketch out Delia's childhood with her eccentric, abusive father.

This introduction suggests that even women who present as "tough" or in control are susceptible to domestic violence. In addition, establishing Delia as a powerful force, at least to her children and outside of her own home, results in the necessity of the narrator's assertion that he can and must "explain" Delia's abuse, indicating an awareness of incongruity and implying that narrative context or an understanding of Delia's background can render abuse, on some level, comprehensible.[3] While nothing in Delia's past seems a specific "cause," the narrator's plea, "let me explain," suggests that the series of exploitations, abuses, indignities, and marginalizations that Delia experienced have led her to expect and tolerate mistreatment.

The film traces Delia's childhood with a father who "occasionally" hit her mother, her mother's abandonment, Delia's alienation from her pubescent body, her use of her sexuality as a teenager, and her marriage to Kurt, who "couldn't stand the idea of any other guy with his hands on Delia, her ass especially.... Delia could stop traffic with that ass. So he married it." That Kurt marries "it," rather than *her*, fragments Delia, her "ass" functioning synecdochally to represent her person. The emphasis on the body presents the undeniability of domestic violence as predicated on objectification of and contempt for women. Her husband's desire to marry Delia's "ass" then, further operates as a form of control and ownership, as well as reflects his participation in heterosexual romance as a form of homosocial competition, as Kurt "couldn't stand the idea of any other guy with his hands on Delia, her ass especially."

Delia's crisis is rooted in her acceptance of her body's objectification and fragmentation. The narrator explains that when she first developed breasts she "felt separated from them" and that she "became the school slut" in part because she enjoyed kissing. As a girl deemed a "slut," Delia learns that she can either be exploited or exploit. Not unlike Slim in *Enough*, Delia embraces the masculine ideals that would otherwise oppress. Thus, the narrator declares that as a sexual being Delia "learned to love her power. It was her vocation."

Thus, while Delia seems to believe she is in control—in her young adult sexual relationships as well as perhaps as an adult—she is consistently revealed as defined and dominated by men. Crucially, it is Delia's maternal identity that provides her with the impetus and power to leave Kurt, to reclaim herself and reconcile these fragments. The narrator explains that, "it was her kids' pain that finally broke through her inertia. Listening to her babies screaming and pleading." The camera cuts to an image of one of her children standing fearfully in a corner. A few moments later, we are told that Delia "imagined going back to Kurt" as she is presented gazing at him asleep on the couch. However, the narrator continues, "this time her body wouldn't follow." In this way, Delia's escape is presented as involuntary; it is the division of body and mind, her alienation from herself, that contains the seeds of her liberation. The abused body rebels.

"I fucking love it here": Survival and Ambivalence in "Delia"

"Delia" is a significant departure from many domestic violence narratives in several respects, including that the vignette does not feature the batterer as a crucial figure. Although Delia remains fearful of him, Kurt's experiences and motivations are not explored—the narrator never interjects to try to "explain" Kurt—and once Delia leaves him, Kurt does not appear again. In addition, the film pursues Delia's attempts to reassemble her life after leaving the abusive home, a crucial aspect of a survivor's story that, as discussed above, is often neglected in media depictions.

The second half of the vignette explores Delia's stay at a domestic violence shelter, her reconnection with a childhood acquaintance and her potentially problematic re-embrace of her own sexual power. Like many media handlings of women fleeing abuse, there is no mention of law enforcement in "Delia." However, Delia does take her children to a shelter, itself a rare sight in mass media. The shelter is portrayed as unattractive, noisy, and a bit sad. Delia, the narrator says, "intimidated the other women with her silence" and he goes on to explain that she was "just being careful…. She felt the women's pain and uncertainty like a vortex pulling her into her own muddled thinking." Here, the narrator justifies Delia's holding herself apart from the other women as self-protection: Delia perhaps fears that connecting with other women will activate her own "pain and uncertainty."

In addition, the shelter scene begins to suggest the difficulties faced by a victimized and traumatized woman, as well as to resist romanticization of the role of community or social services. As Bumiller suggests, many "battered women and rape victims face perilous encounters with the penal/welfare system as an ancillary condition of their protection" (130), systems which insist on compliance with therapeutic professionals (131). In "Delia," Delia is aggressively rude to a social worker, Pam, whom Delia apparently sees as smug and self-righteous. When Pam tells Delia "We all have problems," Delia retorts, "You ever been in love with a man who hits you?" and "Do you have any kids?" Pam's answers—no—seem to confirm for Delia that Pam is incapable of understanding or sympathizing with Delia. When the social worker passive-aggressively informs Delia that she can stay at the shelter as long as she needs to, Delia replies wryly, "Great. I fucking love it here." In this way, the film outlines the ways in which the shelter system is necessary and important, but may nevertheless remain inadequate to the task of truly allowing women to escape and heal from abuse.

As an alternative, the vignette proposes the importance of support and of female allyship. Delia, desperate for a place to stay, contacts an old-acquaintance, Faye. The narrator explains that "Faye had been an outcast like Delia, but in a different category." Images of a teenaged Delia show her pushing a boy who is harassing "Fat Faye," and the narrator states in a voice-over that Delia hadn't liked Faye in high school, but that she had "felt protective of her." This moment suggests that persecution by males—whether bullying harassment or sexual exploitation—is a shared experience for these two girls and Delia's choice to protect Faye suggests, if not solidarity, at least recognition of that shared oppression. While the relationship between Delia and Faye is presented as tense and not a tenable long-term solution—at one point, as Faye passive-aggressively cleans the space that Delia's family is staying in, Delia self-deprecatingly remarks, "Don't bother trying to show you're better than me. I mean, shit, look at me"—this resolution, this momentary stay that allows Delia to get a job and to begin to create a life without her husband, suggests the importance of female community and support.

The film ends with Delia relenting to the advances of a "greasy" young man who constantly harasses her; she aggressively gives him a hand-job, amazing him, and seemingly providing Delia with a sense of her own old power. The scene is intensely uncomfortable to watch as Delia's behavior seems almost predatory, raising the question of whether or not Delia's exploitation has resulted in her exploitation of others. Is this, like *Enough*, a perversion of feminist empowerment and an embrace of the potentially injurious practices of patriarchy, practices that treat others as simply bodies? Or does this moment suggest that unabashedly claiming her sexual power will allow Delia to defuse the potentially harmful advances of arrogant and aggressive males? That the greasy young man appears stunned and awed by Delia, who also seems wryly pleased with herself, suggests that this usurpation of the masculine role of older and dominating sexual partner is one way for Delia to assert herself; perhaps this is her own kind of vengeance.

The conclusion of Delia's vignette is thus ambivalent, just as, perhaps, many survivor's first years away from abusers may seem ambivalent as they grapple with challenges that may include post-traumatic stress, as well feelings of relief, remorse, and shame. Thus, Miller's vignette is an important intervention as it resists clichés surrounding battered women and survivors of violence. In addition, positioned as a selection within a larger film that explores women's stories, "Delia" foregrounds the importance of narratives that deal with women's experiences of oppression. The images against which the opening credits appear provide a key to *Personal Velocity*'s overarching project: the film opens with images of three girls on a swing set. Although all attached to one structure, each child swings independently, at different heights and speeds. This opening may function allegorically to suggest the different experiences of individual women who are nevertheless all operating within the same system. Girls and women may experience different highs and lows, but share structural realities under patriarchy.

Playing Gritball: Overcoming Shame in Madea's Family Reunion

Similarly, Tyler Perry's 2006 film *Madea's Family Reunion* presents an embrace of masculine-coded behavior as well as a turn toward female community as effective responses to intimate partner violence. Perry claims that his goal in filmmaking is to "do a silly character, and put these great messages inside of them so that when children see them, families see them, they can walk away with a great message" (qtd. in Patterson 11). While, as several critics have pointed out, the value of Perry's "great messages" are themselves up for debate,[4] his overt interest in tackling relevant social issues has earned him a loyal audience, most of whom are African American.[5] In particular, while Perry has been rightly criticized for many of his portrayals of African American women[6] as well as his at times ham-handed depictions of domestic violence, *Madea's Family Reunion* departs from the practice of rendering domestic violence as a strictly private affair and instead promotes a renunciation of shame. In *Madea's Family Reunion,* the redemption of the battered woman, Lisa (Rochelle Aytes), is ultimately achieved through a simultaneous declaration of independence and a return to community for support. In depicting isolation or estrangement from one's family as one of the factors that allow violence to flourish, Perry reconnects the personal and the political, suggesting that the public acknowledgment of dysfunction is a crucial step in overcoming it.

In "Lion and Lamb—The Strong Black Woman Gets Abused: 'Afflictions of Specialness' in Post-Feminist and Post-Civil Rights Films," Samantha N. Sheppard contends that *Madea's Family Reunion* is a "post-civil rights and post-feminist film that veils its patriarchal positioning under layers of Black make up" (6). Sheppard astutely critiques many aspects of Perry's film; one of her objections is the film's rendering of Madea's violence against her foster-daughter as both funny and as evidence of Madea's caring. Sheppard writes, "Just as post-feminism uses the language of feminism without linking it to any form of struggle, *Madea's Family Reunion* cheapens its representation of intimate partner violence by making comedic … other forms of violence" (4). She continues, "by making some violence 'fun' or 'funny,' Perry displaces the act of violence as a serious problem, making patriarchal and traditionalist conclusions on 'instructive' violence" (5).

Sheppard's reading is correct; Madea's (Tyler Perry) violent behavior is often framed as justified, her actions as a reassertion of common sense. Her discipline of outrageously disrespectful young people may provide catharsis and humor, as the recipients of Madea's abuse discover that their insolence will not be tolerated. However, in *Madea's Family Reunion* in particular, while females may assault males and other females, male violence against women is not depicted as comedic or tolerable. Thus, when Madea discovers that her foster daughter is being harassed on the school bus, Madea emerges as a righteous defender. Madea boards the bus and, when a young man disrespects Madea, Madea beats him and cries out, "All my life I had to fight. I loves Harpo but I'll kill him dead 'fore I let him beat me." This is a strange moment, particularly as Madea appears earnest in this otherwise absurd and comic situation. But Madea is quoting—and apparently channeling—Sofia in *The Color Purple,* thus positioning the young man's disrespect as part of a larger practice of abusing women—especially women who care for them. Like the

Grandmother in Flannery O'Connor's "A Good Man Is Hard to Find" recognizing the Misfit as one of her "own children," Madea's words re-render the rude young man, at once claiming him and rejecting his violence.[7]

This is also the message that Madea conveys to Lisa. Like *Enough*, *Madea's Family Reunion* suggests that there is a limit to the abuse a woman will suffer; once that limit is exceeded, her retaliation is depicted as understandable. When sisters Lisa and Vanessa (Lisa Arrindell Anderson) ask Madea what their "friend" should do if she is being abused by her husband, Madea is not astounded that a woman might be dealing with domestic violence. Her response instead indicates that this type of violence is all too common and that it is intolerable: she first jokes, "Before or after his funeral?," but continues, "When you get tired of a man hitting on you honey, ain't nothing you can do but cook breakfast for him." Vanessa and Lisa look surprised. Madea explains that once the grits "start to boil like lava," the abused woman should throw them at the man and then hit him with a skillet. Madea physically demonstrates, calling out "throw it an' swat!"

Madea's solution positions women as savvy and self-aware and men as obtuse. That is, the woman's revenge depends on a man underestimating a woman: she can lull him into a sense of normalcy, safety, and dominance by

Figure 9. Madea (Tyler Perry) mimics "playing gritball." Lisa (Rochelle Aytes, seated left) and Vanessa (Lisa Arrindell Anderson) (*Madea's Family Reunion*, Lions Gate Entertainment, 2006, directed by Tyler Perry).

cooking him breakfast, or adhering to a conventional feminine domestic role. In addition, while the scene trivializes violence, it is also a moment of solidarity and connection between the women, who laugh at Madea's antics.

Several critics, however, have taken issue with Perry's deployment of drag, particularly as the Madea character is inserted into female spaces in order to, as Timothy Lyle points out, provide a patriarchal perspective.[8] In "'Check with Yo' Man First; Check with Yo' Man': Tyler Perry Appropriates Drag as a Tool to Re-Circulate Patriarchal Ideology," Lyle argues that Madea "dominates, regulates, and controls" female spaces and conversations (951). Lyle continues, claiming that it's possible that "audience members almost forget that Madea is indeed a male who is proffering a very patriarchal point of view while donning the disguise of a female elder" but that "placing a man in drag as the agent of knowledge" suggests an "inherent assumption that males must teach females how to live their lives. There is a fundamental critique that females cannot see their own situations clearly; rather, Madea (Perry in drag) must point them in the *right* direction" (952).

In addition to espousing a "patriarchal point of view" as Lyle suggests, Madea's advice also reasserts the neoliberal thinking that, Sheppard notes, suggests that a woman must struggle privately with violence in the home. For example, in her advice to Lisa and Vanessa, Madea does not suggest leaving an abusive man. Rather, female violence is framed as corrective; the suggestion is that a woman's violence is an acceptable response to unchecked male violence. In other words, once she has had "enough," the abuse will end.

This thinking is underscored in one of the final scenes when Lisa has fled to Madea's house on Lisa and Carlos' wedding day. When Carlos arrives looking for Lisa, rather than call the police or intervene, Madea tells Lisa, "It's time to stop running, honey, and fight." Madea then leaves (remaining close enough to the house to enjoy the sound of Carlos screaming). Alarmingly, Madea's insistence that Lisa face Carlos alone explicitly positions Lisa in a one-on-one confrontation with a man who had earlier threatened to kill her.

Thus, *Madea's Family Reunion* suggests that, in order to overcome her victimization, a woman's first defense is retributive violence. And again, as seen in other films, in *Madea's Family Reunion* the absence of legal apparatus to protect women from abusers reinforces neoliberal postfeminist thinking that women must transform themselves, rather than society, in order to end men's oppression of women. However, as also discussed above, the lack of social services in *Madea's Family Reunion* may also reflect a reality that is especially relevant in the lives of people of color, that the interventions of the criminal justice system may not always in fact serve women's best interests. As Kimberlé W. Crenshaw argues in "Women, Race and Social Control," "intersectional failures in responding to the underprotection of women of color are linked to the current regime of overpolicing" (1452). Increased criminalization of domestic violence, which includes practices such as mandatory arrests, often have negative consequences, especially for women of color, whose "concerns," Crenshaw argues "were fairly consistently overlooked" in the development of these policies and procedures (1454). For example, not only are women of color more likely to be injured as a result of domestic violence, they are also increasingly likely to be themselves arrested on domestic violence charges (1455).[9]

In "Bruised and Misunderstood: Translating Black Feminist Acts in the Work of Tyler Perry," Nicole Hodges Persley suggests that many critics miss the ways in which Perry's Madea challenges stereotypes, arguing, "With Perry's Madea, you always have to look twice and read between the lines" (225). Certainly, Perry's handling of domestic violence is at once reductive and resonant. On the one hand, in suggesting the necessity of fighting back, Perry's film elides the possibility that a woman's violence may not only further endanger her, but could also subject her to arrest. That Lisa would beat Carlos and that he would not seek his own revenge is improbable, but may be cathartic for audiences, not unlike Slim's violence in *Enough*. On the other hand, *Madea's Family Reunion* does not conclude that violence is the only answer to abuse. First, in confiding in her sister Vanessa, Lisa takes the first step in overcoming shame and isolation. Then, in asking Madea for advice, the sisters widen a circle of support, in addition to evidencing their respect for an older female mentor as well as a larger tradition of women aiding women. Finally, Lisa's plot does not conclude with her assault of Carlos. Instead, Lisa arrives at what would have been her wedding and shares publicly that she has been abused, announcing to the crowd, "I'm not getting married today. I've been beaten every day since we got engaged. And I've tried to make excuses for him ... but it's time for me to start making my own decisions and live for Lisa." Crucially, Lisa is depicted as returning to the community which Carlos has attempted to separate her from; additionally, her public declaration makes clear that although she may have made "excuses" for Carlos, she should not be blamed for her abuse. Further, although the use of the third person may suggest self-alienation, Lisa's words indicate a desire for self-reclamation and a refusal to live in service of someone else.

In part, Lisa's ability to leave Carlos is also possible because, unlike the protagonists in *Enough*, *Waitress*, and *Personal Velocity*, Lisa is neither poor nor dependent on her abuser.[10] Perry's film thus reverses the fairy tale narrative, a move that is emphasized in the depiction of the "appropriate" romance between Vanessa and her boyfriend Frankie, a bus driver.[11] That Lisa allows Vanessa and Frankie to step into the wedding that had been planned for herself and Carlos suggests that the true prince, of course, is not the higher status male, but the dignified working-class male. Perry's treatment of domestic violence in *Madea's Family Reunion* thus overturns the stereotype of the economically disempowered battered woman.

"There are a lot of powerful women around here": Big Little Lies *and the Pervasiveness of Violence*

The 2017 HBO series *Big Little Lies* (based on a novel of the same title) investigates several of the themes discussed here.[12] Perhaps because the series is long-form and allows characters to develop over several episodes, the depiction of violence in the home in *Big Little Lies* is nuanced and evocative. In the *New Yorker*, Emily Nussbaum writes that she was initially skeptical of the series, as it was "written by David E. Kelley, the creator of 'Ally McBeal,' my least favorite anti-feminist fantasia," but that she came to appreciate the series as "a reflection on trauma; at its best moments, it makes risky observations, especially about the dynamics of domestic abuse." Kelley's participation aside, women have also shaped *Big Little Lies* in fundamental ways: it is based on a female-authored novel and several of the producers—including Reese Witherspoon and Nicole Kidman—are women.

In *Big Little Lies,* all women are vulnerable to male exploitation and abuse; all women too are susceptible to the postfeminist thinking that violence in the home remains a source of shame and that only a weak or somehow pathetic woman would identify herself as a "victim." In addition to obvious affluence, characters Celeste (Nicole Kidman) and Renata (Laura Dern) have (or had) high-status careers and those like Madeline (Reese Witherspoon) and Jane (Shailene Woodley) who do not work full-time are depicted as smart and worldly. Thus, the women in *Big Little Lies* evidence some of the success of the second-wave feminist movement: white women, they have access to education, careers, self-expression, and public life. They are sexually liberated and, superficially at least, many seem to enjoy equitable relationships with their husbands. Noting the pressure to succeed in Monterey, one character's daughter remarks, "there are a lot of high-powered women who live here" ("Living the Dream").

Strength and success, however, have not inoculated these women against suffering and gender-based violence. The perilousness is immediately established by the narrative's murder frame; the first episode, for example, is titled "Somebody's Dead" and, after the alternately serene and ominous opening credits (which include the image of a hand holding a gun), the series begins with the flash of police lights, the noise of dully crackling police tape, and the sound of panting breath. That the series immediately establishes that there has been a "victim" before circling back to the weeks leading up to the event renders all off-handed aggressive remarks insidious. For example, in the first episode, Madeline remarks that in Monterey "we pound people with kindness" and Celeste responds, "To death" ("Somebody's Dead"). On other occasions, friends Madeline and Jane joke about punching Madeline's ex-husband's wife Bonnie in the face ("Somebody's Dead"); Madeline's enemy Renata declares that she will "kill" Madeline ("Living the Dream"); Madeline declares that Nathan, her ex, is "obsessed with guns" after learning that Jane herself carries a gun ("Once Bitten"). Although many of the comments are casual and are even meant to be humorous, each incident suggests the extent to which contemporary language has become uncritically violent.

In addition, the series' instantiating event is the violence that takes place among children, thus indicating the ways in which violence is transmitted intergenerationally. An unknown child has choked Renata's daughter Amabella. Although initially unsure of who did it, Amabella, under duress, implicates Jane's son, Iggy. It is revealed at the season's end, however, that one of Celeste's twin sons has been persecuting Amabella all year.

The plot concerning the children raises several issues, including the ways in which male violence against women is often naturalized at a young age and mothers' potential complicity in male violence. Renata's declaration that "little boys don't get to go around anymore hurting little girls" ("Somebody's Dead") isn't exactly true, as Amabella's persecution continues unchecked. Further, while the adults take Amabella's charge seriously (no one offers the old chestnut that boys harass the girls they like), the scene in which Amabella identifies Ziggy, a character the audience may already like and sympathize with, raises questions about who is to believed and why. If Ziggy is innocent, Jane's defense of her son is admirable, but if he is guilty, Jane will appear a parent whose denial enables her son's cruelty. And Jane, of course, has her doubts. Because Ziggy's conception is the result of rape, Jane can't help but wonder if her son has inherited his father's proclivity for violence.

Fear of the intergenerational transmission of violence is also a key to Celeste's narrative. Initially, Max and Josh are never suggested as potential bullies. Rather, their parents, Celeste and Perry (Alexander Skarsgård) resolve to keep the apparent bad influence, Ziggy, away from their sons ("Somebody's Dead"). Max's behavior, however, is the logical outcome of living in a home in which his mother is abused (even though both Perry and Celeste maintain that the children are unaware of the violence). In fact, according to the Unicef report "Behind Closed Doors: The Impact of Domestic Violence on Children," "the single best predictor of children becoming either perpetrators or victims of domestic violence later in life is whether or not they grow up in a home where there is domestic violence. Studies from various countries support the findings that rates of abuse are higher among women whose husbands were abused as children or who saw their mothers being abused" (7).

After telling her that Ziggy has identified Max as the child hurting Amabella, Jane attempts to comfort Celeste saying that children "bully ... they grow out of it"("You Get What You Need"). Celeste responds, "Sometimes they don't," a remark that the audience understands as referring to Perry's behavior. The awareness that Max may develop into an abuser like his father is a primary motivation for Celeste to leave Perry. Thus, Celeste's declaration that, "It's enough.... I have to leave. For them," suggests that her responsibility as a mother is not only to protect herself and her child from abuse but to prevent her child from perpetrating abuse ("You Get What You Need"). Her choice of the word "enough," which of course repeatedly appears in the films discussed here, again suggests that male violence must reach a certain limit before a woman will declare it intolerable.

Even before discovering her son's violence, however, Celeste had resolved to leave Perry, going so far as to rent and furnish an apartment in preparation. In this way, *Big Little Lies* notably departs from the patterns established in many other narratives of domestic violence. First, like Lisa in *Madea's Family Reunion*, but unlike the majority of battered-wife characters, Celeste has the resources to leave her husband. Though she has been a stay-at-home mom, Celeste is an accomplished attorney who apparently has access to money. Thus, Celeste is positioned as a character in no need of the fairy godfather-figure who economically rescues the protagonists in films such as *Enough* and *Waitress*.

If there is any "fairy god" figure in *Big Little Lies*, it is Celeste and Perry's observant and wise marriage counselor, who dispenses frank observations and practical, effective recommendations. Akin to the good witch in *The Wizard of Oz*, who reveals to Dorothy that she had the power to go home all along, Celeste's therapist reveals her own power to Celeste, advising her to think strategically. It is thus through another women's support and encouragement that Celeste is able to take steps to liberate herself. The therapist, for example, tells Celeste to make a record of her abuse and to tell her friends what is happening, warning, "Men like your husband typically go for custody" ("Burning Love"). When Celeste balks, her therapist calls her to competence: "You are a lawyer." In this way, Celeste's therapist functions in the series to suggest that there are ways of approaching intrafamilial violence beyond retributive violence, the embrace of masculinity, or the replacement of one patriarch with another.

However, season one ends with Perry's violent death at the hands of a woman, thus situating *Big Little Lies* within a representational tradition in which the only true solution to men's violence is a man's death. At the same time, the women's group resistance to Perry functions allegorically to suggest women's rejection of men's violence and exploitation. Revealed in the final episode as Jane's rapist, Perry comes to emblematize the ways in which each woman in the series has been victimized: not only has Celeste been beaten and Jane raped, Madeline has been stalked and Renata's daughter physically abused. Each has been injured by patriarchy; each has cause to fear and hate males who seem "nice" and caring and well-mannered, but who are really cruel and selfish and violent.

It is Bonnie (Zoë Kravitz), the only woman of color and a character who is marginalized on the show, however, who, after watching from a distance, is able to perceive something dangerous in Perry's treatment of Celeste at the trivia night party. When Perry is assaulting Celeste as well as lashing out at the other women who attempt to defend her, Bonnie runs—from a literal and metaphorical distance—gaining the necessary momentum to push him to his death.[13]

In an overt celebration of female community, the women band together to protect Bonnie—and perhaps themselves—and the series ends with the women and their children frolicking on a utopic beach. Although still under police surveillance—a skeptical detective watches from a bluff—the ending suggests the communion of women who have also had "enough": enough abuse and sexual assault, enough competition around men and based on appearance, and enough anxiety for their children's safety. In this way, like *Personal Velocity*, and *Madea's Family Reunion*, *Big Little Lies* reinforces the notion of women's shared experiences as a source of strength and healing.

Conclusion: "I'm not a victim"

Celeste's insistence that she and Perry share a "dirty secret" ("Living the Dream"), that she is complicit in the violence, and that she is "not a victim" is an accurate depiction of the ways in which many women understand or even rationalize their own abuse. As Nussbaum argues, the show's "violent sequences also help us understand the story the couple has sold not just to the neighbors but to themselves: that they are simply more passionate than normal people.... As chilling as his character is, Skarsgård makes [Perry] more than a Lifetime monster" (Nussbaum). Unlike many of the depictions of domestic violence discussed in this book, *Big Little Lies* probes the ways in which women are often made to feel responsible for and ashamed of the abuse perpetrated against them. While Celeste's therapist refuses to blame Celeste, she makes clear that both she and Perry participate in the dynamic which keeps them together, saying, "Your husband is ill, Celeste, but so are you" ("You Get What You Need").

Further, Celeste's declaration "I'm not a victim here. I'm not" ("Once Bitten"), reflects the move toward a more widespread discomfort with the label of victim, largely in response to the contempt heaped on victims during the 1980s and '90s backlash to feminism.[14] This disavowal of victimhood persists in much social media. In 2018, one of President Donald Trump's aides, Rob Porter, was forced to resign after multiple allegations of domestic violence against two former spouses became widely acknowledged. Asked if she was concerned about Porter's current girlfriend, Hope Hicks, Trump aide Kellyanne Conway claimed she wasn't, saying that she'd "rarely met somebody so strong with such excellent instincts and loyalty and smarts" as Hicks. Porter's ex-wife, Colbie Holderness, then responded to Conway, writing in a *Washington Post* op-ed that Conway's characterization "implies that those who have been in abusive relationships are not strong. I beg to differ."

Remarks like Conway's further recirculate the notion that those who are battered are perhaps to blame in that they tolerate or fail to prevent abuse. More insidious is the suggestion (not floated here, but often implied), that some women enjoy victim status, that they exaggerate or fabricate abuse in order to receive attention.

Despite the fact that such thinking continues to have cultural currency, Holderness' response, her refusal to be silent and to allow Conway's misconstrual of her story, is possible because of a larger cultural recalibration regarding understanding domestic violence. Holderness' statement, like the very existence of the films discussed in this chapter, evidences a shift in understandings of heterosexual relationships, the status of mothers and wives in our society, and our increasing intolerance for violence against women.

Personal Velocity, Madea's Family Reunion, and *Big Little Lies* also contribute to the dismantling of these injurious myths, exploring the realities of domestic violence as well as the obstacles that many women face in attempting to liberate themselves. In particular, these narratives represent and reject the shame that many battered women feel, as well as begin to propose possible responses to battering beyond retributive violence. Finally, these films reveal that regardless of race or class, even ostensibly "happy" families and communities might harbor dysfunction, oppression and violence, laying bare the myth that the safest place for a woman is in the home. As Bumiller writes of the battered wives she interviewed, "These women have seen it all. None of them harbors illusions about the peacefulness of domesticity. They can't, because they carry around their experience of abuse in their bodies: scars, broken bones, and terrifying memories" (120).

Each film discussed in this chapter concludes with the promise of hope: Delia will potentially recover bodily autonomy, Lisa will return to her family, and Celeste will be sheltered in a female community. In this way, these films not only explode the myth of the patriarchal home as a place in which wives and mothers are protected and cared for, but also seek to replace that patriarchal model with another vision of a female-centered community. The next chapter turns to just such domestic spaces: matriarchal homes as experienced by the children of dauntingly successful mothers.

7
"You're so epic": Matrophilia in Indie Films

The previous chapter notes that narratives including *Madea's Family Reunion* and *Big Little Lies* exist as departures from the more commonly circulated depictions of abused women as poor or economically dependent, instead following the stories of affluent women who are nevertheless vulnerable to abuse and oppression. This chapter also examines representations of professionally successful women, as well as maternal homes which are sites of ambition and strength.

In fact, the mother-figures investigated in this chapter suggest the victories of the women's movement and, in particular, exist as reversals of those mothers dismissed and rejected in young adult franchises; as described in Chapter 3, in signature postfeminist style, movies such as *The Hunger Games* often depict older women as foolish and unnecessary, creating a coming-of-age scenario in which the protagonist must develop her identity in opposition to women who have come before her. The films discussed in this chapter depict adolescent and adult children who admire their mother and seek to please her. Further, particularly in films written and directed by women, young women are depicted as aware of a larger feminist legacy. That is, rather than recirculating the postfeminist narrative that young women are ambivalent about or openly contemptuous of feminism, these films include young women who find significance in their mothers' personal histories, who recognize the gains of earlier feminist movements and who actively participate in the development of the feminist understandings of their own moment.

These films are possible in part because, despite the prevalence of "bad mothers" in much media and despite the social, cultural, economic, and political limitations that may continue to circumscribe women's lives, many post-second wave women enjoy professional, political and educational opportunities hitherto out of reach. Women are now well-represented in high status professions in the law and medical fields and rank among the distinguished artists, authors, and scholars in contemporary culture. Further, these same women often insist on their right to pursue a rewarding family life. Thus, regardless of media hand-wringing over whether or not a 21st century Western woman can really "have it all," many have forged new paths for themselves both professionally and domestically.[1] While in 1977 Adrienne Rich invokes poet Lynn Sukenick's use of the word matrophobia to mean "fear of ... *becoming one's mother*" (ital. orig. 235) and explains that "the mother's self-hatred and low expectations are the binding-rags for the psyche of the daughter" (243), many contemporary mothers find themselves no longer shackled by "self-hatred" and "low expectations."

This is not meant to suggest that equity has been achieved or that women are not disproportionately and unfairly saddled with childcare responsibilities and housework. However, the following chapters focus on media that incorporate or respond to women's changing status. This chapter in particular investigates media depictions of mothers who are also over-achievers, or more generally, the representation of the "liberated" mothers in a post-second wave world. In the work of indie filmmakers Noah Baumbach, Gillian Robespierre, Lena Dunham, and Paul Weitz, mothers are presented as powerful and dauntingly successful.[2] As a result, rather than matrophobia, the children in films including *Margot at the Wedding* (2007), *Tiny Furniture* (2010), *Obvious Child* (2014), and *Grandma* (2015) suffer an excess of matrophilia: they are anxious about failing to live up to the mother's standards and achievements. Further, several of these films present a return to the maternal home as simultaneously sustaining and infantilizing, comforting and challenging, reflecting a larger cultural ambivalence regarding women's increasing social, political, and economic gains, the role of mother, and the promise of the matriarchal home.

Having It All? The Working Mother as Failure or Fantasy

In "'I Hate My Job, I Hate Everybody Here': Adultery, Boredom, and the 'Working Girl' in Twenty-first-Century American Cinema," Suzanne Leonard reviews the feminist position that women's paid labor is crucial to female independence and liberation and remarks that, "One common mantra in feminist theory, and increasingly in postfeminist culture, is that working women are reminders of the vast economic and cultural gains women have made in the past fifty years thanks mainly to their ability to ensure their own means of financial support. Likewise, in previous eras it was precisely the lack of such economic means that often ensured women's dependence on fathers and husbands" (100).

As discussed in previous chapters with regard to domestic violence, economic instability is clearly an obstacle for women—in the real world and in the movies—seeking to leave abusive relationships. In films such as *Enough* (2002) and *Waitress* (2007), women are "rescued" by a benevolent patriarch who endows them with the money they'll need to escape their husbands. While there are a host of issues to address here (including the insufficiency of social safety nets for abused women), the bottom line in these narratives is that these women have limited skills and resources and thus must depend on men.

Several late 20th century/early 21st century American films, such as *Alice Doesn't Live Here Anymore* (1974), *Kramer vs. Kramer* (1979), *Baby Boom* (1987), and *Raising Helen* (2004), grapple with how traditional family life is disrupted—or destroyed—when a mother-figure enters or thrives in the workplace. The protagonist of *Alice*, for example, is presented as a well-meaning if often harried and negligent parent when she is forced to work full-time, while the mother in *Kramer vs. Kramer* outright abandons her son in order to "find some interesting things to do" for her personal fulfillment.[3] The protagonist of *Baby Boom* resolves the crisis instantiated when she becomes a child's guardian by opting for a more family-friendly, less-demanding career path.[4] Similarly, the protagonist of *Raising Helen*, the titular Helen, loses her job after she becomes the guardian to her sister's children. Although the film does provide a subtle critique of the impossible demands faced by many single working parents—Helen, for example, has to walk away from a job that entails a lot of travel—the film ultimately suggests that the experience of parenthood is the catalyst for an overdue reordering of Helen's priorities. The repeated message in each film is that a woman's pursuit of gainful employment, not to mention a passionate commitment to a career vocation, is incompatible with successful motherhood.[5]

More recent media, however, present the "working mother" as a familiar, natural, standard character. In *Enlightened Sexism*, Susan Douglas suggests that media depictions in fact err too much on the side of presenting a world in which women have unfettered access to the highest echelons of power; Douglas contends that on television, at least, we are faced with an endless parade of female surgeons, police chiefs, mayors, and scientists. Douglas writes, "What the media have been giving us, then, are little more than fantasies of power. They assure girls and women, repeatedly, that women's liberation is a fait accompli and that we are stronger, more successful, more sexually in control, more fearless, and more held in awe than we actually are" (5).

Further, as Leonard notes, many media depictions "are predicated ... on the idea that, although the postfeminist working girl benefits from a legacy of feminist critique over the issues of marriage and work, for her these debates have little historical specificity or urgent import" (104). Thus, as both Douglas and Leonard point out, much media shores up a brand of postfeminist neoliberal individualism that suggests that equality has been achieved, that a "successful" woman has no need for feminism or feminist consciousness and that she has gotten where she is solely through hard work. Further, the most obvious manifestation of her success is her consumer power, an idea promoted perhaps most notably by the *Sex and the City* franchise.[6]

It is within this context in which films that present nuanced and realistic depictions of respected and powerful—and sometimes even overtly feminist—mothers emerge as exceptional and exciting. Significantly, the films discussed in this chapter are "independent," a vague category, but one which suggests a degree of freedom from the imperatives of mainstream studios. Three of these films—*Obvious Child, Tiny Furniture,* and *Grandma*—explicitly engage feminist discussions about women, self-expression, work, and inheritance. Thus, rather than recirculating postfeminist thinking that feminism has achieved its goals and thus may be "taken for granted" and dismissed as no longer useful, the films that have female protagonists both recognize the struggles of previous generations and identify the work yet to be done.[7]

Importantly, the films examined in this chapter are not "about" working mothers in the sense of the films mentioned above (*Raising Helen* and *Baby Boom,* for example). Rather, they are primarily focused on the experiences of those women's children. Thus, the protagonists grapple with obstacles such as unplanned pregnancy and identity formation, while the impressive mother figure occupies a secondary but crucial position, functioning as role model, caregiver, and guide, and often providing a feminist critique of contemporary culture.

"Did you see me running?": The Exceptional Mother in Margot at the Wedding

The mother in Noah Baumbach's *Margot at the Wedding*, Margot (Nicole Kidman), is an accomplished author who is beautiful, worldly, and unapologetically brilliant. Claire Perkins, in her discussion of Robert Altman's influence on Baumbach's work, calls Margot "highly narcissistic" and a "classically cynical figure: critical but paralyzed, intellectual but passive-aggressive" (494). Further, Perkins writes that Margot fits in with other Baumbach protagonists: "patterns of judgment are written in overtly intellectual terms, with people and behavior meeting the disapproval of the writer-protagonists when they are not sufficiently serious, engaged, or aspirational" (495). As Perkins suggests, Margot is not simply successful, she is daunting, often mean-spirited, and perhaps impossible to please.

I argue that *Margot at the Wedding* is an exploration of intimacy between mother and son and that the film's central conflict is crystallized in Margot and her son Claude's (Zane Pais) negotiations of each other's physical autonomy. That is, Margot is confounded by Claude's adolescent body (she refuses to let him wear deodorant and waxes his mustache for him), just as Claude manifests the child's desire not only for his mother's complete attention, but for access to her person. Yet successful parenthood is, in part, a process of relinquishment of child and parent's rights to one and another.

The film's final scene presents a synthesis of Baumbach's themes and characters' concerns. Margot urges Claude to board a bus that will take him to join his father on vacation. Claude has asked Margot to come with him, but she's refused. As they approach the bus, Margot tells Claude, "you used to need me to watch you when you played.... When you first started playing with friends, you wouldn't do it unless I was watching you. You were always afraid I was gonna go out the back door." Claude responds by disclosing, "I masturbated last night." Margot says, "You don't need to tell me that, sweetie."

Margot tells Claude he's "acting like a baby" and he climbs onto the bus. Shortly after it departs, however, Margot takes off her sweater, drops her bag, and begins to chase the bus, calling urgently for it to stop. When it does, Margot boards, smiles, and sits next to Claude. "Did you see me running?" she asks as the bus again begins to move, adding, "That was a lot of running." Claude looks impassively out the window.

The movement of the scene evokes the trajectory of parenting itself: the imperative for the child to leave, to be independent, to stop "acting like a baby," but also the parent's longing for the child and the reversal that may occur when the parent begins to seek to the child's approval. Margot is pleased with her athletic performance as it evidences her physical ability and youthfulness despite her age and status as mother. Further, she foregrounds the effort that she has put into "running," and expects her son to be not only impressed, but perhaps grateful. The film suggests that Margot has at last provided what Claude—and perhaps every child—truly desires: the vital mother has abandoned everything in order to devote herself entirely to the child. And yet Claude appears ultimately unmoved.

Further, Margot's question, "did you see me running?," is a request for Claude's attention; that is, just as he once needed her to watch him play, she now asks him to recognize her. In this way, the ending is yet another exchange in the back-and-forth of affection and withholding that is often manifested in attention or lack of attention that seems to mark all of Margot's relationships. Claude's offer of information, "I masturbated last night," is a misguided attempt at intimacy with his mother; as he did when he was a child, he seems to need Margot's approving eye in order to feel secure. That is, an awareness of the mother's absence will create anxiety that will make "play" impossible.

And yet it is not longer appropriate for Claude to remain so close with his mother. Margot's word choice, "You don't need to tell me that," suggests that she recognizes Claude's disclosure as an attempt to fulfill his obligation to her, raising the question of what, if anything, children "need" to share about themselves with their parents. Margot is beginning to recognize that Claude's body no longer belongs to her.

Claude's confusion over boundaries is exemplified in another moment in the film, a moment that, like the films discussed below, includes an attempt to enter the mother's bed, a location with clear resonance in terms of return to the mother's embrace, to childhood, infancy, or even the womb. When Margot rejects his request to sleep with her, Claude counters that he will place a pillow between them. Claude's idea of using a pillow is reminiscent of courtly behavior—laying the sword between a chaste couple—but it is also problematic and absurd. That is, unless there is already something unclear about their relationship, why would they need a barrier between them? Is Claude and Margot's relationship quasi-incestuous or is Claude simply confused by the nature of their relationship? This lack of clarity is also indicated through Margot's sister's remark that Margot prefers Claude. Pauline tells Claude that Margot "always liked you best. More than [Margot's husband] even." Elsewhere, Margot's lover interrogates her about a character in one of her novels, describing a "sexual push-pull" between a father and daughter and suggesting that the father character is based on Margot herself, a comment that deeply upsets Margot, perhaps because of its accuracy.

Not only does *Margot at the Wedding* rehearse the Freudian drama of a son's desire for the mother, but the film also functions as an homage to Margot. As Jennifer O'Meara notes, *Margot at the Wedding*, like Baumbach's earlier film *The Squid and the Whale* (2005), uses a son's perspective: the son's "developing understanding of his family's dysfunction is crucial from the opening scene" (118). However, the title of *Margot at the Wedding* makes clear whom the film is actually about. That is, the film is not called *Claude at the Wedding*. Instead, the film explores Margot as she is experienced by Claude, or a description of the turmoil of the child of the exceptional parent. The intimacy between mother and son is at once enviable and perverse, just as Margot herself is at once charming and cold. Is she a good mother, attentive to her son as well as able to expose him to rigorous and enriching adult experiences, or is she a narcissist who selfishly exposes her son to mature situations he is ill-equipped to understand? Baumbach's film, ultimately, allows her to be both.

The shifting boundaries in Margot's relationship with Claude additionally suggests the ultimate unknowability of the mother. The film takes place at a moment when both Margot and Claude are at transitions in their lives as Claude is embarking on teenage years and Margot is having an affair and considering leaving her husband. The transitional state is also indicated by the bookending of the film with scenes of traveling: just as the film concludes with Margot and Claude traveling on a bus, the film opens with Margot and Claude on a train. In the first scene, Claude leaves Margot's side to go to the food car. On his way back, he sits next to the wrong woman, who turns to reveal Claude's error. Like the final scene, this opening is richly evocative. The child who leaves the mother, embarking on independence, selects the wrong woman upon his return. This experience of the uncanny is, for Claude, deeply embarrassing. Again, however, the scene suggests that Claude is capable of mistaking his mother, that he does not know her as well as he may believe. The awareness that one cannot very fully know one's parents is yet another key discovery on the path to adulthood.

Margot at the Wedding is notable not only as a nuanced investigation of a complex relationship, but also as a rare film to present the exceptional mother. That is, there are countless bad, absent, or one-dimensional mother-figures in movies; in addition, American films have an abundance of movies about how the child of the exceptional father navigates his or her entry to adulthood, including *To Kill a Mockingbird* (1962), several of the *Star Wars* films, *The Weather Man* (2005), *Proof* (2005), and *There Will Be Blood* (2007). There are also numerous films detailing experiences of parents (often mothers) raising exceptional children (often sons), such as *Little Man Tate* (1991), *Simon Birch* (1998), *The Book of Henry* (2017), *Gifted* (2017) and, even, in a different vein, *We Need to Talk about Kevin* (2011). *Margot at the Wedding*, however, is one of a handful of films to take as its focus the impact of the exceptional, intellectual and artistic mother.

"She's your mom? She's a genius": Feminism in Obvious Child

Gillian Robespierre's *Obvious Child* is an overtly feminist romantic comedy that traces the development of a relationship between New York stand-up comic Donna (Jenny Slate) and the man with whom she has casual sex, Max (Jake Lacy); their encounter results in a pregnancy. In *The Atlantic*, Esther Zuckerman writes that *Obvious Child* "is a warm, straightforward romantic comedy, which just happens to have an important political stance. Donna's abortion isn't treated blithely, but her decision isn't an agonizing or melodramatic one either. In fact, the movie makes a point of revealing that abortion is something a lot of women go through."[8] Donna speaks to several characters about her pregnancy and plan to terminate, including her mother, Nancy (Polly Draper). While Nancy is a minor figure, her character nevertheless serves to situate Donna's experiences within a larger feminist context and legacy.

7. "You're so epic" 131

Nancy fits Kathleen Rowe Karlyn's description of the second wave feminist: "educated, white, came of age in the 1960s, and spent much of her life working hard to break through the glass ceiling. And she is a mother" (69). Further, that Nancy refuses "traditional" gender roles is foregrounded by juxtaposed scenes of Donna having dinner with each of her (divorced) parents at their homes. When Donna goes to her father's apartment, he prepares her "favorite" sauce and the two eat pasta. Dinner at Nancy's, however, is shown to be take-out Chinese, perhaps a deliberate rejection of the stereotype of the mother as the individual who provides nurturing and love through meal preparation. Further, it emerges that Nancy is a professor at a business school. Max, who is one of her students, declares her a "genius." Finally, Nancy's own abortion story, which she shares with Donna when Donna tells her that she plans to terminate, echoes the familiar pre–*Roe v. Wade* story of, again, upper-class white girls and women who had access to abortion, although that access itself was tenuous and the circumstances illegal and often dangerous.

Nancy, although often nagging Donna about her life choices, reacts casually to Donna's announcement that she plans to terminate her pregnancy, responding, "Thank God. I thought you were gonna tell me you were moving to LA." This scene, one of the few in which Nancy appears, takes place in Nancy's bedroom, where, like the other protagonists discussed in this chapter, the child has come to ask for permission to get in the mother's bed. Nestled together in the maternal bed, Nancy shares the story of her own abortion. That Donna receives approval for the choice to reject maternity herself in her mother's bed is rich with implications, including that Donna herself is still an "obvious child," that the mother-as-nurturer can still exist even if the mother is "successful" and the daughter grown, or if the mother-daughter relationship is difficult. The mother's bed is thus a site from which one can emerge recommitted to independence and autonomy.

While the inclusion of Nancy's abortion-story is perhaps a bit heavy-handed, one of the more subtle lessons it contains is the notion that, for many women, abortion is not simply a means to free oneself of an unwanted pregnancy, but instead is intricately connected to women's liberation and self-determination. That is, Nancy's abortion makes possible what comes after: Nancy's college education, her career, and Donna's existence. Implicitly, then, Donna's abortion, rather an ending or termination, will make possible Donna's future "success." Like her mother, perhaps Donna will have another, desired, pregnancy, a relationship with a different partner (or even, as the film suggests, a relationship with Max), and her own career in a male-dominated field.

That Donna is a comic is significant, of course, in that it is emblematic of feminist gains generally. While Nancy complains that Donna's work is a disappointment, saying, "you waste that 780 verbal [SAT score] on telling

Figure 10. The mother's bed as a site of safety and support in *Obvious Child*. Nancy Stern (Polly Draper, left) and Donna Stern (Jenny Slate) (*Obvious Child*, A24, 2014, directed by Gillian Robespierre).

jokes about having diarrhea in your pants," it is precisely women's insistence on the right to speak publicly and honestly, to have their artistic expression taken seriously, and to pursue traditionally masculine vocations that have been bedrock goals in each feminist wave. Donna's brand of comedy, in particular, is based on gross-out humor that is frank and, for some, shocking. Donna declares in the routine that opens the film she has a "human vagina" before going on to describe some of what that entails. This radical openness and honesty about bodies and sex is a direct descendent of second wave consciousness-raising groups and third-wave sex radicalism and sex positivity.

In addition, Donna includes abortion in one of her later routines. She tells the audience that she is planning to terminate and then discloses:

> I decided to tell my mom and I thought she was gonna like, you know, be super upset.... But instead she was very relieved and she actually ended up telling me that she herself had gotten an abortion in the 60s.... And I can say that because, you know, once you get an abortion, you can reveal who else has had them. I decided to be on the list of the very many women that have done this.... It's gonna be okay because I'm not alone.... I think it's gonna be okay. And afterwards, I'll just be in my future.

Donna articulates finding comfort and strength in positioning herself as part of a larger group of women who have ended pregnancies. Her joke about being allowed to "reveal" who else has had an abortion is predicated, of course, on the continued secrecy and shame surrounding abortion despite its prevalence in many women's lives. In this way, not only is Donna connecting herself to the larger feminist tradition, but she is also participating in historical and more recent attempts to de-stigmatize abortion through public disclosure, the impetus behind the "We Have Had Abortions" feature of the inaugural issue of *Ms.* in 1972 as well as the more recent "Shout Your Abortion" online campaign which includes a twitter hashtag and a website which reads, in part: "Abortion is normal. Our stories are ours to tell. This is not a debate."

The rejection of shame and secrecy underpins the entire project of *Obvious Child,* as does its endorsement of openness and celebration of the experience of being female. One of the promotional images for the film (which appears on the movie's Tumblr), features a profile of Donna and the text, "Waiting to be ashamed of what I'll probably do this weekend. It's a girl thing!" The film thus goes further than simply accepting abortion as a reality of many women's lives, but also accepts mistakes as part of the maturation process. The copy on the image suggests that being "ashamed" of one's weekend behavior is badge of honor; the tagline "It's a girl thing!" provides an ironic twist on the idea that only men can engage in youthful indiscretions. This too, is a post-third wave way of thinking about young adulthood and crucial to the work of film and television writer discussed in the next section, Lena Dunham.

"Trying stuff out": Maternal Inheritance and the Permission to Fail in Tiny Furniture

Like *Margot at the Wedding,* a central tension in Lena Dunham's debut feature film *Tiny Furniture* is protagonist Aura's (played by Dunham) simultaneous desire for intimacy with her mother Siri (played by Laurie Simmons, Dunham's real-life mother) and her need for differentiation and independence. Also like *Margot at the Wedding, Tiny Furniture* is to a certain extent the child's homage to the mother; a *New Yorker* article about Dunham includes the line: "Laurie Simmons recently figured out that 'Tiny Furniture' is a love letter to her" (Mead). Siri is presented as a serious and accomplished artist as well as a patient and nurturing parent. Aura's uncertainty as to her own artistic vocation as well as her position in her family and, more generally, the world, is inextricable from her keen awareness of her mother's status. Ultimately, it is Siri who provides Aura with the support and assurance that floundering and failure are not only acceptable, but appropriate. The ability to experiment and, at times, to screw up, is a privilege only recently attained for women and still, of course, only truly available to some (usually white and affluent) individuals.

In "Lena Dunham's *Girls*: Can-Do Girls, Feminist Killjoys, and Women Who Make Bad Choices," Anna Backman Rogers identifies an anti-postfeminist worldview in Dunham's HBO series. According to Backman Rogers, *Girls* presents a "world of crisis" and "indicts a particular image of womanhood that serves pernicious structures at large and, moreover, painstakingly examines the mental and physical symptoms caused directly by this aspirational model of selfhood" (46). I follow Backman Rogers and argue that while *Tiny Furniture* also suggests that women's liberation entails the ability to choose freely, such ability must exist within a feminist context which permits a woman's failure. It is through her connection to her mother and to a larger female inheritance that Aura can take authentic risks.[9]

Before she can locate her place in the world, Aura first must determine her place in her family. Aura returns from college to her mother's Manhattan apartment, occupied by Siri, and Aura's sister, Nadine.[10] There is no mention of a father. In fact, the film opens with Aura letting herself in and calling out, "Honey, I'm home," an allusion to the stereotype of the 1950s husband who, reentering the domestic after his time in the public space, announces his intrusion as well as his expectation that he will be greeted and subsequently served (perhaps a martini and a roast). That Aura is not greeted, but instead must set off in search of her family, who are in her mother's studio working on art, suggests the mother-daughter tension that will unfold: like a traditional husband confronted with a professional wife, Aura expects to be needed as well as to be comforted, but while they are supportive of Aura, Siri and Nadine refuse to reorient their existences around her.

Aura's neediness is manifested in her desire to be near her mother and several scenes focus on Aura's violation of Siri's space. In a reversal of the devouring-mother stereotype, Siri is depicted as the character who must protect her body and her time from the child who claims an unending right to both. Thus, Siri allows Aura to sit on her lap, like a child, and when Aura asks, "Am I crushing you?" her mother responds, "A little bit." This exchange presents Siri's honesty with regard to physical discomfort and allegorically suggests that Siri refuses the position of the self-sacrificing, eternal mother.

Siri's bed becomes the primary site for this negotiation. Aura early on articulates a desire to sleep in her mother's bed and Siri responds that Aura may, but that she must first be invited. Aura responds, jokingly, "Like a vampire?" While Siri establishes clear boundaries, Aura's joke acknowledges a reality of the parent-child relationship: the fetus exists parasitically in the mother and, even after birth, the child is sustained if not literally by the parents' body, by the parents' labor. In her insistence on consent, *Tiny Furniture* begins to dramatize a new version of women's physical autonomy. The "good mother" does not have to be always available to the child.

Aura violates her mother's space in allowing a young man to stay in Siri's bed while Siri is away; in another scene, Aura attempts to sleep in her mother's bed only to discover that there is "no room" because her sister Nadine is already there. In many respects, then, the film is a series of thwarted attempts at closeness with the mother (Siri and Nadine go off on a college tour shortly after Aura arrives home) and Aura's violations of Siri's boundaries (she begins to read Siri's journals—and she drinks up all of her wine). This negotiation comes to its conclusion when Aura finally gets to be in her mother's bed at the film's end. In this scene, Aura has returned home after a demoralizing date. Aura massages her mother's back and confesses to having had unprotected sex in a construction pipe; she is clearly upset and ashamed. Although Siri chastises Aura for not using contraceptive protection, she remains unflappable and non-judgmental. When Aura also discloses that she's been reading Siri's journals, Siri remarks that she doesn't "mind." She describes her actions as a young woman: "I was just trying stuff out. Probably kind of like what you're doing."

Siri's connection to her own development as an artist and a woman validates Aura's experimentation, disappointment, and post-adolescent-angst as appropriate and perhaps even useful. In framing Aura's behavior as similar to her own youthful experimentation, Siri renders Aura's mistakes as part of a larger cycle: she is a young woman artist who is "trying stuff out." Earlier in the film, Aura declares she will never be "as successful" as Siri, to which Siri responds, "you will be more successful than me." Siri may be right, particularly as Aura is clearly following in Siri's footsteps.

As in *Obvious Child, Tiny Furniture* posits youthful misadventure as part of the process of growing up. This is important precisely because the flexibility to make mistakes has long been denied girls and women, especially with regard to sexuality and sexual experiences. Further, while of course women of previous generations insisted on "trying stuff out," the pernicious stigma around provocative or unconventional women has resulted in a silencing or disavowal of many of these experiences. Thus, the tagline for Dunham's HBO series *Girls* is also appropriate here: "Living the dream ... one mistake at a time." While perhaps ironically suggesting that the "dream" itself is not all it's cracked up to be, this tag line may also be interpreted to suggest that making mistakes is crucial to "the dream" itself. Dunham has remarked on the decision to center her film on a flawed and difficult character:

> my hope is that the reason she resonates with people is because she feels like a multidimensional woman, she looks like people they might know, and she is behaving in ways we can all certainly relate to even if you haven't committed her specific sins. And I've seen a lot of complex male characters over the years, and there have been some women, but it's probably because there are fewer women making movies.... In some ways, people have been more willing to forgive a male character's flaws. And that's something I'll be unpacking for my most of my career and trying to understand why that is and where you can take female characters that people try to not let you take them ... trying to push those audience boundaries [Silverstein].

In this way, Dunham's film as well as her television series engage with feminist debates beginning in the eighties and persisting today about the role of sex and sexuality in young women's lives. For example, responding to the anti-porn feminists of the 1980s, pro-sex feminists of the 1990s declared that women had a right to pursue sexual experimentation.[11] Ariel Levy's *Female Chauvinist Pigs* (2005) articulated discomfort with what many have termed the "pornification" of American popular culture, asking "Why is this the 'new feminism' and not what it looks like: the old objectification?"[12] Writing a review of Levy's work, Jennifer Baumgardner challenges the assumption that girls and young women who experiment sexually are doing irreparable harm: "If pressed, I'd venture that at least half of my sexual experiences make me cringe when I think about them today ... but if I didn't have those moments, I'm not sure I ever would have found my way to the real long-term relationship I have today. If all my sexual behavior had to be evolved and reciprocal and totally revolutionary before I had it, I'd never have had sex" ("Feminism Is a Failure"). Dunham's work in both *Girls* and *Tiny Furniture* enacts Baumgardner's claims, often featuring the protagonist engaging in demeaning sex under the guise of "trying stuff out." Crucially, however, in both the series and film, the protagonist has the support and understanding of a strong, accomplished, kind mother with whom the protagonist can speak honestly and openly and, again, without shame.

That mothers in Dunham's work are not presented as prudish scolds who uphold patriarchal notions of appropriate behavior for females suggests a move away from stereotypes about older women who don't "get it" or who are out of touch with their daughter's lives and experiences. Siri and Aura's relationship could itself function as an allegory of feminist "generations"; Siri is a representative of an older generation that has established itself and can raise daughters who "take for granted" equal treatment, the right to be sexually active, and who yearn to express themselves, but who are also often self-absorbed and demanding. Yet the mother and daughter's respect for and support of each other are reciprocal.

In the final moments of the film, Siri invites Aura to sleep in her bed. As they lay together, Siri becomes irritated by the ticking of a clock and asks Aura to move it. Aura complies, but when she returns, Siri observes that she can still hear the clock. Aura responds, "Yeah, but only a little bit right?" In addition to the symbolic possibilities of the older woman uncomfortable with a reminder of the passing time and the younger woman who is undisturbed, this scene brings into focus that one of Aura's primary conflicts is the desire for the mother's approval and her own (Aura's) unwillingness to take meaningful steps to ensure that approval. Perhaps Aura wants her efforts—however ineffectual—to be enough to satisfy Siri.

Dunham—who identifies as a feminist—chooses to explore the drama of a female family, to present the mother as a successful artist who is also a nurturing parent, and to trace a young woman's coming of age as an artist herself. The film hews closely to some of the details of Dunham's own life: Dunham's mother, Laurie Simmons, plays Siri (and Dunham's sister plays Aura's sister in the film) and Siri's work in *Tiny Furniture* closely resembles Simmons's work. Both artists recreate the domestic in miniature; in a *New Yorker* profile of Simmons, Calvin Tomkins describes the doll that often appears in Simmons's photographs: "a housewife, goes about her household activities (cleaning, cooking, watching TV) in a nineteen-fifties suburban environment whose claustrophobic loneliness evokes the terrors of the American dream" (36). Framed this way, it becomes clear that both Simmons and Dunham's work critiques the ideals of late 20th, early 21st century femininity, just as Siri and Aura's work as artists are both engaged in the feminisms of their moments.

Simmons has recently begun developing a film and, in the *New Yorker* article, she expressed her anxiety about moving into a field that has already been staked out by her daughter. She reasons, "So you fail, so you embarrass—people don't die from that. And, besides, children are supposed to be embarrassed by their mothers" (Tomkins 41). Thus, like her character in *Tiny Furniture*, Simmons recognizes not only that failure is intrinsic to artistic experimentation, but that failure is also potentially part of artistic, feminist, and maternal legacies as well.

"When I was your age": Intergenerational Connections (or the Matrophor) in Grandma

Like *Obvious Child,* Paul Weitz's *Grandma* (2015) centers on a young woman's plan to procure an abortion. While the film in many ways belongs to Elle, the titular grandma played by Lily Tomlin, it is also in some respects a buddy movie: on their intergenerational quest to raise the money for the termination, Elle's granddaughter Sage (Julia Garner) receives a crash-course feminist education as the two embark on a *Christmas Carol*-esque journey that describes feminism past, present and future.

Discussing his vision, Weitz articulates a consciousness of the importance of including a larger feminist context:

> I've done a couple of movies about mentorship but from the male perspective, and it finally had become clear to me how interesting it would be to me to do a movie about female mentorship. Also the idea that, in not only Lily's character and Julia's but Marcia Gay Harden's character [Sage's mother], that one could check in with different eras of consciousness of women's history, and the idea that there's been an erasure of women's history in the minds of young people now [Eisenbach].

Thus, *Grandma* highlights the achievements of previous feminist movements, as well as the danger of a postfeminist "taking for granted" of women's rights. If Jess Butler's contention is accurate that "while third-wave feminism actively engages with feminist history, if only to deem it inadequate, postfeminism displaces or replaces feminism altogether" (42), a film such as *Grandma* exists as a critique of such dismissals of previous movements. That is, Grandma acknowledges and is at times nostalgic for a feminist past at the same time as it suggests the need for a feminist future.

A lesbian poet and academic, Elle is an Adrienne Rich–type figure. When Sage says that Elle is famous, Elle modestly protests, "I was marginally well-known. Forty years ago." That the legacy of which Elle was a part is no longer recognized or truly valued by a younger generation is brought into focus when Elle develops a scheme to sell first-edition, signed feminist texts including Betty Friedan's *The Feminine Mystique* to raise funds. She is initially confident that this will garner thousands of dollars, but is revealed as out-of-touch with contemporary practices (Sage's quick Internet search shows that the books are sold for much less online) as well as, perhaps contemporary feminism itself.

Elle is also presented as disengaged from a larger feminist political community through her lack of awareness about the current state of reproductive rights. Because neither she nor Sage has the financial ability to pay for Sage's abortion, Elle brings Sage to the site of what had once been a free women's health clinic. They are disappointed, however, to find that the health center has been transformed into a coffee shop. While in the coffee shop, Elle loudly complains, asking, "Where do you get a reasonably priced abortion?" and declaring that six hundred dollars for an abortion is "highway robbery." Here, Elle articulates the platform of second wave radical feminists who argued for the right to free abortion on demand, a goal that had perhaps once seemed achievable in the United States.[13] Now, however, even discussing abortion had become taboo. The manager of the café approaches, saying, "I'm going to have to ask you to leave," and Elle responds, "You're 'going to have to?' When are you 'going to have to' ask us to leave?" Elle's confrontational responses foregrounds the manager's use of euphemism in order to conceal an unpleasant reality. As a feminist poet, Elle is acutely aware of the power of language and the scene overall suggests that not only is liberative health care disappearing, but even frank discussion of reproductive justice is disapproved of, impermissible, erased.

However, Elle's close relationship with a tattoo artist named Deathy, played by Laverne Cox, suggests that she is not completely disconnected from feminist thinking and community. One of the most contentious issues for many 21st-century feminists has been the status of trans women; while many trans women are feminists and while many cisgender women embrace their trans sisters, self-identified gender critical feminists, many of whom are part of an older generation of feminists, have contested the rights of trans women to identify as women.[14] That *Grandma* includes a trans character without making her trans-status the most salient feature of her identity, but rather, allows this status to remain unremarked upon is itself a (small) victory for feminist film. Additionally, it is clear that Elle herself is not trans-exclusionary as her clear embrace of Deathy suggests that she has not allowed herself to settle into entrenched positions.

The current state of feminism is also reflected in the film's depiction of the abortion clinic. While *Grandma* makes clear that the prohibitive cost of abortion is an obstacle to access, the clinic itself appears as almost an oasis after the mayhem of Elle and Sage's quest. The women who work in the clinic are presented as calm, kind, patient, and professional. When Elle, who had an abortion before *Roe v. Wade*, questions the doctor about whether the procedure will be painful, the doctor answers, "Well … like you said. This isn't the dark ages. Not here at least." While acknowledging the shortcomings of adequate health care for women both locally and globally, the doctor's remark also brings into focus the continued existence of access to reproductive medicine (at least for some people, in some places). That is, the fight for reproductive rights did have certain victories; although reproductive rights in the United States, for example, have been compromised in recent years (especially in many rural areas), as of this writing, the right to abortion remains constitutionally protected. American women technically do not have to procure illegal abortions. The doctor's remark, however, that it's not the "dark ages … here," also reflects a colonialist way of thinking about non–Western nations as "dark" or uncivilized, a characterization that is particularly problematic in a film that ignores many of the racial divisions that result in unequal abortion access. Perhaps in some ways this is emblematic of *Grandma's* vision's shortcomings generally: a film that includes several minor characters of color, including Elle's deceased partner, *Grandma* nevertheless remains focused almost exclusively on the problems of relatively affluent white women.

Beyond acquiring the money (which itself turns out to be not really a big deal—all Sage had to do was ask her mother), there are few obstacles to Sage's abortion access. There are two protestors outside of the clinic, but they are comic, ridiculous figures. Notably, the protestors are a mother and her young daughter, suggesting the intergenerational transmission of antifeminist values. The clinic staff seem to tolerate the protestors with a benevolent good humor. On the one hand, this treatment of the protestors allows the focus to remain on Sage's experience and the relationships between the women in her family; on the other hand, this depiction portrays threats to reproductive justice as absurd and rather harmless.

The film's conclusion suggests a reconciliation of the three generations. Judy, Elle's daughter, is a representation of what the second wave has wrought:

the child of liberated, lesbian mothers, Judy is empowered to become some sort of high-powered, "scary" businesswoman who is depicted as cycling through secretaries. Judy tells Elle, "I'm just ... I get so angry. I have so much anger. I don't know where it comes from.... Well ... you gave me good teeth too." Judy indicates that inheriting her mother's rage has been both positive and negative. Equipping their daughters for success in capitalist competition—her anger and drive render Judy and effective businessperson—is not perhaps what many second or third wave feminists might have imagined as their desired legacy, however.

Further, while Sage is perhaps the least-compelling and most underdeveloped character, she is nevertheless also the heir to these extraordinary women. Sage may take her right to abortion for granted, but she has also been given a feminist education over the course of the film. Part of this education is that with support, both in relationships and in larger systems such as health care, public policies, and historical knowledge, one's personal experiences can be placed in a context that makes them comprehensible and manageable. Thus, like *Tiny Furniture* and *Obvious Child*, *Grandma* depicts a young woman's sexual "mistakes" as unpleasant but not necessarily catastrophic. When Sage announces, "I'm such an idiot," Elle replies, "So was I, when I was your age." That Elle was once a foolish young person and yet still was able to develop a long-term fulfilling monogamous relationship, raise a child, and become an accomplished poet and academic suggests the fruition of the labors of the second wave and the promise of a feminist future.

The car that Elle uses to shepherd Sage from place to place may also serve as a metaphor of second-wave feminism. The car, which belonged to Elle's deceased partner Vi, is a classic and clunker, but it gets them where they need to go, until it doesn't. At the point when the car breaks down, possibly as a result of Elle driving too aggressively and pushing it past its limits, Elle and Sage must depend on kind, if potentially politically antagonistic strangers. Similarly, second-wave feminism functioned well to do much for many, but is no longer the appropriate vehicle for achieving feminist goals. Feminists must be resourceful and resilient and must look beyond our inheritance in order to move forward in our journey to equity, community, and empowerment.

Conclusion: "Mom" Has Arrived

The title of the film *Grandma* itself appears as a reclamation of a term that, when not used in relation to a specific person who is literally one's grandmother, is often used sarcastically or as a disparagement (i.e., "Get out of the way, grandma!"). However, in Weitz's film the grandma is possibly the "coolest" character. In the screenplay, she is introduced thus: "She is 70 years old, beautiful, and extremely willful.... There is nothing of the old lady about her. She is selfish and magnetic and smart" (Weitz). This description relies upon the stereotype of the "old lady" in order to define what Elle is not; but again, the title of the film suggests that a "Grandma" can be a daunting, impressive person.

Additionally, once shorthand for patently uncool (as in "mom jeans"), the appellation "mom" has undergone its own cultural reclamation. In 2014, when Kim Kardashian appeared nude in a *Paper* magazine photo spread, singer Lorde tweeted a one-word response: "MOM" (Lindner). Lorde's comment generated controversy and the singer tweeted again to clarify that "among the youthz ... [mom] is a compliment.... It basically jokingly means 'adopt me/be my second mom/i think of you as a mother figure you are so epic" (qtd. in Lindner). Or, as Jessica Bennett put it in the *New York Times*, "these days, 'mom' is the highest form of flattery. And you don't even have to be an actual mother to receive it (nor does the mom you're talking about need to be yours)."

To be a mom, then, is to function as a female role model, an inspirational figure to girls and young women. The notion of the non-biological mother as a caregiver and mentor also manifests in women's prisons, as reflected and perhaps popularized by the Netflix series *Orange Is the New Black,* in which groups of women form "families" headed by "moms."[15] That the valuation of older female mentors has reached the mainstream and has become a central compliment in celebrity culture—many fans call pop stars Beyoncé and Taylor Swift their "mom" (Bennett)—suggests a larger move toward celebrating accomplished, powerful women and recognizing the connection between mothering and success more generally. This is particularly important because while we often talk about the importance of care—especially regarding the very young and very old—our public policies currently do little to support the disproportionately female population that provides both unpaid and often offensively low paid care. And while popular terms such as "boss bitch" reflect the growing power of women in a variety of previously male dominated fields, the endearment "mom" does not connote any sort of masculinization. Instead, "mom" is inherently feminine and the term thus suggests the compatibility of traits such as nurturance and caring, strength and accomplishment, and in the case of Kim Kardashian, for example, "hotness" and overt sexuality.

Thus, perhaps female role models are increasingly available to young people, who themselves perceive role modeling and mentorship as crucial to their development. Rather than someone to be afraid of turning into, the mother may at times, at last, be someone worth emulating. It also perhaps no accident that this embrace of the mother in Western popular culture is occurring synchronously with a re-embrace of the "feminist" label and feminist activism generally.

8

"No wrong way to make a family": Hope and Home in *Tully* and *The Handmaid's Tale*

Michael McCuller's 2008 comedy *Baby Mama* follows protagonist Kate's (Tina Fey) attempt to start a family as a single parent. When visiting the office of Chaffee Bicknell (Sigourney Weaver), an agent who facilitates surrogacy arrangements, Kate expresses reservations. Chaffee reassures her: "We don't do our own taxes anymore. We don't program our computers. We outsource. And what is surrogacy if not outsourcing?" Kate asks, "Wait, you're not saying that my baby would be carried by some poor, underpaid woman in the third world?" Chaffee answers "no" and pauses to make a note; the joke, of course, is that an underpaid woman in the third world is exactly who Chaffee initially had in mind. Continuing to set Kate at ease, Chaffee asserts, "There's no wrong way to make a family."

This scene in *Baby Mama* serves to explicate surrogacy for those who might be unfamiliar with it, as well as to suggest the film's premise (a woman hiring a surrogate) as appropriate for comedy. That is, both Kate and the audience are assured that Kate's choice will not result in another woman's exploitation. However, at the film's crisis, when Kate finds out that Angie (Amy Poehler), the surrogate, has been lying, Kate cruelly describes Angie as "an ignorant white trash woman that I paid to carry my kid." While Kate and Angie later reconcile, Kate's remark cuts through the euphemisms and lays bare the hierarchy upon which many surrogacy arrangements are based, revealing Kate's awareness that this financial/reproductive relationship is based on the other woman's ostensible ignorance and economic precarity and suggesting that there is, perhaps, a "wrong way to make a family."

This chapter examines two generically disparate narratives—Jason Reitman's 2018 film *Tully* and the Hulu series *The Handmaid's Tale* (2017–present)—that trouble the notion that family-building is always a noble endeavor. Rather, in these narratives, the practice of making a family is predicated on women's exploitation, dramatizing the continued expectation that women will provide domestic labor and care that benefit men. Grappling with the ethical complexities surrounding the technologies of household and reproductive labors, *Tully* and *The Handmaid's Tale* present the "outsourcing" of "women's work" as reifying sexist gender roles and upholding patriarchy. At the same time as these narratives present the home as a site of captivity, they also present a longing for an ideal domestic, a site in which women are cared for, valued beyond their maternal functions, and autonomous. Thus, while they critique women's exploitation and suffering, both narratives nevertheless maintain the value of domestic and reproductive work, re-idealizing motherhood and asserting the home as a potential place of hope, healing, and redemption.

New Paradigms for Outsourcing Labor

According to the Barnard Report "Valuing Domestic Work," as a result of privatization and withdrawal of government support from industries including after-school, daycare and elder-care programs, many families employ a variety of cleaners, health care aides, and childcare providers (Nadasen and Williams 5).[1] Increasingly, those doing the work are women of color and their employers are white; they are often "excluded" workers who receive few legal protections (6). The report connects domestic work's "degraded" status to "the gendered and racialized composition of the workforce" (3) and further points out that "the long-standing association of domestic work with women's unpaid household labor has sometimes made it difficult for others to see it as 'real work.'" Similarly, Arianne Shahvisi states that, "The dialectic of feminisation is at work: domestic work is undervalued *because* it is largely performed by women (and, where it is outsourced, usually racialized women), but this is also *why* it is largely performed by women. The devaluation of housework is not merely accidental, rather, it is a natural consequence of social value tracking the interests of the powerful."

In "This Should Be My Responsibility: Gender, Guilt, Privilege and Paid Domestic Work," Amanda Moras also notes that a combination of factors, including worsening economic inequality as well as women's growing participation in the labor market, have resulted in increases in paid domestic labor. While, she contends, "This re-delegation of domestic labor may in some ways represent a threat to privileged women's self image as caring for family has been inextricably part of the ideological construction of what constitutes a good wife and mother" (45), women who employ others often assume a supervisory role. Such a situation, Moras points out, fails to challenge gender roles, instead "displacing housework along raced and classed lines" (45): "This displacement further reinforces the gendered division of labor, continuously ascribing housework and childcare to women. Women contribute to the devaluation of this labor by keeping the occupation underpaid and undervalued" (62). As a result, as Shahvisi points out, some women thus enjoy "the privileges traditionally reserved for men" while men "avoid having those privileges destabilized."

Just as outsourcing of domestic labor may ostensibly liberate certain women at the same time as it reifies entrenched gender, class, and race hierarchies, outsourcing reproductive labor may promise to promote diversity in family structures while it simultaneously upholds those same oppressive hierarchies. Advanced reproductive technologies allow us to imagine a variety of family configurations; for this reason, some second wave feminists imagined that technologies including contraception, abortion, IVF, and surrogacy would liberate women from the biological vicissitudes of pregnancy and childbirth. For example, in 1970, Shulamith Firestone argued that "Nature produced the fundamental inequality—half the human race must bear and rear the children of all of them—which was later consolidated, institutionalized, in the interests of men" and called for "freeing women from the tyranny of the reproductive biology by every means available" (qtd. in Vandenberg-Daves 227).[2]

However, recent practices of surrogacy rely on and shore up understandings of some women as deserving and others as exploitable.[3] In *Brown Bodies, White Babies: The Politics of Cross-Racial Surrogacy*, Laura Harrison writes that while assisted reproductive technologies contain the "potential to transform hegemonic and traditionally restrictive family formations ... the nuclear family has not disintegrated since the advent of reproductive technologies ... indeed, reproductive technologies, including surrogacy, are primarily used in a manner that reinforces the reproduction of the white, heterosexual, married, middle-class family" (2). International surrogacy, in particular, depends upon inequality; as philosopher Francesco Pupa points out, the "process seems to allow the most advantaged members of society to exploit the least advantaged members in one of the most intimate and sensitive areas of life." A woman who opts to gestate another's baby is often doing so as a result of conditions of extreme poverty, a situation that moral philosophers might term a constraint on her freedom.

Much of the current discourse surrounding commercial surrogacy relies upon the erasure of the surrogate's context and personhood. The "new paradigm" in surrogacy, according to Yasmine Ergas, functions thus: one person provides sperm, one person provides ova, and another person carries the pregnancy. In "Babies Without Borders: Human Rights, Human

Dignity, and the Regulation of International Commercial Surrogacy," Ergas writes:

> The provider of ova, stripped of maternal reference altogether, is referred to in the sexually neutralized language of genetic donation ... in the current language of commercial reproduction, the attribute "parent" has been reserved for the commissioning parties, now denominated the "intended parents." These linguistic practices have become so well established that they are routinely reduced to acronyms: "GC" denotes the gestational carrier, "IPs," the intended parents. The recodification entailed is normatively freighted, implicitly indicating how one ought to think.

The surrogate is not only often referred to as a "gestational carrier" or "embryo carrier," but more informally, according to Ergas, is also often described as someone who "rents out" her womb. These phrases reduce the surrogate's body to real estate, or property, in both senses of the word.

Despite this new paradigm, there is increasing discomfort with international surrogacy and several nations, including Nepal and India, have recently banned or limited the practice. Crucially, the limits put on surrogacy often specifically target gay and lesbian couples; India, for example, which had a booming surrogacy industry, banned surrogacy for gays and lesbians in 2012 (Rudrappa). Thus this radical practice, a practice that, again, has the potential to liberate women from physical pregnancy and to allow LGBTQIA+ folks to build genetically related families, becomes a conservative instrument, used to reinforce heteronormativity. Rather than expanding definitions of family, much commercial surrogacy reasserts monogamous heterosexuality as the only legal and socially legible model for parenthood.

Both employing domestic labor and employing reproductive surrogates, then, are predicated on the notion that the work of maintaining a home and creating a family are first, women's work, and second, the kinds of jobs that can be performed by an individual external to the family. The term "outsourcing," of course, originates in the business world and refers to the practice of shipping certain tasks or jobs overseas, away from the company or corporation's national home, to a place with a presumably lower paid work force. The outsourcing of domestic work is also predicated on the existence of those who are exploitable. In addition, the employee is often a national "outsider" and, by definition, an outsider to the conventional family unit. In general, the outsourcing of domestic and reproductive labor as a means to build or maintain the family are practices imbricated in and justified by capitalist ideology as well as a neoliberal, postfeminist attitude that consumption of goods and services is the solution to most, if not all, problems.

The texts discussed below both engage with anxiety over the imperative to family building—as though nothing could be more noble—as well as the high price of family building for mothers and other women.[4] In *Tully* and *The Handmaid's Tale*, a crisis in resources provides the justification for "outsourcing" or the inclusion of non-familial female labor; both also suggest this solution as unworkable. Importantly, however, neither narrative concludes that family-building should be abandoned altogether, but rather reassert mothering as rewarding, positive, and potentially salutary for the mother herself.

"You can't fix the parts without treating the whole": Reconciling Fragmentation in Tully

In the first half of Reitman's *Tully* (written by Diablo Cody[5]), "outsourcing" appears to be the solution to inequity in the home, but this solution is ultimately revealed as an untenable self-deception; it is literally a fantasy. Protagonist Marlo's (Charlize Theron) struggle exemplifies the difficulties many women face in trying to fulfill multiple, sometimes impossible roles, and posits fragmentation, the splitting of the self, as this character's response to the presumably irreconcilable claims made on her for care, attention, and support as well as her own desire for care, attention, and support.

Tully initially appears to explore similar territory as several recent televisions shows, including ABC Australia's/Netflix's *The Let Down* (2016–present) and Channel 4/Amazon's series *Catastrophe* (2015–2019), narratives that delve into the under-discussed indignities, unappreciated sacrifices, and quotidian frustrations new parents often experience. Mothers in these shows are depicted trudging zombie-like to cribs, taken unaware by the vicissitudes of the post-partum body, dealing with a seemingly endless amount of excrement, enacting Simone De Beauvoir's description of housework as "like the torment of Sisyphus" (474). Mining early parenthood for comic moments, these narratives exist in part as rebukes to the earlier practice of either idealizing or ignoring the difficulties and realities of caring for infants and small children.

Similarly, *Tully* begins with Marlo lumbering long-faced through the third trimester and early weeks of her third child's life. Although there are comic moments, Marlo appears on the verge of a severe depression, and is never depicted as smiling or pleased with the new infant. Her brother, who fears "what happened last time" will happen again (thus alluding to an earlier bout with postnatal depression), bemoans that his sister in recent years appears to him as though "somebody snuffed a match."

Tully takes a turn, however, when a night nanny named Tully (Mackenzie Davis), ostensibly hired by Marlo's brother, turns up to rescue the family. Tully tends expertly to both the baby Mia and to Marlo; however, as discussed further below, Tully is ultimately revealed as Marlo's fantasy/hallucination, an embodiment of Marlo's younger-self, returned.[6] While it is Tully's assistance that apparently enables Marlo to "get through the danger zone" of the first postnatal months, Tully is herself both symptom and cause of the problem: Marlo has actually been performing as both herself and as Tully, staying up at night making cupcakes and taking care of Mia, and then moving smilingly through the day, asserting she's well-rested and well-adjusted. The film thus not only depicts the impossible demands often faced by new mothers, but also suggests that the current understanding of successful mothering is itself dangerous to women.

Although it may superficially seem to be yet another exploration of middle-class families' woes, *Tully* exists as a complex critique of the status quo around mothering, families, and gender. Richard Brody, writing in the *New Yorker*, sees *Tully* as devoid of political content, writing that "the film is uninterested in the economic and social demands of motherhood among, for instance, the many working mothers who have no managerial job, no high-earning partner, no rich brother, or, for that matter, no maternity leave. Instead, its vision of freedom from responsibility and self-rediscovery places it all solidly within the hermetically sealed bubble of unquestioned privilege." While Brody is certainly accurate in his description of Marlo's household as, in many ways, quite privileged, Marlo's breakdown is itself an indictment of a sensibility that refuses to see the political in the personal. Postfeminist neoliberal ideology frames motherhood as a personal "choice" regardless of the political and structural forces that promote, for example, the naturalization of an unequal division of domestic labor which persists in our post-second wave world, as men continue to do less housework and childcare than their female partners.[7] Additionally, as Linda Seidel points out in *Mediated Maternity: Contemporary American Portrayals of Bad Mothers in Literature and Popular Culture*, cultural and political trends have resulted in the "potential isolation of the American mother" (Seidel xiv): "Extended families are likely to be far away, neighbors unknown, skillful nannies a luxury for the rich" and yet "Neither government policy nor civil society has attempted to create a collective or communitarian approach to child-rearing—or even to guarantee the existence of safe, affordable child care" (xiv).

Thus, although Marlo is fortunate, within this context, to have maternity leave at all, what does it mean if someone so well-situated is nevertheless isolated, exhausted, and profoundly unhappy? The problem, *Tully* suggests, is limited resources; the solution, initially, seems to be more female labor (rather than the increased participation of Drew, Marlo's spouse). Drew (Ron Livingston) is well-meaning and a generally positive character, but is presented as only marginally available for childcare. Marlo defends Drew, saying that "He works really hard and then he comes home. He does the homework, the reading logs, all that. We make lunches together. And then goes upstairs, puts on a headset, kills zombies and passes out." And yet despite his status as an overall good father, Drew fails to notice his wife's deepening crisis and even initially seems reluctant to employ the night nanny, asking Marlo, "You okay?" in a manner that suggests that there must be something wrong with Marlo, rather than the situation, if she were to need assistance. In this way, then, the film highlights a mundane reality that reflects a structural inequality: individuals may personally believe in domestic equity, but may nevertheless find it hard to actually pull off when confronted with seemingly intractable governmental policies and cultural practices such as the nonexistence of parental leave for many fathers and a persistent gender wage gap coupled with the high cost of child care that, taken together, often makes it more practical for mothers to take extended leaves and/or drop out of the workforce when they have young children.

In short, Marlo, like many women, is doing all of the childcare and domestic work and, in this way, *Tully* brings into focus a "care gap" in the traditional family. Although the labor of caring for others has its own rewards, care in Marlo's home is non-reciprocal: no one provides care to Marlo. The film opens with a tender scene of Marlo "brushing" her son, Jonah, an ostensibly therapeutic practice that will help de-sensitize the "quirky" child. While Marlo later suggests that the exercise might be a bit of quackery, the scene presents the intimacy between mother and son—she lifts his shirt to brush his back and hold his foot as she brushes his sole—that, given the smile on her face, is pleasurable to both mother and child. At the film's end, Jonah suggests that the brushing itself is unnecessary, but says, "I like being by you," demonstrating the importance of this kind of care and physical closeness.

In contrast, immediately after the opening scene of Marlo brushing Jonah, a close-up of Marlo's feet on a personal massage device demonstrates that no one is tending to the hugely pregnant mother-to-be. Rather, she and her husband make plans as Marlo squeezes lotion onto her abdomen and rubs it in. Again, this moment, coming directly after the scene of Marlo brushing her son, suggests that, like a stereotypical eternally self-sacrificing mother, she is expected to uncomplainingly provide while asking for nothing for herself. That Marlo's escape is watching the reality television show *Gigolos*, about men who meet women's physical and sexual needs for money, suggests the extent to which she longs for someone to "take care of" her, as Tully will later vow to do.

It seems that only through the paid employment of another woman Marlo can have her needs met. Upon her arrival, Tully assures Marlo that, "I'm going to take care of you…. You pretty much are the baby" and "I'm here to help with everything. Not just Mia. You can't fix the parts without treating the whole." (She also rehearses au courant clichés such as, "You can't be a good mother if you don't practice self-care," which is itself predicated on old-fashioned ideas that justify women's ostensibly non-maternally focused actions only so far as they serve to make them better mothers). In this way, Tully quickly comes to represent a wish-fulfillment, offering Marlo the kind of companionship and connection that perhaps all people, and maybe new mothers most acutely, desire: someone endlessly curious about her, sincerely devoted to her comfort and happiness, ready to listen, empathize, and assist. In fact, this is the kind of attention most often bestowed upon children by their mothers. In this way, Marlo mothers herself (through Tully).

That Tully is a hallucination thus underscores the lack of this kind of care in many women's lives. In fact, Tully initially presents as "weird," or as an embodiment of the nightmare of the nanny who will disrupt or destroy the family.[8] Before Tully's arrival, Marlo's objection to the notion of hiring help is not predicated on a principled uneasiness with domestic labor generally, but is instead rooted in more personal anxieties: fear of being perceived as a bad mother and fear of an interloper who will endanger the family unit. For example, discussing her brother's offer to hire a night nurse, Marlo says, "you can't outsource your entire life" before jokingly asking if the night nanny will "breastfeed." Underpinning Marlo's exaggeration—equating someone who cares for an infant with asking that person to manage an "entire life"— is the thinking that, for a mother, infant care is or should be one's "entire life." Further, in her remark about breastfeeding, Marlo gestures to a fear of being supplanted or replaced, of the hired help transgressing ostensibly natural boundaries. Drew's response that they aren't living in "feudal China" suggests at least an awareness of the ways in which wet nursing is a practice rooted in exploitation.[9]

Again, however, Marlo's concern is not a reluctance to exploit another woman. Rather, Marlo explains, "I don't want a stranger in my house, bonding with my newborn every night. That's like a Lifetime movie where the nanny tries to kill the family and the mom survives and she has to walk with a cane at the end." Marlo articulates a fear of being displaced; additionally, her remark touches upon a distrust of the kinds of people who would choose to work in another's home. Films such as *The Hand That Rocks the Cradle* (1992) and Lifetime's *Evil Nanny* (2016) capitalize on anxieties about women who are not appropriately maternal or domestic as well as the *type* of person who does domestic work. If she is a single woman (and white), in particular, she is suspect. The Lifetime version of the nanny, according to Marlo, is the insidious interloper.

Yet, at the conclusion of *Tully*, Marlo does in fact walk with a cane as a result of a drunken driving accident (during which Marlo falls asleep at the wheel). The irony is, of course, that Marlo's injury is a result of *not* truly outsourcing or soliciting help. She has not had to "save" her family from Tully (as would perhaps happen in a Lifetime movie); instead, Tully has saved Marlo from her family, or, perhaps, from a larger culture in which family arrangements like Marlo's, in which the mother bears disproportionate responsibility for the well-being of the other family members, is in fact the status quo.

In the end, *Tully* suggests, as currently practiced, family life is bad for women's health. It is only after a crisis, however, that Marlo can articulate her needs and goals as well as discover her own competence. Before she departs, Tully tells Marlo:

> you're convinced that you're this failure, but you actually made your biggest dream come true ... that sameness you despise. That's your gift to them. Waking up every day and doing the same things for them over and over. You are boring, your marriage is boring, your house is boring but that's fucking incredible. That's the big dream, that you grow up and be dull and constant and then raise your kids in that circle of safety.

Here, then, bourgeois family life, stability and familiarity, is presented as an achievement. And, perhaps Tully's assessment is accurate: simply surviving patriarchal motherhood is an accomplishment. Further, Tully's statement is a valorization of home itself, a concept that many superficially endorse but which the realities surrounding childcare (low pay for childcare providers, no pay or social security for stay-at-home mothers, and a lack of federally mandated paid family leave) belie.

However, it is precisely Marlo's attempt to maintain this "boring" life that almost kills her. After her accident, which results from the exhaustion, Marlo says to Drew, "I was doing great. Wasn't I great?" Marlo's version of "great," of course, was always untenable. And yet, Marlo has the ability to literally and metaphorically pull herself out of the wreckage, revealing that Marlo already possessed the resources and perspective she needed. Like Dorothy in *The Wizard of Oz*, whose discovery of the words, "There's no place like home," function to return her to the longed-for domestic, Marlo discovers that she has had the power to save herself all along: it is not some outsider or interloper who identifies and articulates Marlo's mother-work as an accomplishment, but Marlo herself. And in allowing her earlier—more fun, more spontaneous, more exciting—self to reveal this truth, Marlo is also finally capable of reintegrating those two identities: the boring and the fun, the childfree woman and the mother.

Thus, Marlo becomes aware of her own competence and success, just as Drew is called to account for his failure not only to more fully participate in the family, but to perceive Marlo's suffering and his own negligence. At the hospital, when Drew tells the doctor that Marlo's behavior had been "out-of-character" because she'd left with "no one watching the kids," the doctor asks, "Weren't you home?," underlining Drew's failure to identify himself as a functioning parent, even to himself. His awareness heightened as a result of the near-tragedy, Drew apologizes to Marlo, saying, "I wasn't taking care of you." Importantly, Drew does not simply promise to better parent their children, but acknowledges Marlo as an individual in need of care.

Tully concludes with images of Drew's more full participation in the running of the household: Drew is shown independently interacting with the children and holding Mia. Superficially, the ending seems to suggest that a happy resolution is accomplished when men simply realize that they have to do more around the house, and the last scene, in which Drew and Marlo make lunches, suggests a recommitment to partnership at home.

This message, of course, remains problematic if we understand it as propping up the neoliberal imperative to private suffering. Further, the film suggests, perhaps not unrealistically, that change only happens as a result of a near-implosion of the family unit. That is, like many heterosexual American men, Drew has no reason to question the division of labor in his home until its unsustainability becomes undeniable. As Iris Marion Young writes in "The Five Faces of Oppression," "The freedom, power, status and self-realization of men is possible precisely because women work for them. Gender exploitation has two aspects, transfer of the fruits of material labor to men and transfer of nurturing and sexual energies to men" (278). That is, why would men, who are traditionally well-served by the conventional, patriarchal nuclear family structure, seek to change it? Introducing another, female, laborer into the home remains, for many men and women alike, a more palatable solution to a problem of limited resources.

More broadly, *Tully* suggests the necessity of a fundamental rethinking of both the practice and value of mothering and housework. Thus, the point of *Tully* is that because she has resisted outsourcing, or the hiring of another person to help, Marlo feels forced to fragment herself in order to meet the demands placed upon her and keep her family intact and functioning. Ultimately, *Tully* presents not only a longing for an appropriate valuing of the domestic and of mothers' work, for family structures that allow women to be complex, complete human beings, but also a reconfiguration of gender dynamics in the family that would allow mothers, too, to be taken care of, nurtured, and supported.

"Better never means better for everyone"[10]: The Handmaid's Tale *and the Annexation of the Other*

Tully's remark that you "You can't fix the parts without treating the whole" is both accurate and ironic in that Tully, as an aspect or part of Marlo's personality and history, must be reintegrated in order for Marlo to heal. *Tully* posits one of the afflictions of the contemporary woman is the desire to be everything, to everyone, all at once. Marlo, for example, tells Tully that she does not feel capable of sexually connecting with her husband. She explains, "I hold a baby all day and it's me and it's her and it's primal. We're like two gorillas in the zoo. And then nighttime rolls around and I'm supposed to just switch gears? Like, hello, all sexy now. Look at my boobs ... they're all sexual...." Marlo suggests that the intimacy between herself and Mia is natural ("like two gorillas in the zoo"), while her intimacy with Drew is artificial, forced, or inconsistent ("hello, all sexy now"). Marlo's discomfort is rooted in her inability to reconcile the multiplicity of body, or the way in which her breasts, for example, might themselves function differently depending on context. As a result, Marlo's psyche fractures and her persona as Tully allows her to bridge "a gap" (as Tully puts it elsewhere), through dissociation; thus, in a rather jarring scene, Tully seduces Drew as Marlo watches and coaches. This moment suggests that Marlo is ostensibly willing to "outsource" intimacy with her husband in order to keep her family intact and stable.

While stylistically and thematically quite different, the Hulu series *The Handmaid's Tale* is also a narrative in which women's fragmentation results from exploitation in the patriarchal family and, in fact, *The Handmaid's Tale* and *Tully* feature strikingly similar key scenes: a younger woman has intercourse with an older woman's husband, while the older woman/wife looks on. In *Tully,* this scene is relatively benign in that the sex is consensual (and really only includes two people), while these scenes in the *Handmaid's Tale* are scenes of rape and a state-sanctioned exploitation of women's bodies.

The repetition of this tableau reveals that both narratives are centrally concerned with a crisis of resources; that is, one woman in the family simply isn't enough to get the job done. While in *Tully,* there are really only two people in the bedroom (although Marlo believes there are three), in *The Handmaid's Tale* there are three people in the bedroom, although the exploiters pretend that there really are only two. The Handmaids, too, imagine their own absence. In voice-over narration, Handmaids describe their strategies for dissociating: protagonist June (Elisabeth Moss) says, "One detaches oneself" and, after a particularly brutal rape, "I'm not here" ("The Last Ceremony").

The Handmaid's Tale, based on Margaret Atwood's 1985 novel, presents a near-future in which a fundamentalist religious group has taken over the United States, renaming it the Republic of Gilead, and institutionalizing a perverse version of Christianity that permeates every aspect of social, political, and familial life. Framed as a response to an infertility epidemic, women are assessed and sorted: "Wives" are hostesses and comforters to their husbands; "Marthas" are housekeepers and cooks; "Handmaids" are forced surrogates. Women within their groups are apparently interchangeable,[11] as evidenced by how the Handmaids are moved around, living in temporary "postings," their names changed to signify the commanders they serve. For example, June is called "Offred" when she lives in Commander Fred Waterford's home. These practices deprive Handmaids of stable identities and render them homeless. Further, Handmaids are legally reduced to what they can provide in service of the patriarchy: they are "wombs on legs" or "two-legged wombs" ("Birth Day"). Thus, the solution to the problem of limited resources is the institutionalized instrumentalization of women's bodies.

This use of a human body as a means to an end is crystallized in the scenes of rape: the practice is justified through an idealization of reproduction. Children are valued above all in Gilead; as Commander Waterford remarks, "Children. What else is there to live for?" ("Faithful"). However, having children is a good that, according to Gilead's framers, is reserved for the patriarchal family: this is why gay and lesbian families are dismantled and erased and homosexuals persecuted as "gender traitors." It is this overvaluation of the fetus/child that results in the attainment of the child as the motivating factor in both domestic life and national policy in Gilead. As a result, not only are biological mother's bodies less important than adoptive mothers,' but Handmaids's bodies are also clearly deemed less valuable than fetal bodies, a hierarchy also dramatized in the novel: "Separating Offred's rights from those of her potential child, her situation satirizes the idea that women are not only adversely related to the foetus, or to the future child, but are actually much less politically important" (Latimer 220). In this way, although ostensibly rooted in Christian theology, Gilead fully transforms family-building as a consumerist activity; children are the property of the rich, the privileged (and the lucky).[12]

Further, the logic of Gilead relies on a tricky contradiction: it is precisely the Handmaids' humanness that makes them useful, but is it that humanity which renders them inconvenient. The Gileadean rhetoric around exploitation relies upon an elision of the Handmaid herself: she is at once absorbed and erased by the family she is forced to serve. That is, in *The Handmaid's Tale*, families are made through the annexation of less-powerful women's bodies. Serena Joy (Yvonne Strahovski) thus inflicts various punishments whenever June refers to or asks about her daughter Hannah (born before the coup which establishes Gilead) because Hannah represents a threat to Serena's denial of June's personhood. Hannah's existence reveals that June has or had an identity beyond her function as a "womb on legs" in the Waterford household; further, June's maternal identity is itself and affront to Serena. Serena's ordering of the world relies on June's body as functioning as a prosthetic to Serena's own body. As a result, many of Serena's creepiest moments take place when June is pregnant and Serena assumes intimacy with June: in one scene, Serena crawls into bed with June, cradles the other woman's abdomen and says "Mama loves you" ("Other Women"); in another scene, while discussing pregnancy pillows that might aid in June's comfort, Serena remarks, "I'll look in to getting one for us" ("First Blood"). Serena thus attempts to collapse June into herself, to absorb the other, inconvenient woman.

Serena is not unique; throughout, a Handmaid's personhood is treated as an adjunct to the Wife's. As described above, the Handmaids, for example, lie between the Wives' legs during rape/intercourse, an idea proposed by a commander as a way of placating Wives who may have otherwise disapproved of the practice ("Women's Work"). In addition, when a Handmaid goes into labor, the wife she serves performs labor as well, presumably in order to access the experience of childbirth (although their earnest playacting only adds further insult to the Wives' sociopathically inhumane treatment of other women). Serena succumbs to the deceit she herself perpetuates when she attempts to breastfeed the baby Nicole (née Holly). While nursing a non-biological child is possible and is practiced cross-culturally, Serena's attempt is pathetic in part because it reveals how desperately she desires to inhabit June's maternal body, as well as her investment in June as merely an accessory (and a disposable one, at that). Serena says, "I'm sorry," to the infant, apologizing for not being able to physically provide what baby Nicole wants, but also apologizing, perhaps, for her attempt to usurp the role of biological mother ("Postpartum"). (Additionally, Serena's attempt to breastfeed exists as a reversal of Marlo's question, "Does she breastfeed?" in *Tully*. However, rather than anxiety over the ability of a non-biological caregiver's ability to perform as a mother, Serena's action suggests an anxiety over the non-biological mother's ability to perform as a caregiver.)

This erasure of the Handmaid's personhood as separate from the Wife's is what makes possible the violation of the parent-child relationship, which itself is presented as the ultimate injury. As Jennifer Maher points out in "Torture Born: Babies, Bloodshed and the Feminist Gaze in Hulu's *The Handmaid's Tale*," the series valorizes biological motherhood, as well as the restoration of the non-patriarchal family and home. Maher takes issue with this aspect of the series, asking, "in order to most effectively 'warn' us against repressive reproductive futurity does *The Handmaid's Tale* marshal its own kind of neoliberal reproductive fantasies of substance (if not the sanctity) of the nuclear family? ... Gilead is the *most* horrifying of places not only for its cruel gender tyranny but for its distortion of the most 'primary' of human relationships: heterosexual love that produces biological children" (209).

Maher's criticism is valid; *The Handmaid's Tale* certainly emphasizes the importance of romantic and biological relationships. However, in addition to embracing biological motherhood, the series also gestures toward the possibilities of legitimately, humanely, and consensually expanding familial relationships. For example, in the episode "After," June's best friend Moira is depicted as choosing to become a surrogate. Moira's experience is rendered as difficult, but tolerable and potentially positive.

Further, *The Handmaid's Tale* affirms the mother-child relationship as sustaining not simply for children, but for mothers as well. In *The Handmaid's Tale*, June's memories of being with Hannah often focus on times of laughter and play; perhaps a sentimentalized version of the relationship, but one which, again, focuses on the delights of parenthood for the parent. In addition, while the tension of the entire series relies heavily on the threat of family-disruption, this threat is not solely concerned with the damage done to the child. In fact, Hannah is shown to be basically okay when she and June are briefly reunited; although her question for June, "did you try to find me … why didn't you try harder?" ("The Last Ceremony"), suggests her trauma as a result of their separation, it is June's pain—not only at witnessing her daughter's pain, but also at being separated from her daughter—that most clearly registers in this scene.

Additionally, the series, which is so clearly focused on unconventional strategies for the construction of the conventional family, provides counter-examples of alternatives besides the traditional, heteronormative and patriarchal home. First and most superficially, the series includes several interracial families: June and Luke (O-T Fagbenle), Moira (Samira Wiley) and Odette (Rebecca Rittenhouse), and there is also a mixed-raced couple that assists June when she tries to escape. While the show has been criticized for a failure to adequately address race, the depiction of multiracial families is notable, if only because of the sad lack of diversity that persists in so many television and film depictions generally.

Second, the series suggests the possibilities of establishing sustaining, non-traditional family groupings. First, those who are able to escape exploitation in Gilead settle in Canada, in an area called "Little America," indicating longing for their stolen national home. Second, survivors, not unlike some biological families, find themselves bound together by forces beyond their control. Thus, before the coup that establishes Gilead, Luke and Moira are presented as tolerating each other for June's sake and, when she arrives in Canada, Moira reports that she does not have any family to receive her. But at the end of that episode, Luke appears at the refugee center. Asked how he knew where to find her, Luke tells Moira that he was alerted to her entry because she was on his "list." She asks, "List? List of family?" When he answers, "Yeah, of course," she clutches him and weeps with apparent relief and gratitude ("Night"). In their shared love of June, memories of pre–Gilead life, and ongoing grappling with trauma, Luke and Moira are irrevocably connected.

In Season 2, Moira, Luke, and Erin (a woman that Luke met during his own escape) (Erin Wray) cohabitate, forming a family-like unit. In particular, Luke assumes a quasi-parental attitude toward Erin, although, as of this writing, the exact nature of their relationship remains unclear. In addition, in the episode "Baggage," Moira assumes a maternal attitude toward Luke. She cooks him eggs and he says, "Thanks, mom." When she replies, "Fuck you," he counters, "Whoa, my mom used to say the same thing." In this moment, Luke acknowledges their new relationship. In a world in which mothers are in demand, Luke, Moira and Erin have established an alternative currency and sustaining family unit.

Finally, this family unit is further expanded with the arrival of June's daughter Nicole, who is smuggled out of Gilead and delivered to Luke and Moira. Initially, Luke is ambivalent about the child and it seems as though Moira will be forced into a caregiver role. In the episode titled "Mary and Martha," Luke states that June is attempting to save Hannah "cause I couldn't." Here, Luke's discomfort stems from his inability to fulfill the conventional role of the male hero who rescues the vulnerable females. Moira responds that June "had another job in mind for you," indicating that there are other ways of performing heroism and sacrifice and, in particular, that Luke must rise to the occasion and care for a child he is not biologically related to. This act is itself a radical rebuke of the Gileadian system that privileges only male biological connection to offspring and is thus a rejection of the fraudulence of the nuclear families so important to Gilead's national identity.

Further, that Luke does come to care for Nicole, both emotionally and physically, suggests the possibilities for reimagining more expansive familial arrangements. In this way, rather than a depiction of the addition of female labor in order to meet familial needs, *The Handmaid's Tale* gestures to the possibilities for a matriarchal family in which demands might be met through the addition of male laborers and nurturers.[13]

Conclusion: Reproductive Enhancements and the Future of Parenthood

Tully and *The Handmaid's Tale* exemplify many of the contentions in Kate Manne's philosophical investigation, *Down Girl: The Logic of Misogyny*. One of Manne's primary concerns is the ways in which misogyny is the tool used to punish women who fail to perform according to conventional expectations. That is, women who fail to provide nurturing, care, support and attention to men are often penalized, criticized, and otherwise injured. In *Tully* and the *Handmaid's Tale*, outsourcing exists to protect some women from a potential misogynistic backlash, as women who do not or cannot provide certain kinds of female-coded labor hire other women to perform it instead. Thus, rather than an altered ideological approach to domestic or reproductive labor, outsourcing is an extension of the current approach.

However, in addition to depicting the patriarchal response to unsustainable domestic situations as predicated on women's increased exploitation of other women, each narrative maintains the nobility and value of mothering and home-making, a move that some might reject as suggesting an ultimately conservative argument regarding women's roles in society. Yet, these narratives also begin to reveal the limitations of many contemporary family arrangements and suggest the potential of technologies that would facilitate truly radical remakings of the family.

As stated above, in the past fifty years, feminists have debated, critiqued, and speculated about the possibilities of reproductive technologies for reconsidering family formation. While academic feminism has, to a large extent, marginalized mothering studies in recent years, important work continued and continues at the margins and, in particular, many have continued to position the sphere of reproduction as a crucial site for understanding and disrupting the functioning of patriarchy.[14] In 1991, philosopher Susan Moller Okin writes,

> The family is the linchpin of gender, reproducing it from one generation to the next. As we have seen, family life as typically practiced in our society is not just, either to women or to children. Moreover, it is not conducive to the rearing of citizens with a strong sense of justice. In spite of all the rhetoric about equality between the sexes, the traditional or quasi-traditional division of family labor still prevails. Women are made vulnerable by constructing their lives around the expectation that they will be primary parents; they become more vulnerable within marriages in which they fulfill this expectation, whether or not they also work for wages; and they are most vulnerable in the event of separation or divorce, when they usually take over responsibility for children without adequate support from their ex-husbands [170].

Okin concludes that establishing the family as "a just institution" is imperative for a just society (170).

While Okin focuses on changes to social policy that would hasten the existence of a society "without gender" (171) rather than on a change in practices of reproduction, others have pointed to women's reproductive capabilities as precisely the problem.[15] Reading Shulamith Firestone's work in *The Dialectic of Sex*, in which Firestone posits women's liberation as residing in being non-reproductive, Deirdre M. Condit argues that "The result is a devaluation of all things female; an ironic confirmation of patriarchal principles even as [Firestone] desired to dismantle them" (185–6). Condit goes on to argue for the possibilities of androgenesis, or male reproduction:

> Constructivist and postmodern feminists, arguing against the pre-social body (in order primarily to elide the sex differences problem, might I add), have emphasized the possibility of men learning to become caregivers after children are born. Indeed, feminists from Millett to Crittendon have been imploring men to do this for at least the past half-century but with only meager success. It may be that the numbers of men engaging actively in child care remains remarkably low because they are not born into or raised with the expectation that they can one day have an intimate, nurturing, bodily experi-

ence with their offspring. The feminist demand that they "get engaged" simply misses the materialist point [191].

As a result, Condit proposes the development of androgenesis for the means of overcoming patriarchy. Condit points to Marge Piercy's feminist science fiction novel *Woman on the Edge of Time* (1976) as a narrative that explores the possibilities of a world in which men are as physically and emotionally invested in childbirth and childrearing as women traditionally have been.[16] Of Piercy's work, Condit writes, "what we have is a world in which nurturing and caregiving are our most fundamental values, and sex/gender has essentially become irrelevant" (190).

As technologies including uterine transplant become increasingly available, perhaps the possibility of biological motherhood will finally cause a radical shift in men's consciousness and practice, enhancing not only men's reproductive functions, but also empathetic function as they are invited to experience and enjoy physical pregnancy, labor, and childbirth, as well as the emotional experiences that often attend them.[17] Imagining this possibility stands in contradistinction to the imaginative leap taken, for example, by Marlo in *Tully*, who imagines another self into being, as well as the one taken by the founders in Gilead in *The Handmaid's Tale*. That is, both narratives are instantiated when individuals construct a more extreme and sexist version of the world they already inhabit.

Gilead, in particular, comes into existence when the founders narrow their focus in search of remedies to an infertility epidemic. Rather than seeking to expand family structures consensually (that is, for example, imagining roles beside "parent" for adults to play in children's lives), the architects of Gilead instead indulge in nostalgia for a patriarchal past (itself fraudulent), a turn inward and a retreat from the larger world. In general, technological advances are shunned (except, it would seem, for those that men in power favor, such as guns and cars).

The opposite of Gilead would be an embrace of expansiveness, the future, technology and flexibility; the opposite of Gilead—and perhaps to the 21st century world depicted in *Tully*—might manifest as an opening up of the possibilities of motherhood to more parties, inviting more individuals to experience both the rewards and the difficulties of pregnancy, childbirth and parenthood. In this way, *Tully* and *The Handmaid's Tale* are themselves subtle indictments of the status quo of reproduction being exclusively the purview of people with uteruses or those who generally identify as women.[18] If, as both *Tully* and *The Handmaid's Tale* ultimately contend, motherhood is worth the risks, injuries, and dangers, if it is finally the rewarding experience so valued by the women in these narratives, perhaps the experience should be available to all who desire it.

As described above, in addition to presenting the displaced Americans imagining alternative family structures in Canada, *The Handmaid's Tale* in particular suggests that personal experience of oppression—and in particular, parental experience—can motivate those in power to rethink the structures that they uphold. Thus it is only as Nicole's (adoptive) mother, anticipating the ways in which Nicole will be subjugated, that Serena finally recognizes and rejects the oppression which she herself helped institute. Serena's behavior is, again, not unique; notably, studies demonstrate that having a daughter "significantly increases support for policies designed to increase gender equality" among men (Sharrow, et al.).[19] Parenting, for some, is an opportunity to develop increased awareness, compassion, and connection.

Thus, not unlike the founders of Gilead, many of us suffer from the limits of our own imaginations. We might fail to adequately empathize with others and we might fail to develop creative solutions to seemingly entrenched problems, especially at the intersection of public and private. However, the act of imagining more diverse family structures is itself a rebuke of patriarchal motherhood and family life. And perhaps the success of Hulu's adaptation of *The Handmaid's Tale* will result in an increased interest in and recovery of feminist science fiction such as Piercy's *Woman on the Edge of Time*, providing a visual depiction that takes seriously male caregiving.[20] Perhaps in this way, our media will then contribute to an expansion of our imaginations of family, caregiving, and parenthood.

9

"You're such a good mom": Transparenthood, Pain and Privilege

Shelly (Judith Light), the mother-figure in Jill Soloway's HBO series *Transparent* (2014–present), convinced that she has a story to tell, develops a one-woman show about her life, "To Shell and Back." Shelly is generally a rather comic figure on the series and her children often "ridicule" her or smirk behind her back ("Elizah"). Initially, rehearsals for "To Shell and Back" indicate that the show will be no exception, that it will serve mainly to reveal Shelly as pretentious and self-absorbed. But when Shelly finally has a chance to perform for her family on a cruise, the audience—including her former spouse and children—are genuinely moved, giving Shelly a standing ovation ("Exciting and New"). As the audience for the show *Transparent* watches the audience for "To Shell and Back" react to Shelly's performance, the former must recalibrate its assessment of Shelly. Like her family, we are asked to acknowledge her as a complex, sympathetic individual, to recognize that beneath appearances, people have rich, sometimes hidden, and often surprising lives. This, of course, is one of the projects of *Transparent* more generally as, throughout, the audience is provided with a glimpse of that which individuals have felt compelled to conceal both in public and in their own homes. In addition, the surprising revelation that Shelly is intelligent, charismatic, talented, and in her own way, both suffering and strong, is an expansion of the potential of the mother-figure. Shelly moves from punchline to protagonist.

Previous chapters discussed ineffective mothers as well as formidable, admirable mothers. Although in many respects representations of women have remained stagnant and one-dimensional on television (Lauzen),[1] there are nevertheless programs which allow for more flexibility for females and in which mother-roles in particular are becoming more expansive. In this chapter, I argue that recent representations of trans women who are parents before they transition allow for investigations of the ways in which traditional gender roles remain naturalized in mainstream culture, as well as the ways in which parenting roles can be flexible, plastic enough to accommodate and to change with an individual over a lifetime.[2] While the 2005 film *Transamerica* begins to explore the possibility of constructing relationships beyond the dichotomies of mother-son or father-son, more recently, two streaming series, Netflix's *Orange Is the New Black* (2013–present) and Amazon's *Transparent*, suggest the ways in which parenting and trans identities may mutually inform each other; that is, transitioning might change an individual as a parent and being a parent might impact one's transition. In each of these series, the trans-character is a father before she transitions; crucially, in each series, parenthood is deployed at times as a device through which a trans character finds herself confronted with her internalized sexism and is given an opportunity to reflect on her actions and to reconcile who she is now as a parent with who she once was as a patriarch.

Following Judith Butler, Damien W. Riggs identifies the practice of predominantly cis-scholars whose work draws on the narratives or experiences of trans people in order to deconstruct gender.[3] While this chapter argues that stories of trans-parenting can participate in a broader critique of traditional parenting and gender roles, my aim is not to objectify trans people, but to understand how popular culture representation responds to evolving understandings of gender roles in parenting and society more generally. The media discussed here evidence a developing gender-consciousness and acceptance of non-heteronormative families. Further, these series, I argue, go so far as to present transgender individuals as often possessing a unique and valuable parenting vantage point. That is, these characters draw on the social and emotional pain they experience before transitioning in order to comprehend and critique the privileges they may have enjoyed when they were perceived as men.

"Not anybody's mother": The Impossibility of Parenthood in Transamerica

Despite recent gains, transgender individuals remain some of the most marginalized members of society, continuing to face both legal and extralegal discrimination in public and private realms.[4] Further, trans folks are often victimized by groups from across the political spectrum. Some Christian conservatives on the right dehumanize trans folk, suggesting that their existence is "horrifying" and "sad" (Walsh), while some feminists on the left deem trans identity fraudulent. Maintaining that trans women are not "real" women, gender critical feminists, often derogatorily called Trans-Exclusionary Radical Feminists, or TERFS, argue that trans women capitalize on their male privilege as a means to colonize women's experience.[5] Further, some gender critical feminists articulate a critique of trans identity based on a claim that trans women's existence somehow usurps, replaces, or otherwise imperils the identity of cisgender women.[6]

These attitudes underpin many popular depictions of trans folks. Until recently, the prevalent image of a transgender individual in media was the male-to-female transsexual; these characters are often tragic or comic, one-dimensional, and are rarely parents (Bettcher 48).[7] In their qualitative content analysis of scripted U.S. television shows, Jamie C. Capuzza & Leland G. Spencer found that "On the rare occasion transgender people made it to the small screen, depictions were more often than not based on negative stereotypes functioning in a way to ridicule this community via humor, disgust, fear, alienation, and anger" (215). While Capuzza and Spencer acknowledge that "problematic representations are quite likely to persist into the future," they nevertheless close their study by suggesting that media is taking a "new direction" in depictions of trans experience, providing grounds for "cautious optimism" (227).

Duncan Tucker's 2005 film *Transamerica* is notable as an early corrective to offensive, reductive, de-humanizing portrayals of trans people in popular culture in the past thirty years. However, the film, which explores a developing relationship between a trans woman, Bree (Felicity Huffman), and her biological son, Toby (Kevin Zegers), nevertheless shores up many of the offensive transphobic arguments advanced by both conservatives and self-proclaimed radicals. In the film, Bree's therapist forces her to connect with Toby, the son she hadn't known existed until a week before her scheduled gender-affirming surgery.[8] While Bree and Toby learn to accept and perhaps understand each other over the course of the film, *Transamerica* stops short of allowing Bree to inhabit a parental identity, suggesting that Bree exists in a sort of limbo or no-woman's land, neither father nor mother, to Toby.

The film is problematic in several respects, not the least of which is the casting of a cisgender actor as Bree. On the blog *Bitch Flicks*, Stephen Ira eviscerates the film, arguing that the logic for casting Huffman suggests that "transwomen don't look like they could be women." Further, it is only after Bree's surgery that she is depicted as adjusted and ready to engage meaningfully with others. Ira writes, "When we decide that a woman has to have a certain type of genitalia in order to be acceptable for public view and human relationships, that's transmisogyny." Further, as Ira suggests, while Bree's road trip with Toby contributes to her personal evolution, *Transamerica* nevertheless pursues a circular and offensive narrative logic: Bree must develop a relationship with her son in order to be psychologically/emotionally ready for her surgery (which is itself a bizarre and transmisogynistic conception that suggests that trans folks don't really know what's right for them) and it is only after her surgery that she is psychologically and emotionally ready to parent Toby (which suggests that it is only when she is anatomically a "real woman" that she is able to mother).

A key repetition in *Transamerica* highlights Bree's ostensible unfitness to parent: on two occasions Bree is mistaken for Toby's mother and, each time, the error is contemptuously corrected. (Importantly, capitalizing on the dramatic irony, Toby is unaware of his biological relationship to Bree in both instances.) First, soon after Toby discovers that Bree has a penis, a man scolds Toby for how he speaks to Bree, saying, "Watch your mouth around your mother." Toby storms off, shouting, "She is not my mother! She's not anybody's mother! She's not even a real woman. She's got a dick!" In a later scene, when Bree and Toby are out to dinner with Bree's parents and sister, another stranger remarks on Toby's kindness to Bree: "Nice to see a young man treating his mother so nicely." Bree's mother sharply corrects her: "She's not his mother."

Each of these instances highlights the way that Toby and Bree appear to strangers. An adult woman with a young man is "read" as maternal (and perhaps an underlying suggestion is that Bree and Toby somehow resemble each other as a result of their biological connection). In this way, the strangers' assumption that Bree is Toby's parent is accurate; the film posits that they are simply inaccurate with regard to which parent. Further, these scenes suggest that within convention, there are (in)appropriate ways of interacting with one's mother; Toby's behavior might be construed differently if Bree is perceived as simply a friend or even as Toby's father. Toby's remarks demonstrate his limitations in that he cannot see past Bree's genitalia or apprehend Bree as anything but a "fucking lying freak," which gestures to common mainstream representations of trans women as deceitful. In addition, Bree does not correct those who mistake her for Toby's mother or those who correct the strangers; she allows others to construe the relationship. Toby's remark, that she is "not anybody's mother … she's got a dick" draws the focus back to physical femininity as a prerequisite for motherhood. According to Toby, it is Bree's anatomy, not her single or childfree status, that renders a maternal identity invalid.

The repetition that Bree is "not" Toby's mother elliptically positions Bree as an "impostor." She has a maternal relationship to Toby but, unlike an aunt or older mentor, the suggestion that she is his mother is cast as somehow repulsive. That Toby and Bree's mother feel impelled to correct strangers—and that they do so in front of Bree—suggests that contempt and humiliation are the price Bree must pay for appearing female or maternal, as though these are identities that she has no right to claim.

Bree's status in relation to Toby is further complicated by Toby's biological mother's absence. Deceased at the film's beginning, Toby's mother exists as a plot device, her absence providing the opportunity for Bree's intervention.[9] That Bree will potentially fill the vacuum left by Toby's mother is a notion that flirts with the transmisogynistic thinking that trans women's existence threatens to substitute for or supplant cisgender women's existence or roles.

In addition, the film circulates the conservative argument that trans folks are in part responsible for the violence perpetrated against them. For example, unaware of their familial relationship, Toby attempts a sexual relationship with Bree. When Bree reveals that she is Toby's father, Toby flees the bedroom. Bree pursues him through the house and Toby turns and strikes her. While Toby's actions are not inconsistent with his characterization (he is depicted as using sexuality as a means to securing money and attention throughout the film, for example), the scene nevertheless suggests that if Bree had disclosed her relationship to Toby from the start, the potential for incest and Toby's violent response could have been avoided.

As Ira points out, Bree only begin to inhabit a more maternal identity after her surgery. The last scene takes place in Bree's home, suggesting that Bree is herself finally "at home" as well as that Toby is also finally arriving/returning to the maternal home. Bree's interactions with Toby include her acknowledgment of his maturity (she lets him have a beer) as well as his acceptance of her parental role (he submits when she gently scolds him for putting his feet on the coffee table). In addition to relying on clichés about how mothers are supposed to act (fussy and chiding, mildly disapproving but secretly adoring), the scene suggests that Bree is only apparently capable of performing this kind of maternal identity once she has had her gender-affirming surgery, as though the alteration of her genitalia is what allows her to mother Toby after all. Ultimately, while *Transamerica* begins to investigate the intersections of parental and trans identities, the film does not suggest that there are multiple ways of being a mother, instead reconfirming conventional notions that link anatomical femaleness and motherhood.

"You really wanna be a lady in a world where men do that?": Intergenerational Misogyny in Orange Is the New Black

Despite its limitations, *Transamerica* was in many respects a significant and trailblazing film in its relatively nuanced and compassionate depiction of trans experience. The depictions of trans women on recent streaming series such as *Orange Is the New Black* and *Transparent* resist defaulting to cliché or the well-worn narratives that suggest that trans women are tragic, family-less, isolated figures.[10] Instead, characters Sophia Burset (Laverne Cox) and Maura Pfefferman (Jeffrey Tambor) have been in committed marriages to women who clearly love(d) them and both remain invested in their roles as parents. While much of the drama of their storylines occurs because their nuclear families must grapple with their transition, Sophia and Maura are not reduced to their trans status; being trans is just one aspect of their complex identities.

For example, Sophia and Maura are imperfect; they are both depicted as smart and politically conscious, but they are both also depicted as, like all people, flawed. In *Stealing the Show: How Women Are Revolutionizing Television*, Joy Press describes writer Sian Heder's development of Sophia's character: the result was a "character who was 'kind of selfish in some ways,' not to mention a criminal. Heder was worried about the potential for backlash, she says, 'but I think trans people were so relieved to have a three-dimensional person on-screen, warts and all'" (240).

In both *Orange Is the New Black* and *Transparent*, parenthood precipitates the trans-character's confrontation with her past privilege and perhaps continued obliviousness to some of the experiences of marginalized people. As women once identified as men, the characters of Sophia and Maura embrace tolerance and reject sexism, misognyny and transphobia. Yet the conservative structure of the traditional family, of academia, and a culture that is over-reliant on gender dichotomies facilitates sexism, misogyny and homo and transphobia. In overcoming these challenges as trans women, Sophia and Maura must also overcome them as parents.

Sophia is incarcerated and is thus depicted as struggling with her lack of power as she navigates a world, including a prison culture, in which she is multiply marginalized as a trans woman of color.[11] In general, the parents on *Orange Is the New Black* find their power diminished in prison, a situation that reflects the realities of many incarcerated women. They are literally and metaphorically not at home, the ostensible site of many mothers' power. Thus, for example, one character's boyfriend announces he will no longer bring their baby to visit her; angry and heartbroken, her feelings are nevertheless inconsequential to his decision ("Mother's Day"). A scene in which the character Gloria attempts to work on her son's math homework with him during visiting hours serves to highlight how mothers struggle with the same obstacles as non-incarcerated parents, but have an added layer of frustration and disempowerment: Gloria can cajole and threaten and plead, but her authority over her son is severely curtailed ("Tongue-Tied").

As a result of her incarceration, Sophia, whose child Michael is an adolescent, has limited influence over her son. Depicted as a character with great dignity, Sophia refuses to reduce herself or her perspectives in order to conform to others' expectations. Thus, she is presented as at once unapologetically feminine (her space in the prison is the salon, she is an expert on beauty and style, and her full breasts are displayed early in the series) at the same time that she embraces masculine characteristics, for example unequivocally identifying as a father. Sophia describes her expectations of parenthood thus: "I was hoping I could be there, help shape him, you know? Teach him how to shave or change a tire. I might have changed, but I'm still his father" ("Fear, and Other Smells"). Here, Sophia embraces masculine activities she mastered before her transition, suggesting the importance to her of participating in a tradition of father-to-son knowledge transmission. At the same time, she explains that she and her ex-wife "share" Mother's Day ("Mother's Day"), suggesting a comfort with claiming the titles of both father and mother.

For Sophia, her identity as parent is at once crucial and precarious. Sophia's wife becomes involved with the reverend at her church, suggesting that the vacuum left as a result of Sophia's incarceration will be filled by a traditional representative of patriarchal authority. In addition, a conflict between Sophia and another inmate who are both attempting extra-institutional control of their sons reaches its climax when Gloria, the other inmate, taunts Sophia: "I am mothering…. But you wouldn't know anything about that cause you ain't nothing real" ("A Tittin' and a Hairin'") an insult which casts Sophia, like Bree in *Transamerica,* into a parenting no-woman's-land, neither "real" father nor "real" mother. Gloria's insult reveals the profound intolerance of many of the inmates, despite their superficial acceptance of Sophia.

While Sophia seems confident in her parenting identity, her son Michael clearly still struggles with her transition. It is during a period when Michael becomes increasingly rebellious and disrespectful that Sophia retreats to potentially injurious masculine behaviors and habits. Sophia offers Michael romantic advice and, Michael, unsure, asks, "[Advice] from my second mom or my used-to-be dad?" Sophia answers, "From former man to current man" ("Mother's Day"). In this moment, Sophia reasserts her claim to a certain expertise and masculinity. More importantly, the advice that Sophia gives to Michael is problematic:

> SOPHIA: When I was your age, my dad told me, "Find a real insecure girl and practice on her. That way when you meet a girl you really like, you'll be good at it."
> MICHAEL: You really wanna be a lady in a world where men do that?
> SOPHIA: God help me I do. ["Mother's Day"]

Sophia's attempt to bond with her son is perhaps more important to her than any feminist values, or even values that respect girls' and women's basic dignity. Michael himself recognizes the larger, systemic sexism inherent in her advice and her remark, "God help me I do" to Michael's astute challenge of her desire to be a woman in patriarchy is simultaneously flip and almost chilling: this is a world in which trans women of color, in particular, are at great risk of assault and violence. The dehumanization of the other—in this case, girls—and the devaluation of the feminine exist on the same spectrum as the trans and homophobia which fuels such violence. Discussing transphobia, Riggs contends, "there is considerable utility in demonstrating how marginalising speech, hate speech, and murder sit on the same continuum; one that is shaped by normative gender binaries as they relate to embodiment" (158). Sophia's casual misogyny amounts to a dangerous sacrifice of her values and ideals in an attempt to connect with her son.

In subsequent episodes Michael uses a variety of derogatory terms in conversations with Sophia. In one instance, he calls a boy from his school a "pussy" and he openly jokes about putting a bag over an ugly girl's head (presumably so that he can tolerate having sex with her). Michael also justifies having a physical fight with another boy because that boy was "fagging out" ("Where My Dreidel At"). Still an adolescent, Michael is experimenting with various troubling masculine identities, all of which are predicated on the oppression of and contempt for the feminine. Perhaps most striking is Michael's unapologetic homophobia. While Sophia makes attempts to correct or chide Michael, her efforts are tepid and have no discernible results.

Sophia's sexist advice coupled with her failure to deal aggressively with Michael's harmful language highlights the discrepancy between Sophia's identities as a woman and as a father. This is not to suggest that women are incapable of sexism, but rather to suggest that in promoting an exploitative approach to women, Sophia retreats to toxic masculinity, the sexism taught to her by her own "dad," within which respect between men is established through the degradation or exploitation of women. This depiction thus investigates the intergenerational transmission of misogyny, a transmission which may take place even when those involved are indirectly or, in Sophia's case, directly, injured by such misogyny.

It is Sophia's trans-status, however, then, that acts as a disruptive force. Taken to task by her ex-wife for the offensive advice she's given, Sophia is forced to confront her internalized sexism. However, the plot line suggests that Sophia's failure to scrutinize herself sooner—to look critically at how her transition, her commission of a crime, and her injurious advice have affected her son—has disastrous consequences. That is, rather than focusing on her relationship to Michael, Sophia focuses her attention on Gloria's son Benny, repeatedly suggesting that Michael's bad behavior has resulted from his association with Benny. Her misunderstanding of Benny's influence on Michael causes a conflict with Gloria, a conflict which then leads to other inmates to persecute Sophia because of her trans status.

While the argument with Gloria is the catalyst for Sophia's harassment, the series suggests that the specter of abuse is always lurking over Sophia in prison. That is, her conflict with Gloria simply provides an excuse for other inmates to act on their transphobia. Placed in the dreaded segregated housing unit for her own protection, Sophia thus experiences a re-marginalization at the hands of the institution, bringing into focus again the ways in which casual sexism and explicit transmisogyny may result in the grotesque dehumanization and abuse of the "other."

"I hurt people": The Trans Mother's Evolving Identity in Transparent

An exchange during which a father offers his son problematic advice also occurs in *Transparent*. A secondary character, Marcy, has accompanied Maura to a "cross dressing" camp. Unable to be truly themselves at home, in the camp the two find a respite from the performance of traditional fatherhood.

Maura and Marcy, dressed in women's clothes, ride to the camp payphones on their bicycles ("Best New Girl"). They both plan to call home. Maura's friend Marcy calls first. Once on the phone, Marcy assumes a masculine demeanor and posture, spreading his legs wide and hunching over.[12] "Hey man," Marcy begins when his son gets on the phone. The conversation almost immediately turns to sports and it becomes clear that the son is complaining about his coach. Marcy says the coach is a "douchebag" and he tells his son to "man up" and not take "that crap." Maura frowns along and postpones calling her family. She's registered the alteration in her friend; perhaps her discomfort stems from a recognition of the way she too will tailor her behavior in order to more closely conform to conventional ideas of how a "father" should behave.

Part of what makes this scene so effective is that the viewer might recognize that Marcy's behavior isn't logical, laying bare the contradictions that so many live with in patriarchy. That is, not unlike Sophia's advice that Michael explore his sexuality through victimizing a female, Marcy's advice to his son reinforces contempt for the feminine. Thus Marcy either is truly unaware of how he is complicit in the system which prevents individuals like himself from living as they wish or else he is actually acutely and tragically aware of the price he must pay both for his weekend away as well as his maintenance of a traditional, heteronormative, patriarchal domestic life.

While Maura seems, if not disapproving of, at least disappointed by Marcy's behavior, the viewer is aware that it will be decades before Maura is able to come out herself, a fact renders this scene all the more poignant. That is, neither character can be themselves at home, because their homes are

Figure 11. Maura (Jeffrey Tambor, right) and Marcy (Bradley Whitford) at Camp Camellia (*Transparent*, Amazon Studios, season 1, 2014).

extensions of a larger, intolerant mainstream culture. Further, other flashbacks reveal that in "Mort"/Maura's[13] absence, Maura's children embark on potentially dangerous sexual explorations; Maura's son Josh, for example, is victimized by the family's babysitter, which will have a profound and negative impact on Josh's adult sexuality. Thus, although Maura feels she must conceal her activities because of a larger conservative social context and family situation, this deception nevertheless creates the conditions under which her children too will feel they must lie and conceal their "true" selves and activities.

In tracing Maura's transition, *Transparent* investigates not only Maura's personal evolution, but the cultural changes that have made the world more hospitable for people like Maura. By virtue of the focus of this ensemble series, Maura receives more sustained treatment in *Transparent* than Sophia does in *Orange Is the New Black*.[14] As a result, Maura's character appears to experience ongoing development. The series consistently connects the personal to the political, insisting on a recognition that coming out as trans is not an act that happens in a vacuum, but rather an act that is context-contingent. For example, in one episode, Maura receives childhood photographs that have been "regendered" or altered to make boy-"Mort" into girl-Maura. As they look at the photographs together, Maura's daughter Sarah remarks, "Just imagine if you could have been her your whole life" ("Oscillate"), asking both the characters and the viewers to "imagine" the political and personal ramifications of a non-or less-strictly gender binary world.

In some ways, Maura's daughter Ali, depicted as the flaky genius who skitters from one expensive interest to the next, represents the answer to Sarah's conjecture. As she explores her sexuality and gender expression and identity, Ali's freedom is the coming-to-fruition of the battles that feminists and LGBTQIA+ activists and academics have fought in that she is permitted, albeit as an upper-class white woman, to experiment, try on and cast off various identities. And in other ways, Ali is the most like Maura, as Maura suggests in the show's pilot. Although initially uncomfortable with her father's transition, Ali comes to represent Maura's true, if imperfect "ally" and the development of Maura and Ali's relationship is a key narrative strand throughout the series. Maura's transition invites Maura to discover different—and often more positive—ways of being with and relating to all of her children, including Ali.

It is Ali who christens Maura as "Moppa," a combination of the words Mother and Poppa, a title that does the job of recognizing and honoring Maura's history as the family's father, as well as incorporating her transition into a mother-figure. By Season 3, Maura claims the title of "mom" (an assertion that initially troubles Shelly), explaining that she "did" appreciate Moppa, but feels ready to unequivocally embrace a maternal identity. Although all of the children are initially surprised, Ali is clearly comfortable with Maura's new moniker; in Season 4, when Maura is harassed by airport security, Ali insists, "I have the right to know what's going on with my mother," assuming a protective and possessive position toward Maura ("Groin Anomaly"). This moment exists in contradistinction to the moment in *Transamerica* in which Toby disavows the possibility of Bree's maternity, declaring, "she's not anybody's mother."

Thus, *Transparent*'s trajectory is one of increasing understanding of and compassion for Maura (at least in terms of those in her family and community). However, Maura's personal development is not without challenges beyond those of an inhospitable community. A crucial scene and plotline in *Transparent* hinges on how Maura is confronted by the realities of the privileges she had enjoyed as an upper class, high-status white male before her transition. For example, when Ali announces she wants to go to graduate school to study in a women and gender studies program, Maura uses her influence as an established academic to set up a lunch with several scholars. Ali is reluctant, telling Maura, "It feels like nepotism." Maura disagrees: "It's not nepotism, I just want to introduce you to a few of my connections" ("New World Coming").

Maura and Ali meet with Leslie Mackinaw, the head of the Gender Studies program. Leslie recognizes Maura and explains that she had been part of a group of radical feminists who had applied for the editorial board of a reputable journal that Maura (as "Mort"), had run. Leslie charges Maura with "blocking" her from the position. Initially stunned, Maura replies, "I profoundly apologize" and "I don't stand behind what I did back them. I actually don't remember much of it." Leslie responds, "Why would you remember it?" driving home an understanding that although this episode was significant to Leslie, it was inconsequential to Maura. Later in the same episode, in a trans support group, Maura discusses the encounter. She explains, "The radical feminist group ... they thought we were holding them back ... we did. We held them back. That's the truth. I hurt people" ("New World Coming").

Maura's epiphany is established as having arisen precisely because Maura is relying on her former—and to a certain extent continued—privilege as a respected white academic in order to secure privilege for her daughter. The word nepotism of course originates in the practice of showing professional favoritism to a nephew, a male heir. Here, *Transparent* indicates that white women may also be beneficiaries of entrenched privilege, even if the participants are unaware of it.

Maura's honest appraisal of her actions in the support group is a refreshing moment in television narrative in that it allows a character to recognize mistakes, to alter her behavior, and to potentially redeem herself. Audience members too are provided an opportunity to understand how one's intersecting identities might shape one's experiences in the world. Maura is presented as still having significant self-education before her; for example, in Season 2, some of her exchanges with Davina demonstrate a lack of sensitivity and political awareness. However, it is precisely in her role as a parent that Maura is called to account for herself. That is, grappling with her past and confronting her internalized sexism is a crucial component of her own development as a trans woman, but is also a component of her development as Ali's mother.

In this way, *Transparent* refuses reductive narratives that render the trans-character victim or villain, instead grappling with intersectional feminism. In another episode, Leslie, Ali, and Maura attend a women's festival that is clearly based on the trans-exclusionary Michigan Womyn's Music Festival. Maura engages in a debate with a group of older, presumably second-wave feminists, who defend the policy permitting only "women-born women" at the camp ("Man on the Land"). Maura becomes agitated and asserts that before her transition she was in "way too much pain to experience" what the women are "calling privilege." Leslie's response, "Your pain and your privilege are separate" ("Man on the Land") is an assertion that Maura's suffering as a closeted trans woman did not preclude the exercise of privilege in some areas of her life.[15]

This scene, of course, engages directly with the arguments of many gender critical feminists. That is, the episode sensitively portrays both those feminists who participate in or support trans-exclusion as well as the trans woman, Maura, who flees the camp, angry and agitated, ironically shouting "Man on the Land!," alienated by these policies. Maura, of course, is not a threat to these women, but that doesn't mean that her presence at the camp, or her denial of privilege is itself entirely appropriate or accurate. In this scene, then, the series navigates tricky territory, providing a clear picture of an important moment and debate within some feminist communities.

Crucially, again it is the intergenerational parent-child relationship that precipitates these conversations: it is the parent's journey with the daughter that introduces a trans-character to a variety of perspectives, some of which may productively challenge her assumptions about parenting, gender, pain, and, of course, privilege. Perhaps functioning as a metaphor (or matrophor) of the potentially productive conversations and conflict that may take place between feminist generations,[16] these exchanges suggest that the act of calling others to account for former misapprehensions or oppressions while potentially painful, are nevertheless crucial for continued growth, for an expansion of tolerance necessary in order to ensure that all LBTQIA+ folk and women in particular are able to feel at home in their families and in the world.

"Chosen families": Finding a Home for Complex Characters

This chapter demonstrates that media depictions of trans women are increasingly nuanced and that it is precisely through exploring the trans-character's experiences of parenthood that the narratives expand, rather than foreclose on, the possibilities for mother characters. On *Transparent,* for example, Maura is depicted as struggling when she takes a volunteer position answering calls on a suicide hotline; at the same time, when rehearsing for this job, she provides comfort and support for her friend Shea, who is also trans. Shea tells Maura, "You're such a good mom," bringing into focus the notion that Maura plays multiple roles ("Oscillate"). Not only does she function as a mom-figure in her "chosen family" ("To Sardines and Back") but she is also dad, and then moppa, and ultimately mom, to her biological family.

That *Transparent* and *Orange Is the New Black* are both series that found their "homes" on subscription services (Amazon Prime and Netflix, respectively), is of course a crucial aspect that allows their showrunners to develop complex characters over time.[17] These shows can focus on niche audiences. In Hilary Radner's *The New Woman's Film: Femme-centric Movies for Smart Chicks* she writes, "Competition for viewers has encouraged the development of programming that is more challenging in its appeal; premium cable channels such as HBO depend upon subscriptions ... and thus are less vulnerable to pressures from brands that may not wish to be associated with issues that they deem sensitive, including political concerns" (175); she mentions Jenji Kohan (*Orange Is the New Black*) and Jill Soloway (*Transparent*) in particular as showrunners who have been able to operate effectively within this new model. Similarly, in *Mediating Sexual Citizenship: Neoliberal Subjectivities in Television Culture*, Anita Brady, Kellie Burns, and Cristyn Davies observe that in a "post-network" television context, largely freed from concerns about alienating advertisers, writers and directors feel they can take more creative risks (8). They do point out, however, that at the same time and particularly regarding the representation of trans experience, such risk-taking is "inevitably, tied to the extent to which such boundary-pushing produces market value" (155).

Nevertheless, *Orange Is the New Black* and *Transparent* have freedoms denied network television shows, as well as movies, which are subject to a ratings system that may curtail content.[18] Both series have an overt feminist sensibility; in each, this is manifested in the often explicit sex scenes as well as frank talk about issues relating to sex, the body, and sexuality. Additionally, their subject matters reflect attention to that which might otherwise be erased or overlooked in mainstream programming: *Orange Is the New Black* delves into the stories of a women from diverse racial and economic backgrounds, most of whom have been marginalized by a patriarchal, white supremacist society[19] and, in addition to its inclusion of trans folks generally, *Transparent*'s protagonist is an older—even senior—trans woman.

Further, although most of the main characters on *Transparent* are upper-class and white, the show reflects feminist values both in its content and in the production practices surrounding the show.[20] Discussing the show's first two seasons, consultant Zachary Drucker describes a deliberate process in which the creators attempt to remediate the damage of previous representations: "[We] created Maura with a lot of sensitivity to not contribute to the damaging history of representation of trans people, and that has to be done really carefully I think, because there isn't enough out there about us, especially when you consider a mainstream audience ... culturally have been stuck on the transition narrative for so long that the nature, the form, of *Transparent* for both seasons creates this incredible opportunity to transcend that narrative and create a character who is trans, but is a lot of other things as well" (Mey). Additionally, Soloway has made the inclusion of trans folks behind the camera a priority.[21] As Mey writes in "My Day on the Set of "Transparent," Where Trans Voices Actually Get Heard," Soloway's show may "create a new trend in Hollywood. One where trans people get to be a part of their own stories, where trans people get a piece of the money that's being made off of their struggles."

Thus, these streaming services facilitate programming that is deliberately politically progressive in production and in content, allowing popular media to catch up to understandings that there are different kinds of women and ways of being women. In an interview about *Transparent,* Soloway, asked if she has a "pedagogical intent," responds, "Always.... When people say, 'You don't want to be making propaganda,' I'm like, cis-hetero patriarchy has been making propaganda forever. I love the word propaganda. I had to grow up watching fucking white dudes act like women should be competing for them on the basis of their financial success—that's propaganda. So I'm gonna make my propaganda until it's all equal" (Jung). Soloway's attitude, an explicit acknowledgment of popular culture itself as propaganda, is also implicitly an argument that propaganda is effective, that our media works to shape our understandings of people, groups, issues, and practices. According to Soloway, at least, representation matters.

Conclusion: "Switching Teams": Representation Matters

On an April 2016 segment of *60 Minutes,* rather gratingly titled "Switching Teams," Lesley Stahl profiled a Harvard swimmer named Shuyler Bailar who had initially been accepted to Harvard as a female athlete but who subsequently came out as transgender and began transitioning. The segment's positive and sympathetic portrayal of a trans person illustrates changing cultural attitudes, something the producers are keen to emphasize, having Stahl state in the opening: "The story of how Harvard came to be the first men's Division I athletic team in the nation to include an openly transgender young man is also the story of a bigger transformation—in attitudes, acceptance, and the larger conversation about what it means to be transgender."

An exchange between Bailar and Stahl that occurs close to the end of the segment brings into focus a number of interrelated issues, including continued cis-sexism (even among those who consider themselves sympathetic) and the importance of representation. Julia Serano points out in her definition of cissexism, that trans folks' "gender identities, expressions, and sex embodiments are typically viewed as being less valid and natural than those of cissexuals" (114), an attitude that is on display in Stahl's interview. Stahl states that Bailar is "passionate about" answering questions before probing, "What kinds of questions do you get?" When Bailar responds that many ask about his genitals, Stahl pursues this line of questioning, forcing Bailar to disclose that he has a vagina. In a voice-over, Stahl then states that, "in one small matter we discovered, he's leaving his options open." When Stahl states that Bailar will "never get pregnant," Bailar responds, "I don't know about that ... there are trans men that get pregnant because they want to have biological children." Stahl pushes, "So this is in your head, that one day you might give birth?" and Bailar responds, "Might is—is in bold—and underlined and italic-ed. But yes, yeah—I don't know. I'm 19."

That Stahl couches her query about Bailar's genitalia in a question demonstrates at least a vague awareness, perhaps as a result of the fallout after Katie Couric so offensively pursued the subject with Laverne Cox, that asking anyone about their genitalia—and in particular a college students— is inappropriate.[22] And yet Stahl does ask, reaffirming a far-too prevalent attitude that cis-folks have a right to information about trans bodies. Further, this preoccupation with genitals suggests that, for many who avow tolerance or even embrace of trans folks, the notion that one's genitals must align with their gender remains: an individual who chooses not to have "bottom" reassignment surgery transgresses by refusing to situate their experiences as conforming to several reductive contemporary narratives, including the neoliberal/postfeminist myth that surgery is an accessible and pain-free "answer" or "fix" to any number of 21st century problems as well as the dominant narrative of trans experience, that of the individual who has been born into the "wrong body." As writer and advocate Janet Mock argues, the "wrong body" narrative maintains focus on the individual's body, rather than social intolerance. In her article "Trans in the Media: Unlearning the 'Trapped' Narrative and Taking Ownership of Our Bodies," Mock quotes Sass Rogando Sasot: "I am not trapped by my body. I am trapped by your beliefs. And I want to reclaim this body from those who want it to breathe and be fed by their dogmas."

Most crucially for this discussion, however, is Bailar's articulation of self-acceptance, his resistance to the narrative that he finds his body repulsive and needs to change it as soon as possible, as well as his embrace of the potential of female genitalia and organs.[23] Bailar's position throws into question fundamental ideas about maleness and femaleness and pushes back against conservative forces that use trans-identities and narratives to shore up essentialist ideas about men and women. That is, Bailar's choice to keep "his options open" presents a challenge to heteronormative understandings of the gendered division of labor that is traditional parenthood, in which the father is often rendered a secondary, less-important caregiver, the parent who at most serves as support staff as the mother performs the labor of pregnancy and childbirth. Further, Bailar's openness to the possibility of carrying a child challenges the idea that men would not want to experience physical pregnancy or those aspects associated with biological motherhood. To put it another way, on the one hand, Bailar demands that his family, his community, and by virtue of the news program, the world, accept his self-identification as a man at the same time that he insists on his right to what has long been cast as an inherently female prerogative. Bailar shores up his argument by gesturing to other trans men who have already carried and given birth to children, reminding us again of how important representation is generally. For example, a 2016 article in *People* magazine, "Transgender Man Navigates Chest-Feeding and Fatherhood After Giving Birth to a Baby Boy," profiled Evan Hempel and featured an image of him chest-feeding his child (Mazziotta).

Positions and stories like Bailar's and Hempel's suggest that people do not have to accommodate fixed identities, but rather that identities can be expanded to accommodate people. One can be a father and give birth and provide sustenance for a child through chestfeeding. Newsmagazine segments and articles on individuals like Bailar and Hempel, as well as fictional series such as *Transparent* and *Orange Is the New Black* thus participate in the circulation and perhaps normalization of "alternative" ways of being in the world and being parents. While some trans parents do and will of course choose to occupy traditional roles, Bailar's position reflects the more general ways in which trans identities may offer exciting and radical re-conceptualizations of what, to many, were once perceived as unchangeable identity categories such as mother and father. The narratives of trans-parenting presented in *Orange Is the New Black* and *Transparent* suggest that there are different ways of experiencing transgender identity and journeys, perhaps just as there are different ways of experiencing parenting and parenting journeys, motherhood, and mothering journeys.

Conclusion

"Un poco mas doloroso": *Jane the Virgin* and the Home as a Little Less Painful

The previous chapter opened with a description of mother-figure Shelly's (Judith Light) revelatory performance of her one-woman show on the series *Transparent*. As discussed, Shelly is generally a comically self-absorbed, easily mocked character and throughout the episode leading up to her performance, Shelly complains that her children and ex-husband don't consider, understand, or respect her. She asserts, "I am not at home in this family" ("Exciting and New"). That her performance is so powerful and well-received is a fulfillment of Shelly's desire for attention and approval. Additionally, in creating the show, Shelly has mined her past—her experience of childhood sexual abuse, the development of her early romances, and her feelings of betrayal in her marriage—and in this way, Shelly's work has been therapeutic. The title, "To Shell and Back," suggests that, through her art, Shelly is able to make sense of her suffering and to recover herself, or parts of her identity that have been lost or oppressed. In addition, her show allows her to connect with her family and with a larger audience. Ideally, creating and sharing her art might make Shelly feel a little more "at home" in her family and in the world.

An episode of CW's *Jane the Virgin* (2014–2019) explores the therapeutic potential of performance. Xiomara (Xo) (Andrea Navedo) behaves badly at her daughter Jane's (Gina Rodriguez) bachelorette party—making out with Jane's friend's crush—and as a result, the two are involved in a seemingly unresolvable argument ("Chapter Thirty-nine"). Jane's father, Rogelio (Jaime Camil), Xo's on-again-off-again romantic interest, comes to realize that the two are likely fighting because they are both anxious about how Jane's upcoming marriage will affect their relationship. Rather than discuss his revelation with either woman, Rogelio, a telenovela star, organizes a theatrical production and invites Jane and Xo to attend ("Chapter Forty"). In the audience, Jane and Xo see their own lives played out on stage: a mother and daughter are in conflict until a helpful mail carrier (played by Rogelio) enters and explains that they are clearly fighting in order to make the prospect of their impending separation "un poco menos doloroso" ("a little less painful").[1] The viewer of *Jane the Virgin* watches the two women watching. Xo and Jane, who quickly recognize themselves and their situation on the stage, and are both initially annoyed and exasperated by Rogelio's meddling. But registering the emotional truth of the otherwise absurd situation playing out before them, they each begin to cry before they grab hands and reconcile.

Each of these productions—Shelly's show and Rogelio's scene—asserts the role that art can play in promoting healing and a deeper understanding of both self and other. In addition, they both center stories of women often missing in popular culture: Shelly, although affluent and white, is an older woman and Jane and Xo are Latina, a group that is particularly underrepresented in mainstream media (Beltrán 23).[2] Their stories are, in part, stories of surviving in patriarchy: Shelly's narrative is marked by the injuries and repressions that result from unequal and oppressive gender roles, while Jane and Xo's story, although less overtly concerned with gender, asserts the importance of mother-daughter relationships as well as the potential challenges for women negotiating heterosexual conventions. As meta-texts, each illustrates not only how fundamentally popular culture narratives about women have shifted in recent years, but an awareness of the importance of amplifying the stories of women of diverse ages, backgrounds, and experiences.

However, these moments stand out because women generally remain devalued in the larger culture, as do women's stories, a point both series touch on. For example, it's a big surprise that Shelly's one-woman show is actually any good; her family members (and *Transparent* viewers) are primed to expect it to be ludicrous and embarrassing. On *Jane the Virgin,* the network executives watching the scene Rogelio has developed do not find it as compelling as Jane and Xo do. After a writer covers for Rogelio by explaining that the scene serves to set up a "twist" in which the mother and daughter will be revealed as clones, one exec remarks, "Now that makes more sense. I mean, who cares about a fight between a mom and a daughter?" ("Chapter Forty").[3]

This remark brings into focus many of the interrelated concerns explored throughout this book, including the continued dismissal of stories about women's lives. The executive (herself a woman) who suggests that dramas about mothers and daughters aren't interesting or marketable dramatizes a reality described by Joy Press in *Stealing the Show: How Women Are Revolutionizing Television:* "So many aspects of women's lives (as momentous as female friendship, as mundane as period pain) had never been depicted with any depth on a small screen because network executives believed that these things were inherently dull or off-putting" (3).

Home Is Where the Hurt Is has demonstrated, however, that the dramas in women's lives, including their negotiations of their relationships with their mothers and their partners and their children, can be compelling, complex, and important. While the emphasis in this study has been on the ways in which media has responded to increased awareness of the perils and challenges of the domestic for women, as *Jane the Virgin* reveals, the public sphere and perhaps most notably the media industry have also been inhospitable to women. Tarana Burke initially used the phrase "me too" to raise awareness about sexual violence and to give survivors, in particular girls of color, "language" with which to talk about their experiences (Jefferson). Over a decade later, #MeToo was adopted and popularized after news of Harvey Weinstein's predatory behavior became public, drawing attention to rampant sexual harassment and abuse in various fields, but especially the entertainment industry (Garcia). In addition to calling out predators and calling for solidarity, #MeToo brings into focus just some of the obstacles that have prevented complex narratives about women and women's experiences from being developed in larger numbers; in an industry so toxic to women, it is perhaps not surprising that many directors, writers, and producers simply do not value women's stories or that creative women might avoid or flee Hollywood. For example, the idea that men in power have actively suppressed women's stories was substantiated after allegations of sexual harassment arose against CBS CEO Les Moonves. In an article in the *Hollywood Reporter*, *Designing Women* creator Linda Bloodworth Thomason contends that Moonves derailed her career: "People asked me for years, 'Where have you been? What happened to you?' Les Moonves happened to me." Others have noted that a network that had boasted shows including *Designing Women* and *Cagney and Lacey* became, with Moonves as president of entertainment, "a network for men, by men" (Romero). It is hardly surprising that sexist, exploitative men would not seek to promote stories about strong, complex, or fully human women.

Despite the #MeToo movement and despite notable contributions from women such as Jenni Snyder Urman, Jenji Kohen, Jill Soloway, and Issa Rae, multiple studies demonstrate a continued diversity problem. According to the Women's Media Center 2017 report, "Men still dominate media across all platforms" ("The Status of Women"). The report continues: "Women are not equal partners in telling the story, nor are they equal partners in sourcing and interpreting what and who is important in the story." Women's marginalization behind the scenes will logically result in less women on-screen.

Additionally, the Ralph J. Bunche Center for African American Studies at UCLA's "2017 Hollywood Diversity Report" concludes that while women in particular have made some gains, "pronounced underrepresentation is still the norm" (39). In fact, several measures reveal entrenched resistance to the inclusion of central characters and stories about those other than white, cis, heterosexual males. The 2017 GLAAD Studio Responsibility Index documented a "significant decrease" of LGBTQ characters and "the lowest percentage of LGBTQ-inclusive major studio releases since GLAAD began tracking in 2012." Finally, the "Hollywood Diversity Report" found a

> curious disconnect in the Hollywood entertainment industry with respect to the question of diversity. One the one hand, comprehensive analysis of talent in front of and behind the camera consistently revealed the woeful underrepresentation of people of color and women ... on the other hand, each of the reports have also documented the fact that diversity sells: theatrical films and television shows that more closely reflect the racial and ethnic diversity of America tend to excel at the box office and in viewer ratings [5].

That diverse casts and stories appeal to viewers is unsurprising; what is surprising is that it seems to make little difference to those in power in the media industry. Thus, the fight for diversity and for non-stereotypical representation is clearly far from over.

Even in this grim representational landscape, there are still "those moments," as B. Ruby Rich states, that clearly reflect feminist values in media culture. Hope is located here, in the very existence of art that expands representational possibilities. Hannah Gadsby's stand-up comedy special, *Nanette*, for example, not only reflects changing values, but itself is a catalyst for continued change. Gadsby, a self-described "gender not-normal," highlights the connections between concern for men's "reputation," the repression of women's stories, and the ways in which marginalized performers themselves often self-deprecate, edit, and sanitize their stories in order to be heard at all. Gadsby announces that she must renounce comedy, insisting, "I need to tell my story properly." Gadsby's work is so exciting in part because as she calls out a culture which discourages disruption, she enacts just such a disruption, exposing the price many feel they must pay in order to ease tension through jokes. In using the stand-up form, in blending comedy and confession, Gadsby proposes a new, more honest, more feminist, and perhaps more just approach to entertainment.

"*Pretty baseline*": Jane the Virgin *as Women's Studies 101*

I close with a discussion of *Jane the Virgin* because, like *Nanette*, the series brings into focus many of the crucial issues reviewed in this book; in particular, in its engagement with representational politics, social issues, and feminism, *Jane* exists as an example of the ways in which pop culture texts can attempt to promote connection, awareness, and even healing. For example, in terms of racial and ethnic diversity, Diane Martinez writes that *Jane* "so expertly deploys tropes, styles, and themes familiar to Latino audiences—while still being accessible to a broad range of viewers—that it almost seems crass to call it a successful case study of what happens when a network commits to 'diversity.'" Not only is the show anchored in Latinx life and women's experiences, for example developing plots that center on "a fight between a mom and daughter," but like several of the streaming series discussed in chapter 8, *Jane the Virgin*'s female showrunner, Jennie Snyder Urman, includes women's perspectives behind the camera (Brockington), often employing female directors who are women of color. Eva Longoria and Gina Rodriguez, for example, have each directed episodes (Moreno).

In addition, *Jane the Virgin* is a series that directly engages with genre, representational traditions, and contemporary politics. The show is feminist in content and, in some respects, in form, embracing those practices, conventions, and interests often devalued precisely because they are deemed feminine. In the *New Yorker,* Emily Nussbaum writes that *Jane* reclaims many of the genres, "the soap, the rom-com, the romance novel ... that get dismissed as fluff, which is how our culture regards art that makes women's lives look like fun. They're 'guilty pleasures,' not unlike sex itself.... *Jane the Virgin* is more like a joyful manifesto against that very putdown, a bright-pink filibuster exposing the layers in what the world regards as shallow."

Adapted from a Venezuelan telenovela (Sava), *Jane* is a self-referential, postmodern parody/homage to the genre it descends from, simultaneously participating in and critiquing postfeminist media culture. For example, the narrator, voiced by Anthony Mendez, will often comment on the action or encourage the characters—"Deep breaths, Jane!"—("Chapter Forty") or, when plot twists are particularly outrageous, knowingly comment, "Just like a telenovela." At other moments, the narrator references the world beyond the show; in one episode, when a character casually announces that he sides with someone by saying, "I'm with her," the narrator remarks, "I was too ... along with the rest of the popular vote" ("Chapter Fifty-Two"), thus referencing one of Hillary Clinton's presidential campaign slogans and her 2016 loss to Donald Trump.

These moments draw attention to the show's constructedness as well as its engagement with larger cultural and political forces. The call-out to Clinton in particular reveals a liberal/progressive perspective, an identification with the "rest of" the audience who might still smart over Clinton's loss. As Diana Martinez points out in *The Atlantic,* unlike U.S. soap operas, telenovelas often engage directly with political and social issues such as immigration. Thus, *Jane* confronts injustices large and small—class inequities in the public school system ("Chapter Sixty-Six"), abortion ("Chapter Forty-Six"), gender power dynamics in academia ("Chapter Seventy-Five"), and racism and discrimination ("Chapter Sixty-One").

Further, tackling issues of central concern to the community it is anchored in, *Jane the Virgin* also attempts to use narrative as a force for the promotion of understanding and compassion. For example, when Jane's grandmother is hospitalized and her family informed that she will be deported once she awakes from a coma, Xo exclaims, "That can't be legal!" Captions on the screen appear, reading: "Yes, this really happens. Look it up. #immigrationreform" ("Chapter Ten"). The appearance of the captions is unexpected—an intrusion of "reality" into a dramatic scene—and confronts the viewer with the notion that, in a world of outlandish events, in which, for example, one disgruntled twin paralyzes and takes the place of her "beautiful sister," some of the most inhumane and unbelievable twists are themselves based on things that "really" happen.

Snyder Urman explains the decision to include a plotline about immigration: "it affects so many families in the Latino community, the community we're representing; it's something our country is grappling with, and it's something that we feel strongly about in our writer's room." In addition to potentially resonating with Latinos, the inclusion of this story might prove revelatory for non–Latinos; Gina Rodriguez remarks that this episode "educates others on issues that may not arise in their area or community.... Why not use our art to inspire thought?" (Moreno).

Further, by including the hashtag "#immigrationreform" and the narrator's imperative "look it up," the show urges viewers not only to self-educate, but to take political action around this often quite divisive issue. While it is unclear as to whether or not this advocacy is effective, the embrace of political positions as well as the dramatization of an issue that may otherwise remain abstract for many non-immigrant viewers on a show centrally concerned with the domestic—concerned with romance and with the relationships between mothers, grandmothers and daughters—exists as a potential rebuke of the postfeminist severing of the personal and political.

Finally, *Jane* responds to and engages directly with feminism, incorporating feminist debates and grappling with pressing feminist issues in a manner that suggests an ease and familiarity. As Amy Richards and Jennifer Baumgardner have suggested of the larger culture generally, on *Jane the Virgin,* feminism is "like fluoride ... it's in the water" (17). For example, when negotiating various aspects of their soon-to-be married life, Jane's fiancée Michael texts Jane that "Feminism = women can take the garbage to the street just as easily as men can" ("Chapter Forty-Four"). Michael's equation of feminism with the performance of unpleasant tasks may be reductive (it is, of course, communicated via text message), but nevertheless reveals feminism as a value that Jane embraces (and that Michael thus also values in their relationship). Further, Michael's text acknowledges the negotiation of gender roles in the home and in marriages as a fraught issue for many U.S. families. While women have increasingly taken on more public roles and work outside the home in greater numbers, they continue to perform the bulk of domestic labor and much of that labor falls into gender stereotypical roles (Covert). Ultimately, while Michael's point may seem trivial, it in fact alludes to systemic sexism, potentially confronting viewers with a radical challenge to the status quo.

In a different episode, Jane learns about the Bechdel test from her graduate school advisor and, as the concept is both explained and dramatized, viewers are provided with a lesson on the importance of representation.[4] Jane is an aspiring romance writer, but her grad school advisor, apparently a feminist, is dismissive of the genre generally. She informs Jane that Jane's novel will only be acceptable if it passes the Bechdel test: "Does the work feature two female characters, with names, who talk about something other than a man?" ("Chapter Thirty-Seven").

Later in the episode, the show's narrator applies that Bechdel test to a scene in Jane's grandmother Alba's kitchen. A large × appears on the screen (accompanied by a buzzing sound) each time Jane, Xo and Alba discuss various love interests. After it happens twice in a row, the narrator remarks, "Jeez, this thing is tough." Enacting the Bechdel test illustrates how women on screen often spend their time, making visible some of the sexist practices that are so common as to have come to seem natural. In addition, just as the narrator's commentary draws attention to *Jane the Virgin* as a construction, so too does the advisor's advice to Jane. That is, both *Jane* and Jane's novel are creations that are informed by their cultural moment, as well as by the demands of the market and finally, by the biases, backgrounds, and interests of their authors or creators. Jane revises her manuscript based on her new consciousness; implicitly, this moment suggests that other writers, directors, showrunners can do so too.

The Bechdel test, of course, has its limitations. As others have observed, the test does not reveal if a text is feminist or not; it simply assesses representation. On the blog *Depths of TV*, Shreya Dervasula writes that the inclusion of the Bechdel test is a "clever conceit which encapsulates *Jane the Virgin*'s ability to gently mock a trope while embracing it at the same time." Thus, even Jane's advisor doesn't take the test too seriously. When Jane meets with her again and points out that the latest draft of her novel passes the Bechdel test, her advisor shrugs it off: "Yeah, big whoop. That's pretty baseline, right?" ("Chapter Thirty-Seven"). On the one hand, then, it is stunning how many popular narratives fail the test—and a show that boasts several strong female characters, *Jane*, almost has difficulty passing. On the other hand, it is "baseline" in that equal representation, or asking that a narrative have named female characters who aren't only interested in talking about men, is only the beginning. The advisor's comment suggests that we can and should be asking more from our media.

In this way, *Jane the Virgin* provides an example of a pop culture text that draws on and even informs the conversations happening among academic and activist feminists. As Janelle Hobson has written in her discussion of "celebrity feminism":

> certain celebrities are articulating and, dare I say, *theorizing* critical issues pertaining to gender and its intersections with race and class for a mass audience.... There is a massive consciousness-raising underway concerning women's potential empowerment and the gender inequities that still inhibit their rise to collective power. These messages exist in our commercial and alternative music, films, and art and have the potential to complement, not replace, the feminist manifestos, academic monographs, policy briefs, and grassroots missions that have come to represent feminist theorizing and practice [ital. orig.].

Jane and other shows including *Insecure, Transparent, Orange Is the New Black, My Crazy Ex-Girlfriend,* and *UnReal* are thus mainstream programs that not only deliberately engage with feminist thinking, but come from a context in which the folks working behind the cameras are themselves feminists.[5] While I have elsewhere departed from her assessment of the shortcomings of some feminist critique, I follow Joanne Hollows who, in *Feminism, Femininity and Popular Culture,* writes that "Instead of popular culture being the object of a feminist 'make-over,' analyzing the popular could teach feminist how to 'make-over' feminism" (203). That is, many feminist celebrities, writers, showrunners, and directors have much to offer our current conversations. That celebrities and media creators as diverse as Gina Rodriguez, Jill Soloway, Diablo Cody, Issa Rae, Lena Dunham, Beyoncé, Janelle Monáe, Amber Tamblyn, and Terry Crews have understood feminism as a tool that has improved their lives and that has potentially enabled them to more productively engage in a larger, unjust world should not only be perceived as a feminist victory, but should galvanize our ongoing commitment to feminist projects.

Home Is Where the Healing Is?

While the texts discussed in this book, at the minimum, focus on women's experiences, many nevertheless shore up injurious notions of femininity, suggesting either that a woman's place is, ultimately, the home or that the only way for a woman to thrive is to surrender to patriarchy or to embrace traditionally masculine values. However, the narratives discussed here all begin the interrogation of the domestic, at times exploring the fraught territory of the home and at other times suggesting a way forward to a world in which women are safe both at home and in the public sphere.

Women can be safe at home when they are not at risk of violence from other family members and instead are nurtured in an environment of mutual aid and respect. Women can be safe at home when they can rest assured that government agencies work to ensure the health and well-being of all individuals, regardless of class and race. Finally, women will be safe at home when they are able to leave the home: when they are able to participate freely in public life and when they feel supported to pursue their vocations.

On *Jane the Virgin*, Alba's matriarchal home represents a fulfillment of these requirements. Both Jane and Xo grow up in Alba's house and both return to it in times of trouble. A stay against the chaos of the outside world, Alba's home exists in distinction to the other central setting on *Jane the Virgin*: the Marbella hotel. A hotel, of course, exists as a place of escape from the home. Upscale and inviting, the Marbella is nevertheless populated by sociopaths and crime lords and evil twins. Most of the murders and betrayals on *Jane the Virgin* occur in or around the Marbella, signaling a moral depravity and lawlessness beyond the maternal home.[6]

Alba's house is also where Jane first develops her love—with her mother

Figure 12. Alba (Ivonne Coll, left), Jane (Gina Rodriguez, center), and Xo (Andrea Navedo) form a mutually supportive family unit (*Jane the Virgin,* The CW, season 1, 2014–2015).

and grandmother—of telenovelas. Several episodes open with the three of them sitting on a couch, reacting to what they are watching on the screen. The emphasis on their shared enjoyment of telenovelas suggests that media can facilitate a common experience and an opportunity for multi-generational bonding. Further, that the scene Rogelio stages takes place in a set meant to approximate Alba's home thus suggests that in *Jane the Virgin,* home—the place in which Americans increasingly consume most of our media (Feldman, "Do You Prefer?")—can be where the healing is.

Finally, the scene in which Jane and Xo recognize themselves functions allegorically to suggest the importance and possibilities of mass media representation. Although we all at times enjoy the dramas of characters who are distinctly unlike us, like Jane and Xo, we may also find it incredibly powerful to see ourselves and our experiences depicted on the stage, the page, or the screen. Rogelio's scheme, presenting a thinly veiled version of Jane and Xo's life in order to facilitate their reconciliation, is predicated on the concept that art, even not especially skillful art, can catalyze self-awareness, empathy, and even healing. Narrative can have an impact on people and on attitudes. Popular culture that strives to include diverse perspectives and to present nuanced, complex portraits of all people's lives may make our own homes, experiences, and culture "un poco menos doloroso."

Chapter Notes

Introduction

1. See the Introduction to Kim A. Loudermilk's *Fictional Feminism: How American Bestsellers Affect the Movement for Women's Equality* for an overview of the 1980s and 90s media accounts of feminism's alternating obsolescence and resurgence as well as the ways in which feminists began to embrace various definitions of feminism during this time (2, 11).

2. See also Sarah Ahmed's blog post "Selfcare as Warfare" for a discussion of the ways in which self-care is a radical political act for many individuals. In addition, back in 1987, bell hooks argued that the "anything goes" definition of feminism "has rendered it practically meaningless" ("Feminism" 62).

3. One might argue that the term "postfeminist," discussed later in this introduction, more accurately describes what is passing as feminism lately. That is, many of the qualities now attributed to feminism are those that scholars such as Gill, Tasker, Negra, and McRobbie have outlined as characteristic of postfeminism. However, none of the individuals mentioned (Beyoncé, hooks, Swift, Ahmed, West, Clinton, Garza, or Trump) use "postfeminist" to identify themselves or their commitments. The word feminist, then, seems to be undergoing a renaissance following decades during which feminism was often announced as "dead" or no longer necessary.

4. See Susan Douglas' *Enlightened Sexism: The Seductive Message That Feminism's Work Is Done* (2010), Yvonne Tasker and Diane Negra's *Interrogating Postfeminism: Gender and the Politics of Popular Culture* (2007), Hilary Radner and Rebecca Stringer's *Feminism at the Movies: Understanding Gender in Contemporary Popular Cinema* (2011), Rosalind Gill's *Gender and the Media* (2007), Rebecca Feasey's *From Happy Homemaker to Desperate Housewives: Motherhood and Popular Television* (2012) and Elizabeth Nathanson's *Television and Postfeminist Housekeeping: No Time for Mother* (2013).

5. Throughout this text, my use of the words "woman" and "women" are meant to indicate those who identify as women. Although I wish to resist them, the vast majority of the pop culture texts I discuss themselves uncritically reify gender binaries.

6. See also discussions of how chemicals are stored in fatty tissue in Florence Williams' *Breasts: An Unnatural History* (2013).

7. While the impact of American media is a contested issue, U.S. popular culture exports remain pervasive. See Lane Crothers' updated *Globalization and American Popular Culture* (2017).

8. See Charlotte Brunsdon, "Feminism, Postfeminism, Martha, and Nigella."

9. In deploying the metaphor of the "funhouse mirror," Ames and Burcon are drawing on Todd Gitlin's work in *The Whole World Is Watching: Mass Media in the Making & Unmasking of the New Left* (2003).

10. David Harvey has defined neoliberalism as a global embrace of "deregulation, privatization, and withdrawal of the state from many areas of social provisions" (3). Jess Butler points out, "The shift to neoliberal forms of governance in the West nonetheless provides fertile ground for the development of discourses that emphasize consumer citizenship, personal responsibility, and individual empowerment" (41).
11. Swiffer apologized and pulled the ad after widespread criticism (Cullers).
12. Tasker and Negra write that "postfeminism suggests that it is the very success of feminism that produces its irrelevance for contemporary culture" (8).
13. See Adrienne Trier-Bieniek's Introduction to *The Beyoncé Effect: Essays on Sexuality, Race and Feminism*, for further discussion of Beyoncé's career and influence.
14. Beyoncé's feminism has been the subject of much critical debate. For example, in her critique of "Lemonade," bell hooks argues that Beyoncé's "construction of feminism cannot be trusted. Her vision of feminism does not call for an end to patriarchal domination. It's all about insisting on equal rights for men and women. In the world of fantasy feminism, there are no class, sex, and race hierarchies that breakdown simplified categories of women and men, no call to challenge and change systems of domination, no emphasis on intersectionality" ("Moving Beyond").
15. As *The Hunger Games* and *Twilight* movies both closely follow the books they are adapted from, this chapter discusses the novels and films. In-text page number citations make clear when a novel is being referred to in each instance.
16. Nancy Felipe Russo coined this term in 1976.

Chapter 1

1. While the women depicted in *What to Expect* are superficially diverse (three are white, one is Latinx; two appear wealthy and two struggle financially), they are in fact fairly homogenous; they are heterosexual and bourgeois.
2. The character Wendy, who owns a shop devoted to facilitating breastfeeding and has authored a children's book on the subject, is depicted as an expert on pregnancy and childbirth. Her extensive knowledge, however, proves useless as she struggles in pregnancy and has to abandon her birth plan when an emergency C-section becomes necessary.
3. Clearly, attitudes have shifted significantly. A pivotal moment was Demi Moore's appearance, seven-months pregnant and without clothing, on the cover of *Vanity Fair* in 1991. Since then, many high-profile celebrity pregnancies have been part of the normalization of the pregnant body.
4. See Dawn Keetley's discussion of the ways in which "Murder House" "overtly registers contemporary fears about impending social collapse brought about by the recent housing crisis in the US and the subsequent, sustained recession" (92). Keetley, following Stephen King's observations in *Danse Macabre*, points out that the *Amityville Horror* movies of 1979 and 2005 explore a similar theme.
5. Seidel also argues that "neoliberal mothering" also creates conflicts for mothers in that they feel an imperative to work outside the home at the same time as childcare becomes increasingly privatized and social and familial support decreases (xv).
6. In "Seasons, Family and Nation in *American Horror Story*," Derek Johnston studies the inclusion of Halloween and Christmas in the series.
7. While most of the texts included in this study are of U.S. origin, *The Babadook* is Australian.
8. For an overview of the behaviors of abusive parents, see Al Odhayani, Watson, and Watson's "Behavioural Consequences of Child Abuse."
9. For an overview of the discussion, see Jarman, who argues that many of these critics "reinforce the intensely negative stereotypes about large bodies and remobilize some of the very elements of objectification and dehumanization that the film sets out to condemn" (169).

10. See Tracy Royce's "Unfit Mothers? Mother-Blame and Moral Panic Over Obesity." For a discussion of fat stigma in relation to critical discussions of *Precious*, see Scott Stoneman's "Ending Fat Stigma: *Precious*, Visual Culture, and Anti-Obesity in the 'Fat Moment.'"

11. Mary embodies the stereotypical "welfare mother," a figure described by Susan Douglas and Meredith W. Michaels in *The Mommy Myth* as "an omniscient icon of motherhood gone wrong, a nationally recognized media villain" (181).

12. See Pimpare's chapter "Social Workers and Charity Reformers" for an overview of depictions of social workers in film.

13. Seidel points out that the novel gestures toward a context for Mary's behavior (62).

14. The movie *Girls' Trip* does feature a mother-character, Lisa (Jada Pinkett-Smith), who is depicted as needing to learn to be more carefree and sexually uninhibited in order to be a happier person.

Chapter 2

1. *Gilmore Girls* has experienced a recent resurgence in popularity. In *Stealing the Show: How Women Are Revolutionizing Television,* Joy Press writes, "the year 2014 was the big bang for *Gilmore Girls* fandom: that's when Netflix began streaming all seven seasons, introducing Stars Hollow to a new generation of viewers who had been too young to watch the first time around, as well as to those who had previously snubbed it" (99). Then, in 2016, Netflix aired four new episodes of the series.

2. For example, Phylicia Rashad was only ten years older than Sabrina LeBeauf, who played her daughter on *The Cosby Show* (1984–1992); more recently, on *Boardwalk Empire* (2010–2014), actress Gretchen Mol has been cast to play the mother to Michael Pitt, an actor who is only 9 younger than she. See also Doug Barry's "Shockingly, Hollywood Still Refuses to Let Actresses Age At All."

3. See Lauren Rabinovitz's "Sitcoms and Single Moms: Representations of Feminism on American T.V." for a discussion of women on *The Mary Tyler Moore Show, Alice* and *One Day at a Time*.

4. This dynamic also exists between Jane and her mother Xiomara on *Jane the Virgin*, a series that showrunner Jenni Snyder Urman has described as "somewhere between *Ugly Betty* meets *Gilmore Girls*" (Villarreal). *Jane the Virgin* is further discussed in the conclusion of this book.

5. While my claims apply to all seasons of all the shows referenced here, my analyses are largely focused on the first seasons of *Parenthood* and the *Gilmore Girls,* and the second seasons of *16 and Pregnant* and *Teen Mom 2*.

6. See, for example, Medea, Gertrude in *Hamlet,* Mary Johnson in *Maggie: A Girl of the Streets,* the films *Mommy Dearest* and *Precious* (based on the novel *Push*), as well as media depictions of Brittany Spears and "octomom" Nadia Suleman. *New York Daily News* TV critic David Hinckley has also pointed out a proliferation of "bad moms" on TV, including Cersei Lannister on *Game of Thrones* and Gemma Teller on *Sons of Anarchy*.

7. In "Ralph, Fred, Archie, Homer, and the King of Queens: Why Television Keeps Re-Creating the Male Working-Class Buffoon," Richard Butsch describes a tendency to depict working-class men as incompetent, particularly in contrast to their "sensible" wives. Additionally, in the Introduction to *The Tube Has Spoken: Reality TV and History,* Julie Anne Taddeo and Ken Dvorak point out that despite TV shows focusing on "supernannies and wife swapping [that] take place in a postfeminist society in which families farm out parenting and domestic duties," reality programming narratives "nevertheless still cling to traditional notions of motherhood" (1).

8. Roseanne Barr's character on *Roseanne* (1988–1997, 2018) provides an exception and corrective to this.

9. See, in particular, Gill's "Culture and Subjectivity in Neoliberal and Postfeminist Times."

10. See Chapter 1 for a discussion of racism and classism in the assessment of mothers as "good" or "bad."

11. Further collapsing the distinction between mother and daughter is the repetition of plot lines for each character. Both Sarah and Amber embark on affairs with their bosses (Seasons 1 and 3). While this parallel might simply suggests similarities between mother and daughter (or a lack of ideas in the writer's room), it also suggests that Sarah is not so far removed from the types of relationships—and mistakes—that her nineteen year-old daughter might make. (However, in a wonderful and surprising moment on primetime television, Sarah defends her teenage daughter's choices, declaring, "if she's gonna learn that it's not right to date your boss, she's gonna learn it on her own" ("Remember Me, I'm the One Who Loves You"), suggesting that Sarah respects Amber as an intelligent, resilient, and self-aware person.)

12. See, for example, George Will's remarks that children born outside of wedlock are more of a threat to minority communities than lack of civil rights ("Black Single Mothers") and the attempts of the Wisconsin legislature to pass a bill condemning single parents (Pollitt). At the same time, however, the teen birth rate in the United States is declining: after a consistent downward trend, there was a brief uptick in 2007 that was followed by another 42 percent decrease for all groups (Patten and Livingston).

13. In the final season of *Parenthood*, Amber also becomes a young and unmarried mother; at the conclusion of the 2016 Netflix *Gilmore Girls* reunion, Rory too announces she is pregnant. While Rory is in her 30s, the identity of the father is unknown, suggesting that Rory, like Lorelai, may decide to single parent.

14. Lorelai runs away from home as a teen mom; her employer allows Lorelai and Rory to live in a cottage on the grounds of the inn where Lorelai works. See Season 1, episode 19, "Emily in Wonderland."

15. While Emily Gilmore is a powerful matriarch, Richard holds the literal and metaphorical checkbook.

16. In later seasons, Rory's father Christopher offers to pay her college tuition.

17. In the final season of *Parenthood*, Sarah's daughter Amber also becomes a young and unmarried mother; at the conclusion of the 2016 Netflix *Gilmore Girls'* reunion, Rory too announces she is pregnant. While Rory is in her 30s, the identity of the father is unknown, suggesting that Rory, like Lorelai, may decide to be a single parent.

18. See also *How to Live with Your Parents (For the Rest of Your Life)* (2013), a short-lived sitcom that documented the experiences of young single mother forced to move back in with her parents.

19. In "Reality TV and the American Family," Leigh H. Edwards defines reality TV as "factual programming with key recurring generic and marketing characteristics (such as unscripted, low-cost, edited formats featuring a mix of documentary and fiction genres, often to great ratings success)" (125).

20. The vast majority of these episodes are focused on females, with male protagonists featured only rarely. Interestingly, when a male is the focus of the show, he is often the child of a celebrity or a celebrity himself.

21. Responding to charges that the programs glamorize teen pregnancy, Lauren Dolgen, the creator of *16 and Pregnant* and the *Teen Mom* series, has written, "These documentary series tell the honest, unpleasant truth of teen pregnancy in America—the whole truth.... These young women struggle to make ends meet. They make mistakes as they try to navigate an adult life too soon. Relationships with their partners, parents and friends often crumble, and the pressure of raising a child is often too much to bear" (Dolgen).

22. In her article "Juno for Real: Negotiating Teenage Sexuality, Pregnancy, and Love in MTV's *16 and Pregnant/Teen Mom*," Tanja N. Aho writes that Pinksy is a "manifestation of patriarchal capitalism's interest in policing these young women's bodies and minds, and his paternalistic role diminishes the young mothers from active producers of truth claims and subjective knowledge about motherhood to infantilized dependents awash in emotions" (215).

23. Aho writes that, "each homologous episode is narrated by the teenage mother in

question, which not only serves reality TV's purpose of immediacy and intimacy, but also establishes and aura of authenticity—and, not to forget, provides a modicum of agency for the young women portrayed, even though questions surrounding scripting, censure, and silencing remain" (209).

24. I use the title *Teen Mom* to refer to all three series: *Teen Mom*, *Teen Mom 2*, and *Teen Mom 3*.

25. Chelsea is described as a "Daddy's Girl" in the episode description for "No Looking Back" on MTV.com. For examples of baby talk, see Chelsea's interactions with her boyfriend Adam in "So Much to Lose."

26. Since her *16 and Pregnant* episode, Jenelle has been involved in at least two abusive relationships, has struggled with substance abuse, (including addictions to marijuana and heroine) and has been arrested multiple times on drug charges (Morrisey). She has been diagnosed as bipolar, and yet this diagnosis has seemed to do little in terms of enabling her to get the help she needs.

27. Fallas also observes that "bad" moms are "often featured laying down and not directly interacting with their children … their struggles with the expectations and demands of parenting are not shown as normal difficulties that many people face but are rather framed as personality deficiencies in these girls" (56).

28. The transformation of the girls into moms, Caryn Murphy argues, is consistent with the tropes regularly seen on reality makeover shows, suggesting that the pre-pregnancy life is the "before," while the "after" image (at least on *16 and Pregnant*) remains "vague … episodes spend the most time on the transitional period" (93). Murphy's point is that after the child's birth, the protagonists are divided into "can-do" or "at risk" girls and for "can-do" girls, "Giving birth is marked as a re-making of the self … although many express regret over the adolescent experiences they have missed, successful subjects embrace new identities and responsibilities" (94).

29. Jenelle is widely reviled on the Internet. See for example, the comment section of virtually any article discussing her, including "I Swear I'll Leave Teen Mom 2."

30. $200,000 a year is Melanie Ann Stewart's estimate.

Chapter 3

1. In the film, Peeta says, "They'd turn me into something I'm not … another piece in their game" (*The Hunger Games*).

2. As *The Hunger Games* and *Twilight* movies both closely follow the books they are adapted from, this chapter discusses the novels and films. In-text page number citations make clear when a novel is being referred to.

3. Discussing absent mothers in children's literature, author Catherine Gilbert Murdock writes that, "It is by definition the absence of a mother … that makes the adventure feasible. The simple act of eliminating mom provides a venue where anything dangerous or magical or gallant can happen."

4. In "Literary Traditions on Fire: Mimetic Desire and the Role of the Orphaned Heroine in Suzanne Collins's *Hunger Games* Trilogy," Alison L. Bewley calls Katniss an "honorary orphan" (372) and presents a helpful overview of the different narrative treatments of male and female orphan protagonists.

5. Collins leaves Katniss' race ambiguous (Katniss suggest she has "olive skin" (Collins, *The Hunger Games*, 8), resulting in some controversy when a white actress was selected to portray her in the movie. See Sarah Seltzer's "The Imminent Whitewashing of *The Hunger Games* Heroine."

6. In the novel, *Mockingjay*, Katniss's mother opts to live in a different district, starting a hospital at which she will care for other damaged people (instead of her own daughter).

7. One exception in the novels is Katniss' friend Madge; this character does not appear in the films.

8. Many of the male residents of the Capitol are presented as feminine and foppish.

9. Additionally, in the novels Katniss articulates a rejection of the Capitol's beauty standards, including their embrace of hairlessness. In this way, Collins denaturalizes beauty practices common in both the Capitol and in early 21st century America, such as the imperative to remove hair and to use makeup, which is particularly interesting as many of her younger readers themselves may be just beginning to participate in—and may feel ambivalent about—these practices.

10. General Paylor, who ascends to the presidency at the conclusion of the series, is an exception. She is depicted as a competent and reasonable woman warrior.

11. In "Violence, Agency, and the Women of *Twilight*," Ann Torkelson provides a helpful overview of feminist responses to the series. Several critics point to Edward's troublingly dominant behaviors as evidence of Meyer's glorification of violence against women. In "Maybe Edward Is the Most Dangerous Thing Out There: The Role of Patriarchy," Melissa Miller argues that *Twilight* "promotes a dangerous and damaging ideology of patriarchy that normalizes and rationalizes the control of women by men" (165) and quotes Cynthia Enloe's concept of a "Culture of Imminent Danger" (166).

12. Bella, unlike Katniss, is depicted as genuinely fond of her mother, whom she refers to as her "best friend" (105); she happily acknowledges, "My mom looks like me, except ... with laugh lines" (4) and tells Edward "She looks a lot like me, but she's prettier" (105).

13. On the one hand, *Twilight* and *The Hunger Games* are emblematic of girl culture; on the other, *Twilight* in particular is often dismissed as bad art or not worthy of study. The disparagement of narratives associated with women is not new; in 1996 Charlotte Brunsdon observed: "I have always been conscious of the way in which what women and girls like is somehow *worse* than the equivalent masculine pleasures" (Brunsdon, *Screen Tastes* 2). This sentiment persists; Carol Stabile, discussing the particularly passionate hatred directed at the *Twilight* franchise in particular asks, "Imagine a Facebook group organized around participants' abhorrence of *Halo*'s Master Chief or thousands of antifans devoted to loathing *Lost*'s Sawyer or *Star Wars*' Boba Fett or Michael Jordan and you get some sense of the sexism directed at the mass-produced girl culture so many girls and women love" (E 4).

14. In Anna North's article "Breaking Dawn: What to Expect When You're Expecting ... a Vampire," North critiques Meyer's "disturbingly rosy account of teen marriage and pregnancy, vampire-style" and goes on to mock the fact that "Because she is now a vampire, Bella is even hotter than she was before pregnancy, and after a short recovery period she's able to have all-night sex sessions with her husband while her extended family takes care of the perfectly behaved, telepathic baby ... teen motherhood just makes your life rad."

15. See "Team Bella: Fans Navigating Desire, Security and Feminism" by Ananya Mukjerjea for a discussion of paternalism in the novels.

16. These choices are also consistent with teachings of Mormon church. For further discussion, see Margaret M. Toscano's "Mormon Morality and Immortality in Stephenie Meyer's *Twilight* Series."

17. Kelly makes a similar point in her discussion of *Twilight* in *Abstinence Cinema: Virginity and the Rhetoric of Sexual Purity in Contemporary Film*.

18. Hila Shachar notes, however, that "Bella's 'power' highlights that her new immortal body's eternal function is to be useful to others: to protect them, to nurture them, to hide them" (154).

19. Kelly notes that "in the *Twilight Saga*, vampires no longer represent illicit sexual desire but instead offer a reprieve from a society polluted by desire and destabilized by feminism" (27).

20. See Peretz's "Inside the Trump Marriage: Melania's Burden" and Wong's "17 of the Most Absurd Things Donald Trump Has Said About Marriage."

21. See Sarah S. Richardson's "Don't blame the mothers: careless discussion of epigenetic research on how early life affects health across generations could harm women."

22. Women are often excoriated online for their perceived failures as mothers. Rachel Garlinghouse maintains that social media shaming has increased: "Moms are used to opin-

ions, often unsolicited, from relatives, friends, neighbors, co-workers, and sometimes more annoying and intrusive from strangers" but more recently, even strangers feel emboldened: "taking a photo of a mom and her children and using it to crucify her for her decisions.... These are moms doing everyday things: eating, browsing merchandise at a store, walking down a sidewalk." See also Salaky "People can't stop shaming moms, and it's causing 'maternal anxiety.'"

23. For more discussion of the pronatalist "motherhood mandate," see Gotlib, "'But You Would Be the Best Mother': Unwomen, Counterstories, and the Motherhood Mandate."

Chapter 4

1. See also the "Second National Report on Human Exposure to Environmental Chemicals" (2003) from the Centers for Disease Control and Prevention and "Why a Woman's Organization" from *Women's Voices for the Earth*. In addition, some investigators associate the almost 50 percent increase in cancer rates between 1950 and 1990 with the introduction of thousands of new chemicals into consumer, commercial, and industrial use during that time period (Knopper 40).

2. See Lisa Yakas' "Nasty Germs are Lurking in Your 'Clean' Home" or Darla Carter's "Harmful Germs Lurking in Your Kitchen Can Make You Sick."

3. Significantly, reviewing Davis' *The Secret History of the War on Cancer* (2006), Ezekiel J. Emanuel writes that Davis' book is "*hysterical* and exasperating" (italics added, 33).

4. MCS, also termed "chemical AIDS," was described as an "acquired disorder" impacting "multiple organ systems" as a result of "demonstrable exposure to many chemically unrelated compounds at doses far below those established in the general population to cause harmful effects" (Cullen 57).

5. For a discussion of hysteria, see Elaine Showalter's *Hystories: Hysterical Epidemics and Modern Media*.

6. For example, Hooker Chemicals, the company responsible for the toxic waste at Love Canal, is owned by a corporation that, among other activities, produces pharmaceuticals, disinfectants, and detergents. The pharmaceuticals, in particular, may relieve certain kinds of suffering, but their by-products certainly contributed to the suffering of residents at Love Canal.

7. *The Incredible Shrinking Woman* was "suggested by" Richard Matheson's science fiction novel *The Shrinking Man* (1956). Unlike the film, the novel takes seriously the protagonist's diminishment as the result of pesticide exposure.

8. Disability studies scholars have identified a tradition in which disabled bodies are often deployed as "visible symptom[s] of social disorganization and collapse" (Mitchell 348). See also Garland-Thomson's "Introduction" to *Freakery: Cultural Spectacles of the Extraordinary Body* and Sara Hosey's "'One of Us': Identity and Community in Contemporary Fiction."

9. See Robert D. Bullard's *Dumping in Dixie: Race, Class, and Environmental Quality* and *The Quest for Environmental Justice: Human Rights and the Politics of Pollution*, as well as Dorceta E. Taylor's "Women of Color: Environmental Justice, and Ecofeminism" and the United Church of Christ's report "Toxic Wastes and Race at Twenty."

10. For discussion of Carol's whiteness, see also Danielle Bouchard and Jigna Desai's "'There's Nothing More Debilitating Than Travel'": Locating U.S. Empire in Todd Haynes' *Safe*" and Susan Potter's "Dangerous Spaces: *Safe*."

11. See also Sharon O'Dair's "Horror or Realism? Filming Toxic Discourse in Smiley's *A Thousand Acres*" and Potter's "Dangerous Spaces: *Safe*."

12. See Rosalind Gill's "Postfeminist Media Culture: Elements of a Sensibility" for a discussion of the "makeover" as a component of the postfeminist sensibility.

13. See also Gaye Naismith's "Tales from the Crypt: Contamination and Quarantine in Todd Haynes' *Safe*" and Amy Taubin's "Nowhere to Hide."

14. Wein directed; he and Lister-Jones co-wrote the film.

Chapter 5

1. In addition, there are numerous television movies—too many to include in this chapter—particularly movies made for the Lifetime network, that use domestic violence as a narrative trope. For a discussion of Lifetime movies, see Emily L. Newman and Emily Witsell's *The Lifetime Network: Essays on "Television for Women" in the 21st Century.*

2. For a discussion of the backlash against the "victim label" see Rebecca Stringer's "Rethinking the Critique of Victim Feminism" in Ellen Faulkner and Gayle MacDonald's *Victim No More: Women's Resistance to Law, Culture and Power.*

3. While I also use the terms "battering" and "intimate partner violence" in this chapter, I choose the phrase "domestic violence" because it reinforces the notion that much male violence against women takes place in the home or is related to concepts of the patriarchal home as a site of male dominion.

4. Saint Hoax has also developed a campaign "When did she stop treating you like a hero?" featuring images of the princes/heroes of Disney films, as well as a "Pr*incest* Diaries" campaign meant to draw attention to incest.

5. See Reidy, et al., "Man Enough? Masculine Discrepancy Stress and Intimate Partner Violence."

6. Interestingly, Charles' assistant acts alarmed when he suspects that Marisa is "Spanish" (presumably he means Hispanic or Latina). Both Marisa and her son, Ty, are olive-skinned; the assistant's comment underscores the thinking that, when dressed the part, Marisa can pass as upper-class and potentially of European descent.

7. Radner notes in *Neofeminist Cinema* that *Maid* "draws upon the persona of an already established star, Jennifer Lopez, who outside the film's narrative offers an exemplar of neofeminist achievement that extends the ethos of the film beyond the cinematic experience" (98).

8. See Kozol's "Fracturing Domesticity: Media, Nationalism, and the Question of Feminist Influence" for an overview of how the feminist movement raised awareness of domestic violence.

9. Early Hollywood films depict men hitting romantic interests/partners/wives for laughs or as the natural result of heightened emotion. See for example, the "grapefruit scene" in *The Public Enemy* (1931).

10. Of *Raging Bull*, Duncan Wheeler writes, "Although spousal abuse is not condoned, the battered wife is never developed as a three-dimensional character; Jake's outbursts are primarily construed as a tragic symptom and cause of his decline, equivalent in both narrative and ethical terms to his increasing dependence on junk food" (156).

11. See Jenny Platz's "Subversion of the Final Girl in Rape Revenge Narratives and the Normalization of Violence Against Women in *The Tenth Circle* and *The Assault*" in Newman and Witsell's *The Lifetime Network.*

12. Stasia also makes this connection, as does Finley. There are numerous films that depict women taking revenge against their rapists. See Alexandra Heller-Nicholas' *Rape Revenge Films* (2011).

13. In "Enduring Themes and Silences," Patricia Easteal, Kate Holland and Judd Keziah review the work of feminist theorists who argue that news media handlings of domestic violence render it as an individual problem, rather than a social problem facilitated by patriarchy (1425).

14. See Kimmel's *"Gender Symmetry" in Domestic Violence A Substantive and Methodological Research Review.*

15. According to the ACLU's "Words From Prison—Did You Know?": "Women receive harsher sentences for killing their male partners than men receive for killing their female partners." Additionally, many incarcerated women report being victims of domestic violence: "The vast majority of women in prison have been victims of violence prior to their incarceration including domestic violence, rape, sexual assault and child abuse" ("Words from Prison"). See also Victoria Law, "How Many Women Are in Prison for Defending Themselves Against Domestic Violence?"

Chapter 6

1. In "Fracturing Domesticity: Media, Nationalism, and the Question of Feminist Influence" Wendy Kozol quotes Kathleen Ferraro, who argues that the criminal justice system is "designed to protect and reinforce the social order through punishment of individual deviants. It is, therefore, fundamentally at odds with a structural, gendered analysis of woman battering" (qtd. in Kozol 652).
2. *Personal Velocity: Three Portraits* is based on Miller's book, *Personal Velocity*.
3. In his *Salon* review, Jeff Stark remarks on the use of a narrator: "oddly enough, each story is narrated by a male voice. (You know, because it's a book.)"
4. In her *Crunk Feminist Collective* article "Tyler Perry Hates Black Women" Brittney Cooper identifies problematic representations in Perry's TV show *The Haves and Have Nots*; after Perry called her up to discuss her criticisms, Cooper published a more "generous" discussion of his film *The Single Moms Club* in *Salon* ("How I Confronted").
5. According to *Variety*, 80–90 percent of the audience for Madea movies are African American (Lang). In addition, Ronald L. Jackson and Jamel Santa Cruze Bell urge us to remember that at this time, Perry exercises more power "to shape images and representations of African Americans" than any other African American in Hollywood (5).
6. See, for example, Stephane Dunn's "Cool Drag: Black Masculinity in Big Mama Disguise," in which Dunn argues that the Madea character "reinforces stereotypes of both Black masculinity and femininity" (67).
7. Perry alludes to *The Color Purple* in several of his films and plays; see Whitney Peoples' "(Re)Mediating Black Womanhood: Tyler Perry, Black Feminist Cultural Criticism, and the Politics of Legitimation."
8. See, for example, Hilton Als' "Mama's Gun," in which he writes that Perry's "movies condescend to their audience, conveying lazy cultural stereotypes about blackness."
9. See also, "Arrest Policies for Domestic Violence" and "INCITE! Critical Resistance Statement."
10. Carlos is, however, wealthy. Similar to the treatment of the male abuser in other films, Carlos is an uncomplicated villain; his only redeeming qualities seem to be his good looks and his money. The repeated depiction of male abusers as wealthy suggests a naturalization of the connection between physical and financial power and control.
11. There are significant differences between Perry's play *Madea's Family Reunion* (2002) and the film, including that in the play, the Lisa character leaves her wealthy fiancée on their wedding day in order to marry her working-class ex-boyfriend.
12. The discussions thus far in this chapter have been limited to film. While *Big Little Lies* is a television series, its handling of domestic violence is relevant in the way in which it points perhaps to the direction of representations to come.
13. In Moriarity's book it is revealed that Bonnie recognizes Perry's violence in part because she grew up in a home in which her father beat her mother.
14. For a discussion of the backlash against the "victim label" see Rebecca Stringer's "Rethinking the Critique of Victim Feminism" in Ellen Faulkner and Gayle MacDonald's *Victim No More: Women's Resistance to Law, Culture and Power*.

Chapter 7

1. For further discussion, see Susan J. Douglas and Meredith Michaels' *The Mommy Myth: The Idealization of Motherhood and How It Has Undermined All Women* (2005); more recently, see Ann Marie Slaughter's book, *Unfinished Business: Women, Men, Work, Family* (2016) and the responses to Slaughter's initial article for *The Atlantic*: "Why Women Still Can't Have it All."
2. I group these films as "indies" because of their writer/director's relative independ-

ence from big studios. For a discussion of indie or "smart" cinema, see Jeffrey Sconce's "Irony, Nihilism and the New American 'Smart' Film," Claire Perkins' *American Smart Cinema,* and Geoff King's *American Independent Cinema.*

3. Notably, Ted Kramer, who takes custody of his son in the film, is also penalized for parenting and loses his advertising job.

4. In *Manchester by the Sea,* a deeply disturbed male character becomes his nephew's guardian. The film resolves with his rejection of this role.

5. Women, of course, have always worked and parented. Leonard writes, "As a feminist icon, the modern woman worker is, predictably, white and upper or middle class, as were the women whose discourse fomented the working woman as a feminist model in the 1960s and 1970s. Narrating the story of working women only through the construction of such privileged and educated women is problematic, however, for it ignores the long history that working-class women and women of color have had in the labor force" (101).

6. See Jane Arthurs' "Sex and the City and Consumer Culture."

7. For discussions of postfeminism, see Yvonne Tasker and Diane Negra's *Interrogating Postfeminism: Gender and the Politics of Popular Culture* (2007), Hilary Radner and Rebecca Stringer's *Feminism at the Movies: Understanding Gender in Contemporary Popular Cinema* (2011) and Rosalind Gill's *Gender and the Media* (2007). See also Rosalind Gill's article, "Post-Postfeminism? New Feminist Visibilities in Postfeminist Times" for a discussion of the resurgence of popular feminism in maintsream media.

8. Initially, *Obvious Child* was a short that Robespierre wrote with Anna Bean and Karen Maine; the full length film was developed with producer Elizabeth Holm (Angelo).

9. That the privilege to experiment and fail is not available to all people equally is perhaps (subconsciously) reflected by the strikingly white palette of the home in *Tiny Furniture.*

10. Laurie Simmons' apartment is used in the film.

11. See Jess Butler's "For White Girls Only" for further discussion of how pro-sex feminists responded in part to anti-porn feminists.

12. A more recent example of debate over the boundaries between liberation and pornification is the discussion of the reclamation of the word "slut." See, for example, Leora Tanenbaum's *I Am Not a Slut* (2015).

13. See Katha Pollitt's *Pro: Reclaiming Abortion Rights* (2014).

14. For overviews of the debate between trans-exclusionary and trans-inclusionary groups, see Sally Hines' "The Feminist Frontier: On Trans and Feminism" and Cristan Williams' "Radical Inclusion: Recounting the Trans Inclusive History of Radical Feminism."

15. See Kyra Hunting's "All in the (Prison) Family: Genre Mixing and Queer Representation"; see also Taylor Glogiewicz's "Psuedo-Families: Group Formations in Women's Prisons."

Chapter 8

1. Many households have long employed domestic workers; in fact, rates of domestic employment decreased in the mid-20th century. See Maggie Caldwell's "Invisible Women: The Real History of Domestic Workers in America" and Ester Bloom's "Maids in America: The Decline of Domestic Help."

2. The Feminist International Network of Resistance to Reproductive and Genetic Engineering (FINRRAGE) was a radical group on the other side of the feminist spectrum. In *Pandora's Box: Feminism Confronts Reproductive Technology,* Nancy Lublin describes FINRRAGE as an organization critical of the application of patriarchal reproductive interventions (xiv).

3. The point of this section is not to argue that surrogacy is inherently unethical. As asserted in Chapter 9, cultural definitions of mothers and motherhood are increasingly diverse and expansive; I suggest this is a positive development. Surrogacy can be an affirming experience for many of those, including children, who participate in or benefit from it.

4. Each text in its own way elides discussion of the racialization of domestic labor. That is, rather than even marginally addressing the history of U.S. and European exploitation of women of color's bodies as surrogates, wet nurses, caregivers, and domestic workers, both *Tully* and *The Handmaid's Tale* problematically present post-racial worlds.

5. Reitman and Cody's earlier collaboration, 2007's surprise hit *Juno*, also explores variety within the family unit: *Juno* focuses on the relationship between a teenage mother and the married couple who plan to adopt her child.

6. For discussion of the controversy surrounding *Tully*, in particular its handling of perinatal mental illness, see Christina Caron's "Diablo Cody, Responding to Criticism, Says 'Tully' is Meant to be Uncomfortable."

7. See Khazan's "Emasculated Men Refuse to Do Chores—Except Cooking" and Rebecca M. Horne's "Time, Money, or Gender? Predictors of the Division of Household Labour Across Life Stages."

8. Tully at first presents as an eccentric, swooping in as what Rand Richards Cooper calls a "postmodern Mary Poppins" and Richard Brody calls a "Manic Pixie Dream Nanny."

9. Drew's remark locates reproductive exploitation elsewhere, beyond the United States, further erasing the United State's long history of white families exploiting non-white women's reproductive capabilities. See Harrison's *Brown Bodies, White Babies* for discussion of the racialization of reproductive technologies, including wet-nursing, in the United States.

10. This is a remark that June makes in the episode titled "Baggage."

11. An episode that features a wife (Marisa Tomei) who has been shipped off to work and die in "the colonies" suggests that even women at the top of the hierarchy are subject to replacement ("Unwomen").

12. The "Econopeople" are apparently permitted to have and keep their own children, perhaps as a result of their conduct before the coup. June remarks that she might have been an Econowife if she hadn't been "an adulteress" ("Baggage").

13. Additionally, as of this writing, the love triangle that includes Luke, June and Nick (Nicole's biological father), has not been resolved. While Nick begins to feature less prominently in Season 3, that June had avowed her love for both men and that she has children with both men might allow the series to depict a true reversal of the non-consensual ménage à trois that defines Gilead. That is, is it possible that June, Nick, and Luke could engage in a consensual polyamorous relationship?

14. In "New Directions in Motherhood Studies," her overview of developments in research and writing about mothering, Samira Kawash writes that, despite a focus on mothering, motherhood, and the maternal in the 1970s and 80s, motherhood became "an embarrassing theoretical relic of an earlier naive view of the essential woman and her shadow, the essential mother" (972). As a result, discussions of motherhood largely disappeared from academic journals, publications, and conferences (973).

15. Anna L. Weissman writes that women's reproductive capabilities continue to provide rationale for subordination, writing that the division of sexuality from reproduction is "dangerous" because "if the means of reproduction that (re)create certain values are changed, values can change ... patriarchy can potentially be dismantled or displaced" (292).

16. In *Woman at the End of Time,* reproduction takes place asexually, but men are depicted as breastfeeding and as otherwise tending to children.

17. While the possibilities are obvious for trans women, Alghrani suggests that, for cisgender men, a uterine transplant might serve as "an 'enhancement' of reproductive function" (305).

18. The first uterus was successfully transplanted in 2014 (in Sweden), with the United States following in 2017 (Alghrani 302).

19. Interestingly, a father's support for such policies only increases if his first child is a daughter; having a daughter or daughters after sons does not appear to have the same effect.

20. Male pregnancy is also depicted in the 1994 film *Junior,* as well as the 1978 comedy *Rabbit Test.*

Chapter 9

1. In the report "Boxed In 2016–2017: Women on Screen and Behind the Scenes in Television," Martha M. Lauzen finds that *"Regardless of platform, gender stereotypes on television programs abound.* Female characters were younger than their male counterparts, more likely than men to be identified by their marital status, and less likely than men to be seen at work and actually working" (ital. orig.).
2. See Sally Hines' "Intimate Transitions: Transgender Practices of Partnering and Parenting" for discussion of how trans parents' experiences and practices can illuminate changes in contemporary family and social structures.
3. Similarly, Julia Serano observes: "Cissexual feminist fascination with transsexuality (where it has occurred) has typically been motivated not by a concern for transsexual individuals but by an interest in how the existence of transsexuality might impact, or provide support for, gender artifactualist perspectives and politics" (117).
4. See Dejean's "Transgender Rights Are Under Attack in These 11 States," Ford's "Housing Discrimination Against Transgender People Is Even Worse Than We Thought," Burns' "How a New Trump Policy Enables Anti-Trans Discrimination" and Teeman's "Why Are So Many Transgender Women of Color Being Killed in America?"
5. See Williams' "Gender Critical Feminism, the Roots of Radical Feminism and Trans Oppression." See also the controversy over the term "TERF" as described in Flaherty's "TERF War."
6. See Goldberg's "What is a Woman?"
7. See, for example, depictions in *Ace Ventura* (1994), *The Hangover: Part II* (2011), *The Crying Game* (1992), and *Boys Don't Cry* (1999). Further, as Cael Keegan points out in "How *Transparent* tried and failed to represent trans men," trans men remain underrepresented: "The increased visibility for trans women has not necessarily meant increased visibility for transgender men."
8. In *"Transamerica* (2005): The Road to the Multiplex after New Queer Cinema" Gary Needham says that the film "*Transamerica*'s queering of the road movie utilizes the tried-and-tested generic tropes of the genre as a ruse to see bodily transformation and identity as another type of journey" (in Radner and Stringer 55).
9. It is revealed that Toby was sexually abused by his stepfather, suggesting that Toby's mother was herself was not an ideal parent. Additionally, Toby's hatred for his stepfather further positions Toby as alone in the world (and in need of a parent).
10. Hilary Malatino writes that the depiction of Sophia is "subtle, humanized" (97).
11. Like Maura, Sophia must parent at a remove; that is, while Maura occupies an important role in her children's lives, they are grown and she is no longer a custodial parent.
12. I use a male pronoun here because Marcy identifies as a man.
13. I use "Mort" to indicate moments, such as in flashbacks, when Maura is identified as such.
14. However, Evan Read Armstrong in *The Acisted Eye: Transgender and Intersex Bodies in International Cis-Authored Film and Television* argues that *Transparent* is not actually about a transperson's story, but is "a series that follows a story that is trans-adjacent" as "the camera does not spend much time on Maura herself but instead sticks closely to the reactions and consequences that her three children experience" (62). That is, much of the first season is really about how Maura's children deal with her transition as well as how they struggle in other areas of their lives, areas that may or may not be impacted by Maura's transition.
15. In "*Transparent* Is Radically Selfish, and That's Why It Matters" Jamieson Cox forwards a similar assertion: "Maura isn't a saint, and she's not a martyr either; she's condescending, secretive, obstinate, emotionally manipulative, and blinded by privilege." Further, as Brady, Burns, and Davies argue, the show refuses "sympathetic portrayal" at the same time it "insists on an ethical empathy" (158).
16. For discussion of the "matrophor," see Astrid Henry's *Not My Mother's Daughter: Generational Conflict and Third-Wave Feminism.*

17. In the *New Yorker*, Ariel Levy calls *Transparent* a "radical exploration of gender and sexuality, unlike anything that preceded it on television."

18. Amanda D. Lotz argues that "narrowcasting" is particularly relevant for women viewers: "In an environment characterized by narrowcast competition, smaller, specific audiences gain value, which makes demographic groups such as women—and even more specific groups, such as eighteen-to-forty-nine-year-old working women, African Americans, and other subgroups of the overall heterogeneous audience—increasingly important" (26).

19. In an interview on NPR's *Fresh Air*, Kohan contended: "Piper [the protagonist] was my Trojan horse. You're not going to go into a network and sell a show on really fascinating tales of black women and Latino women and old women and criminals. But if you take this white girl, this sort of fish out of water, and you follow her in, you can then expand your world and tell all those other stories. But it's a hard sell to just go in and try to sell those stories initially" ("Orange Creator").

20. However, in 2017, allegations of sexual harassment emerged against Jeffrey Tambor; in March 2018, Amazon announced that Tambor would not be returning to the show (Goldberg).

21. See Mey's "My Day on the Set of *Transparent*, Where Trans Voices Actually Get Heard." In addition, in her book *Stealing the Show: How Women Are Revolutionizing Television*, Joy Press describes Soloway's implementation of "what she called a 'transfirmative action program,' actively seeking out trans personnel for the crew and even leading a trans screenwriting workshop to train new writers" (266).

22. See McDonough "Laverne Cox Flawlessly Shuts Down Katie Couric's Invasive Questions About Transgender People."

23. Almost ten years earlier, Thomas Beatie, a pregnant trans man interviewed by Oprah Winfrey, was unequivocal in his rejection of the "wrong body" narrative, saying, "I don't feel like I was born in the wrong body. I felt like I was meant to be exactly who I am today," a claim that Damien W. Riggs suggests Winfrey is skeptical of.

Conclusion

1. Rogelio speaks in Spanish; English subtitles translate for non–Spanish speakers.

2. In "Latina/os on TV!: A Proud (and Ongoing) Struggle Over Representation and Authorship," Beltràn notes that "Latinos unfortunately have been marginalized in English-language television story-worlds to a degree that's only beginning to be countered. We have often been invisible—simply not there—and misrepresented when we do appear in prime time programming" (23).

3. As discussed in Chapters 4 and 7, mother-daughter relationships are often underrepresented on screen; relationships between mother and daughters of color are even more rare.

4. I have, in fact, used this clip in my WST 101 class in order to demonstrate the Bechdel Test.

5. However, Press argues the election of Donald Trump revealed that television, in particular, "was transmitting a vision of an America that was racially vibrant and sexually progressive, a vision that turned out to be too far ahead of the actual reality of much of America, which was still attached to traditional values and traditional inequities of power" (15).

6. As a self-appointed custodian of Jane's virginity, Alba is in many respects a delegate of the patriarchy. Further, in particular in its initial premise, *Jane* defaults to a heterosexist and narrow understandings of sex; however, over the course of the series, sexual desire is often handled with honesty and complexity.

Works Cited

"After." *The Handmaid's Tale*, created by Bruce Miller, Hulu, 30 May 2018.

"Afterbirth." *American Horror Story: Murder House*, created by Brad Falchuk and Ryan Murphy, FX, 21 Dec. 2011.

Ahmed, Sarah. "Selfcare as Warfare." *Feminist killjoys*, 25 August 2014, https://feministkilljoys.com/2014/08/25/selfcare-as-warfare/. Accessed 3 March 2018.

Aho, Tanja N. "Juno for Real: Negotiating Teenage Sexuality, Pregnancy, and Love in MTV's 16 and Pregnant/Teen Mom." *Television and the Self: Knowledge, Identity, and Media Representation*, edited by Kathleen M. Ryan and Deborah A. Macey, Lexington Books, 2013, pp. 205–226.

Akin, Stephanie. "Long-Ignored Hero of Flint Water Crisis: I'm Just a Mom.'" *Rollcall*, 4 February 2016, https://www.rollcall.com/news/flint-resident-ignored-months-now-hero-congressional-hearing-water-crisis. Accessed 28 May 2018.

Al Odhayani, Abdulaziz, William J. Watson, and Lindsay Watson. "Behavioural Consequences of Child Abuse." *Canadian Family Physician*, vol. 59, no. 8, 2013, pp. 831–836.

Alghrani, Amel. "Uterus Transplantation in and Beyond Cisgender Women: Revisiting Procreative Liberty in Light of Emerging Reproductive Technologies." *Journal of Law and Bioscience*, 10 July 2018, pp. 301–328.

Alice. Created by Robert Gretchel, D'Angelo-Bullock-Allen Productions and Warner Brothers, 1975–1985.

Alice Doesn't Live Here Anymore. Directed by Martin Scorsese, performances by Ellen Burstyn and Kris Kristofferson, Warner Brothers, 1974.

Allmark, Panizza. "Pushing Boundaries: *Weeds*, Motherhood, Neoliberalism and Postfeminism." *Outskirts, Feminisms Along the Edge*, vol. 35, November 2016, pp. 1–23.

Als, Hilton. "Mama's Gun." *The New Yorker*, 26 April 2010, https://www.newyorker.com/magazine/2010/04/26/mamas-gun. Accessed 1 May 2011.

Ames, Melissa, and Sarah Burcon. *How Pop Culture Shapes the Stages of a Woman's Life: From Toddlers-in-Tiaras to Cougars-on-the-Prowl*, Palgrave Macmillan, 2016.

Angelo, Megan. "A Rom-Com Path Less Traveled." *New York Times*, 30 May 2014, https://www.nytimes.com/2014/06/01/movies/jenny-slate-in-gillian-robespierres-obvious-child.html. Accessed 13 June 2017.

Armstrong, Evan Read. *The Acisted Eye: Transgender and Intersex Bodies in International Cis-Authored Film and Television*. Thesis, Carleton University, Ontario, 2016.

"Arrest Policies for Domestic Violence." *Stop Abusive and Violent Environments*, 2010.

Arthurs, Jane. "Sex and the City and Consumer Culture: Remediating Postfeminist Drama." *Feminist Media Studies*, vol. 3, no. 1, 2004, pp. 83–98.

Ashcraft, Donna Musialowski. *Deconstructing Twilight: Psychological and Feminist Perspectives on the Series*. Peter Lang, 2013.

Atwood, Margaret. *The Handmaid's Tale*. Houghton, Mifflin, Harcourt, 1986.

"Audrey." *My Super Sweet 16*, directed by

Lucy J. Lesser and David L. Bowles, MTV, 18 June 2007.

The Babadook. Directed by Jennifer Kent, performances by Essie Davis and Noah Wiseman, Screen Australia, 2014.

Baby Boom. Directed by Charles Shyer, performance by Diane Keaton, United Artists, 1987.

Baby Mama. Directed by Michael McCullers, performances by Tina Fey and Amy Poehler, Universal Studios, 2008.

Bacchiocchi, Gina. "What MTV Didn't Show: Teen Mom' Kailyn Lowry Reveals How She Hid Homelessness, Cheating, and Medical Scares from Reality TV Cameras in New Tell-All." *Radar Online*, 17 April 2014, https://radaronline.com/exclusives/2014/04/mtv-didnt-show-teen-mom-2-kailyn-lowry-hid-homelesness-cheating-medical-scares/. Accessed June 17, 2014.

Bad Moms. Directed by Jon Lucas and Scott Moore, performances by Mila Kunis, Kristen Bell and Kathryn Hahn, STX Films, 2016.

A Bad Moms Christmas. Directed by Jon Lucas and Scott Moore, performances by Mila Kunis, Kristen Bell, and Kathryn Hahn, STX Films, 2017.

"Baggage." *The Handmaid's Tale*, created by Bruce Miller, Hulu, 2 May 2018.

Barry, Doug. 2013. "Shockingly, Hollywood Still Refuses to Let Actresses Age at All." *Jezebel*, 21 September 2013, https://jezebel.com/shockingly-hollywood-still-refuses-tolet-actresses-ag-1361159199. Accessed 23 September 23 2013.

Baumgardner, Jennifer. "Feminism Is a Failure, and Other Myths." *Alternet*, 16 November 2005. https://www.alternet.org/story/28237/feminism_is_a_failure%2C_and_other_myths. Accessed 4 November 2017.

———, and Amy Richards. *Manifesta: Young Women, Feminism, and the Future*. Farrar, Straus, Giroux, 2000, 2010.

Beam, Cris. *To the End of June: The Intimate Life of American Foster Care*. Mariner Books, 2014.

"Behind Closed Doors: The Impact of Domestic Violence on Children." *UNICEF*, 2006, pp. 1–14, https://www.unicef.org/media/files/BehindClosedDoors.pdf. Accessed 1 September 2018.

Beltràn, Mary. "Latina/os on TV!: A Proud (and Ongoing) Struggle Over Representation and Authorship." *The Routledge Companion to Latina/o Popular Culture*, edited by Frederick Luis Aldama, Routledge, 2016, pp. 23–33.

Bennett, Jessica. "On the Internet, to Be Mom Is to Be Queen." *New York Times*, 3 December 2016. https://www.nytimes.com/2016/12/03/fashion/how-teens-use-the-wordmom online.html. Accessed 30 May 2017.

"Best New Girl." *Transparent*, created by Jill Soloway, Amazon Studios Studios, 26 September 2014.

Bettcher, T.M. "Evil Deceivers and Make-Believers: On Transphobic Violence and the Politics of Illusion." *Hypatia*, vol. 22, no. 3, 2007, pp. 43–65. JSTOR, www.jstor.org/stable/4640081.

Bewley, Allison L. "Literary Traditions on Fire: Mimetic Desire and the Role of the Orphaned Heroine in Suzanne Collins's Hunger Games Trilogy." *Children's Literature Association Quarterly*, vol. 40, no. 4, Winter 2015, pp. 371–385.

"Birth." *American Horror Story: Murder House*, created by Brad Falchuk and Ryan Murphy, FX, 14 December 2011.

"Birth Day." *The Handmaid's Tale*, created by Bruce Miller, Hulu, 26 April 2017.

"Black Single Mothers Are 'Biggest Impediment' to Progress Journalist George Will Says (Video)." *The Huffington Post*, 26 August 2013, https://www.huffingtonpost.com/2013/08/26/black-single-mothers-biggest-impediment_n_3818824.html. Accessed 21 August 2014.

Bloom, Ester. "Maids in America: The Decline of Domestic Help." *The Atlantic*, 23 September 2015, https://www.theatlantic.com/business/archive/2015/09/decline-domestic-help-maid/406798/. Accessed 4 November 2018.

Bonner, Mehera. "Farrah Abraham Had Complete Creative Control Over Her Sex Film!" *Wetpaint*, 13 May 2013, http://www.wetpaint.com/farrah-abraham-had-complete-creative-790861/. Accessed 23 September 2013.

Bouchard, Danielle, and Jigna Desai. "'There's Nothing More Debilitating Than Travel': Locating US Empire in Todd Haynes' Safe." *Quarterly Review of Film*, vol. 22, no. 4, 2005, pp. 359–370.

Brady, Anita, Kellie Burns, and Cristyn

Davis. *Mediating Sexual Citizenship: Neoliberal Subjectivities in Television Culture*. Routledge, 2018.

Briefel, Aviva. "Parenting Through Horror: Reassurance in Jennifer Kent's *The Babadook*." *Camera Obscura, 95*, vol. 32, no. 2, 2017, pp. 1–27.

Broad, Katherine R. "'The Dandelion in Spring': Utopia as Romance in Suzanne Collins's *The Hunger Games* Trilogy." *Contemporary Dystopian Fiction for Young Adults: Brave New Teenagers*, edited by Balaka Basu, Katherine R. Broad, and Carrie Hintz, Taylor and Francis, 2013, pp. 117–130.

Brockington, Ariana. "Top Female Showrunners Talk TV Industry Battles, Opening Doors for Others." *Variety*, March 2018, https://variety.com/2018/scene/news/female-showrunners-barbara-hall-jennie-snyder-urman-1202735962/. Accessed 1 June 2018.

Brody, Richard. "*Tully* Reviewed: Diablo Cody's Blinkered View of Motherhood and Mental Illness." 6 May 2018, *The New Yorker* https://www.newyorker.com/culture/richard-brody/tully-reviewed-diablo-cody-blinkered-view-of-motherhood-and-mental-illness. Accessed 4 September 2018.

Brunsdon, Charlotte. "Feminism, Postfeminism, Martha, and Nigella." *Cinema Journal*, vol. 44, no. 2, 2005, pp. 110–115.

———. *Screen Tastes: Soap Opera to Satellite Dishes*. Routledge, 1997.

Buell, Lawrence. *Writing for an Endangered World: Literature, Culture, and Environment in the U.S. and Beyond*. Harvard University Press, 2003.

Buerger, Shelley. "The Beak That Grips: Maternal Indifference, Ambivalence and the Abject in *The Babadook*." *Studies in Australasian Cinema*, vol. 11, no. 1, 2017, pp. 33–44.

Bullard, Robert D. *Dumping in Dixie: Race, Class, and Environmental Quality*. 3rd Ed., Westview Press, 2000.

———, editor. *The Quest for Environmental Justice: Human Rights and the Politics of Pollution*. Sierra Club Books, 2005.

Bumiller, Kristin. *In an Abusive State: How Neoliberalism Appropriated the Feminist Movement Against Sexual Violence*. Duke University Press, 2008.

The Burning Bed. Directed by Robert Greenwalk, performance by Farah Fawcett, Tisch/Avnet Productions, Inc., 1984.

"Burning Love." *Big Little Lies*, created by David E. Kelley, HBO, 26 March 2017.

Burns, Katelyn. "How a New Trump Policy Enables Anti-Trans Discrimination." *Vice*. 6 October 2017, https://www.vice.com/en_us/article/kz79z9/how-a-new-trump-policy-enables-anti-trans-discrimination. Accessed 21 May 2018.

Butler, Jess. "For White Girls Only?: Postfeminism and the Politics of Inclusion." *Feminist Formations*, vol. 25, no. 1, 2013, pp. 35–58.

Butsch, Richard. "*Ralph, Fred, Archie, Homer, and the King of Queens: Why Television Keeps Re-Creating the Male Working-Class Buffoon*." *Gender, Race, and Class in the Media: A Critical Reader*, edited by Gail Dines and Jean M. Humez, Sage, 2011, pp. 87–98.

Caldwell, Maggie. "Invisible Women: The Real History of Domestic Workers in America." *Mother Jones*, 7 February 2013, https://www.motherjones.com/politics/2013/02/timeline-domestic-workers-invisible-history-america/. Accessed 4 November 2018.

"The Canary Report Website." *Daily Strength*, 2018, https://www.dailystrength.org/group/multiple-chemical-sensitivities/discussion/the-canary-report-website. Accessed 1 June 2018.

Caplan, Paula. "Don't Blame Mothers: Then and Now." *Gender and Women's Studies in Canada: Critical Terrain*, edited by Margaret Hobbs and Carla Rice, Women's Press, 2013, pp. 99–106.

Capuzza, Jamie C., and Leland G. Spencer. "Regressing, Progressing, or Transgressing on the Small Screen? Transgender Characters on U.S. Scripted Television Series." *Communications Quarterly*, vol. 65, no. 2, 2017, 214–230.

Caron, Christina. "Diablo Cody, Responding to Criticism, Says 'Tully' Is Meant to Be Uncomfortable." New York Times, 2 May 2018, https://www.nytimes.com/2018/05/02/movies/tully-postpartum-depression-charlize-theron.html. Accessed 3 September 2018.

Carson, Rachel. *Silent Spring*. Houghton Mifflin, 1962, 2002.

Carter, Darla. 2013. "Harmful Germs in Your Kitchen Can Make You Sick." *USA Today*, 26 September 2013, https://www.usatoday.com/story/news/nation/2013/09/26/health-kitchen-germs/2880125/. Accessed 1 December 2016.

"Chapter Ten." *Jane the Virgin*, developed by Jennie Snyder Urman, The CW, 19 January 2015.

"Chapter Thirty-seven." *Jane the Virgin*, developed by Jennie Snyder Urman, The CW, 21 March 2016.

"Chapter Thirty-nine." *Jane the Virgin*, developed by Jennie Snyder Urman, The CW, 11 April 2016.

"Chapter Forty." *Jane the Virgin*, developed by Jennie Snyder Urman, The CW, 18 April 2016.

"Chapter Forty-four." *Jane the Virgin*, developed by Jennie Snyder Urman, The CW, 16 May 2016.

"Chapter Forty-six." *Jane the Virgin*, developed by Jennie Snyder Urman, The CW, 24 October 2016.

"Chapter Fifty-two." *Jane the Virgin*, developed by Jennie Snyder Urman, The CW, 23 January 2017.

"Chapter Sixty-one." *Jane the Virgin*, developed by Jennie Snyder Urman, The CW, 1 May 2017.

"Chapter Sixty-six." *Jane the Virgin*, developed by Jennie Snyder Urman, The CW, 20 October 2017.

"Chapter Seventy-five." *Jane the Virgin*, developed by Jennie Snyder Urman, The CW, 2 March 2018.

Chase & Sanborn Coffee. "If Your Husband Ever Finds Out." *Life*, 11 August 1952.

"Chelsea." *16 and Pregnant*, created by Lauren Dolgen, MTV, 9 March 2010.

Chidgey, Red. "Feminist Protest Assemblages and Remix Culture." *The Routledge Companion to Media and Activism*, edited by Graham Meikle. Routledge, 2018, pp. 196–204.

"Child Care Is Fundamental to America's Children, Family, and Economy." National Women's Law Center, December 2016, https://nwlc-ciw49tixgw5lbab.stackpathdns.com/wp-content/uploads/2017/01/Child-Care-101-1.17.17.pdf. Accessed 1 December 2017.

Clorox. "For a Healthier Home." www.clorox.com, 2014.

Collins, Suzanne. *Catching Fire*. Scholastic Press, 2009.

———. *The Hunger Games*. Scholastic Press, 2008.

———. *Mockingjay*. Scholastic Press, Scholastic Press, 2010.

Condit, Deirdre M. "Reproducing Possibilities: Androgenesis and Mothering Human Identity." *Twenty-First Century Motherhood: Experience, Identity, Policy, Agency*, edited by Andrea O'Reilly, Columbia University Press, 2010, pp. 181–196.

Consumed. Directed by Daryl Wein, performance by Zoe Lister-Jones, MarVista Entertainment, 2015.

Coontz, Stephanie. *A Strange Stirring: The Feminine Mystique and American Women at the Dawn of the 1960s*. Basic Books, 2012.

———. *The Way We Never Were: American Families and the Nostalgia Trap*. Basic Books, Revised 2016.

Cooper, Brittney. *Eloquent Rage: A Black Feminist Discovers Her Superpower*. St. Martin's Press, 2018.

———. "How I Confronted Tyler Perry: A Surprisingly Frank Phone Call Yields Real Results." *Salon*, 18 March 2014. https://www.salon.com/2014/03/18/my_surprisingly_frank_phone_call_with_tyler_perry. Accessed 21 April 2016.

———. "Tyler Perry Hates Black Women: Thoughts on the Haves and Have Nots." *Crunk Feminist Collective*, 29 May 2013. http://www.crunkfeministcollective.com/2013/05/29/tyler-perry-hates-black-women-5-thoughts-on-the-haves-and-have-nots/. Accessed 21 April 2016.

Cooper, Rand Richards. "Ambivalence and Oblivion: *Tully* and *Lean on Pete*." *Commonweal*, 18 May 2018, https://www.commonwealmagazine.org/ambivalence-oblivion. Accessed 31 October 2018.

Correll, Shelley J., Stephen Benard, and In Paik. "Getting a Job: Is There a Motherhood Penalty?" *American Journal of Sociology*, vol. 112, no. 5, 2007, pp. 1297–1338. JSTOR, www.jstor.org/stable/10.1086/511799.

Covert, Bryce. "Why It Matters That Women Do Most of the Housework." *The Nation*, 30 April 2014, https://www.thenation.com/article/why-it-matters-women-do-most-housework/. Accessed 1 June 2018.

Cox, Jamieson. "*Transparent* Is Radically Selfish, and That's Why It Matters." *Verge*, 9 December 2015, https://www.theverge.com/2015/12/9/9878202/transparent-season-2-review-Amazon Studios-jeffrey-tambor. Accessed 5 May 2018.

Crenshaw, Kimberlé W. "From Private Violence to Mass Incarceration Thinking Intersectionally About Women, Race, and Social Control." *UCLA Law Review*, vol. 59, 2012, pp. 1418–1472.

Crispin, Jessa. *Why I Am Not a Feminist: A Feminist Manifesto*. Melville House, 2017.

Crothers, Lane. *Globalization and American Popular Culture*. 4th Edition, Rowan and Littlefield, 2017.

Cullen, Mark R. "The Worker with Multiple Chemical Sensitivities: An Overview." Occupational Medicine, vol. 2, no. 4, 1987, pp. 655–661.

Cullers, Rebecca. "Swiffer Feels the Heat After Putting Rosie the Riveter Back in the Kitchen." *Adweek*, 5 June 2013, https://www.adweek.com/creativity/swiffer-feels-heat-after-putting-rosie-riveter-back-kitchen-150027/. Accessed 25 November 2018.

"Curveball." *Teen Mom 2*, created by Lauren Dolgen, MTV, 13 December 2011.

Davis, Devra. *The Secret History of the War on Cancer*. Basic Books, 1990.

DeaVault, Rodney M. "The Masks of Femininity: Perceptions of the Feminine in *The Hunger Games* and *Podkayne of Mars*." *Of Bread, Blood and the Hunger Games: Critical Essays on the Suzanne Collins Trilogy*, edited by Mary F. Pharr and Leisa A. Clark, McFarland, 2012, pp. 190–198.

De Beauvoir, Simone. *The Second Sex*. 1949. Vintage, 2011.

Dejean, Ashley. "Transgender Rights Are Under Attack in These 11 States." *Mother Jones*, 27 January 2017, http://www.motherjones.com/politics/2017/01/transgender-rights-bathrooms-state-legislature-texas-arizona-wyoming-kansas/. Accessed 1 March 2017.

Dervasula, Shreya. "*Jane the Virgin*: Beyond the Bechdel Test." *Depths of TV*, 4 April 2016, http://depthsoftv.com/blog/2016/3/28/jane-the-virgin-feminist-or-no, Accessed 1 June 2018.

Devries, Karen, Mak, J.Y., Garcia-Moreno, C., et al. "The Global Prevalence of Intimate Partner Violence Against Women." *Science*, vol. 340, no. 6140, 2013, pp. 1527–1528.

DiChiro, Giovanna. "Nature as Community: The Convergence of Environment and Social Justice." *Uncommon Ground: Toward Reinventing Nature*, edited by William Cronon, W.W. Norton and Company, 1995, pp. 298–320.

"Do You Prefer to See Movies in a Theater or Wait for Them to Come Out on Home Release?" *Statista*, 2018, https://www.statista.com/statistics/264399/preferred-place-of-movie-consumption-in-the-us/. Accessed 2 June 2018.

Dolgen, Lauren. "Why I Created MTV's *16 and Pregnant*." *CNN*, 5 May 2011, http://www.cnn.com/2011/SHOWBIZ/TV/05/04/teen.mom.dolgen/index.html. Accessed September 23, 2013.

Douglas, Susan. *Enlightened Sexism: The Seductive Message That Feminism's Work Is Done*. Times Books, 2010.

_____, and Meredith W. Michaels. *The Mommy Myth: The Idealization of Motherhood and How It Has Undermined All Women*. Free Press, 2005.

Dubrofsky, Rachel E., and Emily D. Ryalls. "*The Hunger Games*: Performing Not-Performing to Authenticate Femininity and Whiteness." *Critical Studies in Media Communication*, 2014, vol. 31, no. 5, pp. 395–409.

Dunn, Stephane. "Cool Drag: Black Masculinity in Big Mama Disguise." *Interpreting Tyler Perry: Perspectives on Race, Class, Gender and Sexuality*, edited by Jamel Santa Cruze Bell and Ronald L. Jackson II, Routledge, 2014, pp. 57–68.

Easteal, Patricia, Kate Holland, and Keziah Judd. "Enduring Themes and Silences in Media Portrayals of Violence Against Women." *Women's Studies International Forum*, vol. 48, 2015, pp. 103–113.

Easteal, Patricia, and A. Carline. *Shades of Grey: Domestic and Sexual Violence Against Women*. Routledge, 2014.

Edwards, Leigh H. "Reality TV and the American Family." *The Tube Has Spoken: Reality T.V. and History*, edited by Julie Taddeo, University of Kentucky Press, 2010, pp. 123–144.

Eisenbach, Helen. "*Grandma*'s Paul Weitz Talks Secrets, Surprises and Channeling Lily Tomlin." *The Huffington Post*, 4 September 2015, https://www.huffingtonpost.com/helen-eisenbach/the-secret-grandmas-paul-_b_8029228.html. Accessed June 17 2017.

Eligon, John. "A Question of Environmental Racism in Flint." *New York Times*, 21 January 2016, https://www.nytimes.com/2016/01/22/us/a-question-of-environmental-racism-in-flint.html. Accessed 28 May 2018.

"Elizah." *Transparent*, created by Jill Soloway, Amazon Studios, 23 September 2016.

Elman, Julie Passanante. "'Nothing Feels as Real': Teen Sick-Lit, Sadness, and the Condition of Adolescence." *The Journal of Literary and Cultural Disability Studies*, no. 6, vol. 2, 2012, pp. 175–191.

Emanuel, Ezekiel J. 2006. "Will Your Cell Phone Kill You?" *The New Republic*, vol. 9, April 2006, pp. 28–34.

"Emily in Wonderland." *Gilmore Girls*, created by Amy Sherman-Palladino, The WB, 26 April 2001.

Enough. Directed by Michael Apted, performance by Jennifer Lopez, Columbia Pictures, 2002.

Ergas, Yasmine. "Babies Without Borders: Human Rights, Human Dignity, and the Regulation of International Commercial Surrogacy." *Emory International Law Review*, 18 November 2012

Eschner, Kat. "The Story of the Real Canary in the Coal Mine." *Smithsonian Magazine*, 30 December 2016, https://www.smithsonianmag.com/smart-news/story-real-canary-coal-mine-180961570/.

"Exciting and New." *Transparent*, created by Jill Soloway, Amazon Studios, 25 September 2016.

"Faithful." *The Handmaid's Tale*, created by Bruce Miller. Hulu. 10 May 2017.

Fallas, Jennifer A. "Othering the Mothering: Postfeminist Constructs in *Teen Mom*." *MTV and Teen Pregnancy: Critical Essays on* 16 and Pregnant *and* Teen Mom, edited by Letizia Guglielmo, Scarecrow Press, 2013, pp. 49–64.

Faulkner, Ellen, and Gayle MacDonald. *Victim No More: Women's Resistance to Law, Culture and Power*. Fernwood, 2009.

"Fear, and Other Smells." *Orange Is the New Black*, created by Jenji Kohan, Netflix, 11 June 2015.

Feasey, Rebecca. "Absent, Ineffectual, and Intoxicated Mothers: Representing the Maternal in Teen Television." *Feminist Media Studies*, no. 12, pp. 155–159, 2012.

_____. *From Happy Homemaker to Desperate Housewives: Motherhood and Popular Television*. Anthem Press, 2012.

_____. "From Soap Opera to Reality Programming: Examining Motherhood, Motherwork, and the Maternal Role on Popular Television." *Imaginations*, vol. 4, no. 2, 2013, pp. 25–45.

Feldman, Dana. "Hulu: How America Watched Television in 2017." *Forbes*, 18 December 2017, https://www.forbes.com/sites/danafeldman/2017/12/18/hulu-how-america-watched-television-in-2017/#5a64dce91588. Accessed 2 June 2018.

Finley, Laura L. *Domestic Abuse and Sexual Assault in Popular Culture*. Praeger, 2016.

Firestone, Shulamith. *The Dialectic of Sex*. William Morrow and Company, 1970.

"First Blood." *The Handmaid's Tale*, created Bruce Miller, Hulu, 23 May 2018.

Flaherty, Colleen. "TERF War." *Inside Higher Ed*, 29 August 2018, https://www.insidehighered.com/news/2018/08/29/philosophers-object-journals-publication-terf-reference-some-feminists-it-really. Accessed 2 September 2018.

"For Better or for Worse." *Teen Mom 2*, created by Lauren Dolgen, MTV, 1 April 2013.

Ford, Zack. "Housing Discrimination Against Transgender People Is Even Worse Than We Thought." *ThinkProgress*, 3 April 2017, https://thinkprogress.org/trans-housing-discrimination-study-889129c40c1b/. Accessed 12 April 2018.

Fricker, Miranda. *Epistemic Injustice: Power and the Ethics of Knowing*. Oxford University Press, 2007.

Friedman, May. "'100% Preventable': Teen Motherhood, Morality, and the Myth of Choice." *MTV and Teen Pregnancy: Critical Essays on* 16 and Pregnant *and* Teen Mom, edited by Letizia Guglielmo, Rowan and Littlefield, 2013, pp. 67–78.

Fuller, Bonnie. 2014. "'Teen Mom' Jenelle Evans: Defying MTV by Getting Breast Implants." *Hollywood Life*, 26 April 2012, http://hollywoodlife.com/2012/04/26/teen-mom-jenelle-evans-breast-implants/. Accessed 1 May 2014.

Gandal, Keith. *Class Representation in Modern Fiction and Film*. Palgrave Macmillan, 2007.

Garcia, Sandra E. "The Woman Who Created #MeToo Long Before Hashtags." *New York Times*, 20 October 2017, https://www.nytimes.com/2017/10/20/us/me-too-movement-tarana-burke.html. Accessed 1 June 2018.

Garcia-Moreno, C. et al. "WHO Multi-Country Study on Women's Health and Domestic Violence Against Women." *World Health Organization*, 2005, www.who.int. Accessed 1 June 2017.

Garland-Thompson, Rosemarie. Introduction. *Freakery: Cultural Spectacles of the Extraordinary Body*, New York University Press, 1996, pp. 1–22.

Garlinghouse, Rachel. "A New Wave of Mom-Shaming: Posting Photos Online." *The Huffington Post*, 13 July 2015. https://www.huffingtonpost.com/rachel-garlinghouse/a-new-wave-of-mom-shaming-posting-photos-online_b_7765548.html. Accessed 8 September 2017.

Gay, Roxane. *Bad Feminist: Essays*. Harper Perennial, 2014.

Genius, Stephen J. "Sensitivity-Related Illness: The Escalating Pandemic of Allergy, Food Intolerance and Chemical Sensitivity." *Science of the Total Environment*, vol. 408, 2010, pp. 6047–6061.

Gibbs, Lois. *Love Canal: The Story Continues*. New Society Publishers, 1998.

Gill, Rosalind. "Culture and Subjectivity in Neoliberal and Postfeminist Times." *Subjectivity*, vol. 25, 2008, pp. 432–445.

_____. *Gender and the Media*. Polity, 2017.

_____. "Post-Post Feminism: New Feminist Visibilities in Postfeminist Times." *Feminist Media Studies*, vol. 16, no. 4, 2016, pp. 610–630.

_____. "Postfeminist Media Culture: Elements of a Sensibility." *European Journal of Cultural Studies*, vol. 10, no. 2, 1 May 2007, pp. 147–166.

Gilmore Girls. Created by Amy Sherman-Palladino, performances by Lauren Graham and Alexis Bledel. The CW. 2000–2007.

Glogiewicz, Taylor. "Psuedo-Families: Group Formations in Women's Prisons." *Incarcerated Interactions: A Theory-Driven Analysis of Applied Prison Communication*, edited by Erik D. Fritzvold and Jonathan M. Bowman, Peter Lang Publishing, 2016, pp. 51–58.

Glynn, Sarah Jane. "Fact Sheet: Child Care." *Center for American Progress*, 16 August 2012, https://www.americanprogress.org/issues/economy/news/2012/08/16/11978/fact-sheet-child-care/. Accessed 8 September 2017.

Goldberg, Leslie. "Jeffrey Tambor Officially Dropped from *Transparent* in Wake of Harassment Claims." *The Hollywood Reporter*, 17 February 2018, https://www.hollywoodreporter.com/live-feed/jeffrey-tambor-officially-fired-transparent-wake-harassment-claims-1085236. Accessed 2 April 2018.

Goldberg, Michelle. "What Is a Woman?" *The New Yorker*, 4 August 2014, https://www.newyorker.com/magazine/2014/08/04/woman-2. Accessed 1 May 2018.

Good Will Hunting. Directed by Gus Van Sant, performances by Matt Damon and Minnie Driver, Miramax Films, 1997.

Gotlib, Anna. "But You Would Be the Best Mother: Unwomen, Counterstories, and the Motherhood Mandate." *Bioethical Inquiry*, vol. 13, 2016, pp. 327–347.

Grandma. Directed by Paul Weitz, performance by Lily Tomlin, Sony Pictures Classic, 2015.

Gregson, Joanna. *The Culture of Teenage Mothers*. SUNY Press, 2009.

"Groin Anomaly." *Transparent*, created by Jill Soloway, Amazon Studios, 21 September 2017.

Hamilton, Cynthia. "Women, Home, and Community: The Struggle in an Urban Environment." *Reweaving the World: The Emergence of Ecofeminism*, edited by Irene Diamond and Gloria Feman Orenstein, Sierra Club Books, 1990, pp. 215–222.

Harding, Sandra. *Whose Science? Whose Knowledge?* Cornell University Press, 1991.

Harrison, Laura. *Brown Babies, White Babies: The Politics of Cross-Racial Surrogacy*. NYU Press, 2016.

Harvey, David. *A Brief History of Neoliberalism*. Oxford University Press, 2007.

Haynes, Todd. "Commentary." *Safe*, directed by Todd Haynes, Good Machine, 1995.

Hazlett, Maril. "'Woman Vs. Man Vs. Bug': Gender and Popular Ecology in Early Reactions to *Silent Spring*." *Environmental History*, vol. 9, no. 4, 2004, pp. 701–722.

Heffernan, Virginia. 2013. "Job Title: The Gilmore 'Noodge.'" *New York Times*, sec.

Arts, 23 January 2005, https://www.nytimes.com/2005/01/23/arts/television/job-title-the-gilmore-noodge.html. Accessed 20 August 2013.

Heitler, Susan. "When Your Mother Has a Borderline Personality." *Psychology Today*, 31 October 2012, https://www.psychologytoday.com/us/blog/resolution-not-conflict/201210/when-your-mother-has-borderline-personality. Accessed 1 December 2017.

Heller, Dana. "Wrecked: Programming Celesbian Reality." *Reality Gendervision: Sexuality and Gender on Transatlantic Reality Television*, Duke University Press, 2014, pp. 123–148.

Heller-Nicholas, Alexandra. *Rape-Revenge Films*. McFarland, 2011.

Hempel, Jessi. "My Brother's Pregnancy and the Making of a New American Family." *Time*, 12 September 2016, http://time.com/4475634/trans-man-pregnancy-evan/. Accessed 2 December 2017.

Henry, Astrid. *Not My Mother's Sister: Generational Conflict and Third-Wave Feminism*. Indiana University Press, 2004.

Hinckley, David. "The June Cleaver Type of Mother Is Slowly Fading from Television." *New York Daily News*. 11 May 2014, http://www.nydailynews.com/entertainment/tv/moms-tv-bad-article-1.1781820. Accessed 14 May 2014.

Hines, Sally. "The Feminist Frontier: On Trans and Feminism." *Journal of Gender Studies*, 18 December 2017.

Hobson, Janell. "Celebrity Feminism." *Signs*, Summer 2017, http://signsjournal.org/currents-celebrity-feminism/hobson/. Accessed 1 June 2018.

Holderness, Colbie. "Rob Porter Is My Ex-Husband. Here's What You Should Know About Abuse." *The Washington Post*, 12 February 2018, https://www.washingtonpost.com/opinions/rob-porter-is-my-ex-husband-heres-what-you-should-know-about-abuse/2018/02/12/3c7edcb8-1033-11e8-9065-e55346f6de81_story.html?noredirect=on&utm_term=.658ef35f772f. Accessed 1 March 2018.

Hollows, Joanne. *Feminism, Femininity and Popular Culture*. Manchester University Press, 2000.

_____, and Rachel Moseley. "Popularity Contests: The Meanings of Popular Feminism." *Feminism and Popular Culture*, edited by Joanne Hollows and Rachel Moseley, Oxford, 2006: 1–22.

hooks, bell. "Moving Beyond Pain." *Bell Hooks Institute*, 9 May 2016. http://www.bellhooksinstitute.com/blog/2016/5/9/moving-beyond-pain. Accessed 1 June 2017.

Horne, Rebecca M., et al. "Time, Money, or Gender? Predictors of the Division of Household Labour Across Life Stage." *Sex Roles*, September 2017, pp. 1–13.

Hosey, Sara. "'One of Us': Identity and Community in Contemporary Fiction." *Journal of Literary and Cultural Disability Studies*, vol. 3, no. 1, 2009, pp. 35–50.

The Hunger Games. Directed by Gary Ross, performance by Jennifer Lawrence, Lionsgate, 2012.

The Hunger Games: Catching Fire. Directed by Francis Lawrence, performance by Jennifer Lawrence, Lionsgate, 2013.

The Hunger Games: Mockingjay—Part I. Directed by Francis Lawrence, performance by Jennifer Lawrence, Lionsgate, 2014.

The Hunger Games: Mockingjay—Part II. Directed by Francis Lawrence, performance by Jennifer Lawrence, Lionsgate, 2015.

Hunting, Kyra. "All in the (Prison) Family: Genre Mixing and Queer Representation." *Feminist Perspectives on* Orange Is the New Black, edited by April Kalogeropoulos Householder and Adrienne Trier-Bieniek, McFarland, 2016, pp. 111–127.

"I Swear I'll Leave Teen Mom 2!!! MTV Screwed Me in Editing." *TMZ*, 19 October 2017, http://www.tmz.com/2017/10/19/teen-mom-2-jenelle-evans-threatens-to-leave-mtv-season-8-edits/. Accessed 1 June 2018.

"*Orange* Creator Jenji Kohan: Piper Was My Trojan Horse.'" *National Public Radio*, 13 August 2013, https://www.npr.org/templates/transcript/transcript.php?storyId=211639989. Accessed 1 April 2018.

"Incite! Critical Resistance Statement." *Incite*, 2001. mail.incite-national.org/page/incite-critical-resistance-statement. Accessed 21 July 2017.

The Incredible Shrinking Woman. Directed by Joel Schumacher, performance by Lily Tomlin, Universal Studios, 1981.

Ira, Stephen. "LGBTQI Week: *Transamer-*

ica." *Bitch Flicks*, 27 June 2012, http://www.btchflcks.com/2012/06/lgbtqi-week-transamerica.html#.Wgm1K7aZPq0. Accessed 4 November 2017.

Jackson, Ronal L. II, and Jamel Santa Cruze Bell, Eds. *Interpreting Tyler Perry: Perspectives on Race, Class, Gender and Sexuality*. Routledge, 2014.

Jacobo, Julia. "Flint Mother Gives Emotional Testimony of How Water Crisis Affected Her Children's Health." *ABC News*, 29 March 2016, https://abcnews.go.com/US/flint-mother-emotional-testimony-water-crisis-affected-childrens/story?id=38008707. Accessed 15 December 2016.

Janicker, Rebecca. *Reading American Horror Story: Essays on the Television Franchise*. McFarland, 2017.

Jarman, Michelle. "Cultural Consumption and Rejection of Precious Jones: Pushing Disability Into the Discussion of Sapphire's *Push* and Lee Daniels' *Precious*." *Feminist Formations*, vol. 24, no. 2, Summer 2012, pp .163–185.

Jefferson, J'na. "A Long Road Ahead: MeToo Founder Tarana Burke on Sexual Assault, Stigmas, and Society." *Vibe*, 3 April 2018, https://www.vibe.com/featured/tarana-burke-me-too-feature/. Accessed 1 June 2018.

"Jenelle." *16 and Pregnant*, created by Lauren Dolgen, MTV, 16 February 2010.

Johnston, Derek. "Seasons, Family and Nation in *American Horror Story*." *Reading American Horror Story: Essays on the Television Franchise*, edited by Rebecca Janicker, McFarland, 2017.

Jung, E. Alex. "Jill Soloway Wonders What the Word 'Woman' Is for and Revisits an Old Debate (With Jenji Kohan)." *Vulture*, 26 September 2017, http://www.vulture.com/2017/09/jill-soloway-transparent-israel-female-gaze.html. Accessed 15 January 2018.

Juno. Directed by Jason Reitman, written by Diablo Cody, performance by Ellen Page, Fox Searchlight Pictures, 2007.

Kaplan, Amy. "Homeland Insecurities: Reflections on Language and Space." *Radical History Review*, no. 85, Winter 2003, pp. 82–93.

Karlyn, Kathleen Rowe. *Unruly Girls, Unrepentant Mothers: Redefining Feminism on Screen*. University of Texas Press, 2011.

Kawash, Samira. "New Directions in Motherhood Studies." *Signs*, vol. 36, no. 4, Summer 2011, pp. 969–1003.

Keegan, Cael. "How *Transparent* Tried and Failed to Represent Trans Men." *The Advocate*, 2014, http://www.advocate.com/commentary/2014/10/22/op-ed-how-transparent-tried-and-failed-represent-trans-men. Accessed 5 May 2018.

"Keeping Hope Alive." *Teen Mom 2*, created by Lauren Dolgen, MTV, 20 November 2012.

Keetley, Dawn. "Stillborn: The Entropic Gothic of *American Horror Story*." *Gothic Studies*, vol. 15, no. 2, November 2013, pp. 89–107.

Kelly, Casey Ryan. *Abstinence Cinema: Virginity and the Rhetoric of Sexual Purity in Contemporary Film*. Rutgers, 2016.

Khazan, Olga. "Emasculated Men Refuse to Do Chores—Except Cooking." *The Atlantic*, 24 October 2016, https://www.theatlantic.com/health/archive/2016/10/the-only-chore-men-will-do-is-cook/505067/. Accessed 21 September 2018.

Kidd, Briony. "Umbilical Fears: Jennifer Kent's *The Babadook*." *Metro Magazine: Media and Education Magazine*, vol. 180, Autumn 2014, pp. 6–12.

Kimmel, Michael. "'Gender Symmetry' in Domestic Violence: A Substantive and Methodological Research Review." *Violence Against Women*, vol. 8, no. 11, 2002, pp. 1332–1363.

King, Geoff. *American Independent Cinema*. Indiana University Press, 2005.

King, Stephen. *Danse Macabre*. Gallery Books,1981, Reprint 2013.

Knabe, Susan. "Suffer the Children: National Crisis, Affective Collectivity, and the Sexualized Child." *Canadian Review of American Studies*, no. 1, 2012, pp. 82–104.

Knopper, Melissa. "Everything Gives You Cancer." *E: The Environmental Magazine*, vol. 16, no. 5, 2008, pp. 40.

Knowles, Beyoncé. "We Can Do It." *Instagram*, 22 July 2014. Accessed 1 June 2018.

Kozol, Wendy. "Fracturing Domesticity: Media, Nationalism, and the Question of Feminist Influence." *Signs*, vol. 20, no. 3, 1995, pp. 646–667. JSTOR, www.jstor.org/stable/3174837.

Kramer Vs. Kramer. Directed by Robert

Benton, performance by Dustin Hoffman, Columbia Pictures, 1979.

Lakoff, George, and Mark Johnson. *Metaphors We Live By*. University of Chicago Press, 1980.

Lang, Brett. "Box Office: Madea Halloween' Edges Out 'Jack Reacher 2' with $27.6 Million." *Variety*, 23 October 2016, http://variety.com/2016/film/news/box-office-madea-halloween-edges-out-jack-reacher-2-with-27-6-million-1201898150/. Accessed 21 October 2017.

"The Last Ceremony." *The Handmaid's Tale*, created by Bruce Miller, Hulu, 20 June 2018.

Latimer, Heather. "Popular Culture and Reproductive Politics: *Juno*, *Knocked Up* and the Enduring Legacy of *The Handmaid's Tale*." *Feminist Theory*, vol. 10, no. 2, 2009, pp. 211–226.

Lauzen, Martha M. "Boxed in 2016–2017: Women on Screen and Behind the Scenes on Television." *Center for the Study of Women in Television & Film*, San Diego State University, September 2017, https://womenintvfilm.sdsu.edu/wp-content/uploads/2017/09/2016-17_Boxed_In_Report.pdf.

Law, Victoria. "How Many Women Are in Prison for Defending Themselves Against Domestic Violence?" *Bitch Media*, 18 September 2014, https://www.bitchmedia.org/post/women-in-prison-for-fighting-back-against-domestic-abuse-ray-rice. Accessed 12 April 2017.

Lee, Felicia R. "To Blacks, *Precious* Is 'Demeaned' or 'Angelic.'" *New York Times*, 20 Nov. 2009, https://www.nytimes.com/2009/11/21/movies/21precious.html. Accessed 1 December 2017.

Leonard, Suzanne. "'I Hate My Job, I Hate Everybody Here': Adultery, Boredom, and the 'Working Girl' in Twenty-First-Century American Cinema." *Interrogating Postfeminism: Gender and the Politics of Popular Culture*, edited by Yvonne Tasker and Diane Negra, Duke University Press, 2007, pp. 100–131.

Levin-Epstein, Jodie & Angie Schwartz. "Improving TANF for Teens." *Clearinghouse Review Journal of Poverty Law and Policy*, 2005, pp. 183–94.

Levy, Ariel. *Female Chauvinist Pigs: Women and the Rise of Raunch Culture*. Free Press, 2006.

_____. "The Radical Mind Behind *Transparent*." *The New Yorker*, 14 December 2015, https://www.newyorker.com/magazine/2015/12/14/dolls-and-feelings. Accessed 15 April 2018.

Lindner, Emilee. "Lorde Explains Her 'MOM' Tweet About Kim Kardashian, Calls Her a 'Fine-Ass Wine.'" MTV.Com 14 November 2014. http://www.mtv.com/news/1998000/lorde-kim-kardashian/. Accessed 21 December 2017.

Littler, Jo. "The Rise of the 'Yummy Mummy': Popular Conservatism and the Neoliberal Maternal in Contemporary British Culture." *Communication, Culture, and Critique*, vol. 6, no. 2, June 2013, pp. 227–243.

"Living the Dream." *Big Little Lies*, created by David E. Kelley, HBO, 5 March 2017.

Lonow, Claudia, creator. *How to Live with Your Parents for the Rest of Your Life*. Twentieth Century–Fox Television, 2013.

"The Lorelais' First Day at Chilton." *Gilmore Girls*, created by Amy Sherman-Palladino, The WB, 12 October 2000.

Lotz, Amanda D. *Redesigning Women: Television After the Network Era*. University of Illinois Press, 2006.

Loudermilk, Kim. *Fictional Feminism: How American Bestsellers Affect the Movement for Women's Equality*. Routledge, 2004.

Lublin, Nancy. *Pandora's Box: Feminism Confronts Reproductive Technology*. Rowan and Littlefield Publishers, 1998.

Lyle, Timothy. "'Check with Yo' Man First; Check with Yo' Man': Tyler Perry Appropriates Drag as a Tool to Re-Circulate Patriarchal Ideology." *Callaloo*, vol. 34, no. 3, Summer 2011, pp. 943–958.

Madea's Family Reunion. Written and directed by Tyler Perry, performance by Tyler Perry, Lionsgate, 2006.

Maher, Jennifer. "Torture Born: Babies, Bloodshed and the Feminist Gaze in Hulu's *The Handmaid's Tale*." *Communication, Culture and Critique*, vol. 11, no. 1, 1 March 2018, pp. 209–211.

Maid in Manhattan. Directed by Wayne Wang, performance by Jennifer Lopez, Sony, 2002.

Malatino, Hilary. "The Transgender Tipping Point: The Social Death of Sophia Burset." *Feminist Perspectives on* Orange is the New Black, McFarland, 2016, pp. 95–110.

"Man on the Land." *Transparent*, season 2,

episode 9, 11 December 2015, *Amazon Studios*.

Manchester by the Sea. Directed by Kenneth Lonergan, performance by Casey Affleck, Roadside Attractions, 2016.

Manne, Kate. *Down Girl: The Logic of Misogyny*. Oxford University Press, 2017.

Margot at the Wedding. Directed by Noah Baumbach, performance by Nicole Kidman, Paramount Vintage, 2007.

Martin, Nina. "U.S. Has the Worst Rate of Maternal Deaths in the Developed World." *National Public Radio Investigates*, May 12, 2017, https://www.npr.org/2017/05/12/528098789/u-s-has-the-worst-rate-of-maternal-deaths-in-the-developed-world. Accessed September 8, 2017.

Martinez, Diana. "*Jane the Virgin* Proves Diversity Is More Than Skin Deep." *The Atlantic*, 19 October 2015, https://www.theatlantic.com/entertainment/archive/2015/10/janethe-virgintelenovelas/409696/. Accessed 1 June 2018.

"Mary and Martha." *The Handmaid's Tale*, season 3, episode 2, Hulu, 5 June 2019.

Mazziotta, Julie. "Transgender Man Navigates Chest-Feeding and Fatherhood After Giving Birth to Baby Boy." *People*, 2 September 2016, https://people.com/bodies/transgender-man-navigates-fatherhood-after-giving-birth-to-baby-boy/. Accessed 1 September 2018.

McDonald, Brian. "The Three Faces of Evil: A Philosophic Reading of the *Hunger Games*." *The Politics of Panem*, edited by Sean P. Connors, Sense Publishers, 2014, pp. 65–84.

McDonough, Kate. "Laverne Cox Flawlessly Shuts Down Katie Couric's Invasive Questions About Transgender People." *Salon*, 7 January 2014, https://www.salon.com/2014/01/07/laverne_cox_artfully_shuts_down_katie_courics_invasive_questions_about_transgender_people/. Accessed 7 April 2018.

McRobbie, Angela. *The Aftermath of Feminism: Gender, Culture, and Social Change*. Sage Publications, 2008.

Mead, Rebecca. "Downtown's Daughter: Lena Dunham Cheerfully Exposes Her Privileged Life." *The New Yorker*, 15 November 2010, https://www.newyorker.com/magazine/2010/11/15/downtowns-daughter. Accessed 28 June 2017.

Meloy, Michell L., and Susan L. Miller. *The Victimization of Women: Law, Policies, and Politics*. Oxford University Press, 2011.

Mey. "My Day on the Set of *Transparent*, Where Trans Voices Actually Get Heard." *Autostraddle*, 13 December 2015, https://www.autostraddle.com/transparent-wants-to-give-trans-people-power-over-their-own-stories-and-in-the-industry-320237. Accessed 1 March 2018.

Meyer, Stephenie. *Breaking Dawn*. Little, Brown Books for Young Readers, 2010.

———. *Eclipse*. Little, Brown Books for Young Readers, 2009.

———. *New Moon*. Little, Brown Books for Young Readers. 2008.

———. *Twilight*. Little, Brown Books for Young Readers. 2006.

Miller, Clare Cain. "The Motherhood Penalty Vs. the Fatherhood Bonus." *New York Times*, 6 September 2014, https://www.nytimes.com/2014/09/07/upshot/a-child-helps-your-career-if-youre-a-man.html. Accessed September 8, 2017.

Miller, Danny. "LAFF '15 Interview: Zoe Lister-Jones and Daryl Wein Tackle GMOs in Their New Thriller 'Consumed.'" *Cinephiled*, 15 June 2015, http://www.cinephiled.com/laff-15-interview-zoe-lister-jones-daryl-wein-tackle-gmos-new-thriller-consumed/. Accessed 26 October 2017.

Miller, Laura. "*The Hunger Games* Vs. *Twilight*." *Salon*, 5 September 2010, https://www.salon.com/2010/09/05/hunger_games_twilight/. Accessed 24 August 2017.

Miller, Melissa. "Maybe Edward Is the Most Dangerous Thing Out There: The Role of Patriarchy." *Theorizing Twilight: Critical Essays on What's at Stake in a Post-Vampire World*, edited by Maggie Park and Natalie Wilson, McFarland, 2011, pp. 165–177.

Miller, Rebecca. *Personal Velocity: Three Portraits*. Grove Press, 2002.

Mitchell, David. "Modernist Freaks and Postmodern Geeks." *The Disability Studies Reader*, edited by Lennard Davis, Routledge, 1997, pp. 348–365.

Mock, Janet. "Trans in the Media: Unlearning the 'Trapped' Narrative and Taking Ownership of Our Bodies." JanetMock.com, 9 July 2012, https://janetmock.com/2012/07/09/josie-romero-dateline-transgender-trapped-body/. Accessed 1 December 2017.

Moras, Amanda. "'This Should Be My Responsibility': Gender, Guilt, Privilege and Paid Domestic Work." *Gender Issues*, 34, 2017, pp. 44–66.

Moreno, Carolina. "*Jane the Virgin* Officially Adds Another Latina Director to Its Ranks." *The Huffington Post*, 10 January 2018, https://www.huffingtonpost.com/entry/jane-the-virgin-officially-adds-another-latina-director-to-its-ranks_us_5a566ef6e4b0a300f90563fe. Accessed 1 June 2018.

Moriarty, Liane. *Big Little Lies*. Berkley, 2015.

Morrisey, Tracie Egan. "*Teen Mom*'s Jenelle Evan's Is Pregnant Again. Let's Take a Look at Her Year of Bad Choices." *Jezebel*, 18 January 2013, https://jezebel.com/5976870/teen-moms-jenelle-evans-is-pregnant-again-lets-look-back-at-her-year-of-bad-choices. Accessed 23 September 2013.

"Mother's Day." *Orange Is the New Black*, created by Jenji Kohan, Netflix, 11 June 2015.

Mr. and Mrs. Smith. Directed by Doug Liman, performances by Angelina Jolie and Brad Pitt, Twentieth Century–Fox, 2005.

Mukjerjea, Ananya. "Team Bella: Fans Navigating Desire, Security, and Feminism." *Theorizing Twilight: Critical Essays on What's at Stake in a Post-Vampire World*, edited by Maggie Park and Natalie Wilson, McFarland, 2011, pp. 70–86.

"Murder House." *American Horror Story: Murder House*, created by Brad Falchuk and Ryan Murphy, FX, 19 Oct. 2011.

Murdock, Catharine Gilbert. "The Adventures of Mommy Buzzkill." *The Horn Book: Publications About Books for Children and Young Adults*, 13 March 2009, https://www.hbook.com/2009/03/opinion/the-adventures-of-mommy-buzzkill/. Accessed 21 September 2017.

Murphy, Caryn. "Teen Momism on MTV: Postfeminist Subjectivities in *16 and Pregnant*." *Networking Knowledge*, vol. 5, no. 1, February 2012, pp. 84–99.

Murphy, Mekado. "That Book! It's…It's… Aaaaaaahhhh…" *New York Times*, 20 November 2014, https://www.nytimes.com/2014/11/23/movies/inside-the-horror-pop-up-book-in-the-babadook.html. Accessed 10 December 2017.

Nadasen, Premila, and Tiffany Williams. "Valuing Domestic Work." *The Barnard Center for Research on Women, New Feminist Solutions Series*, 14 May 2010, http://bcrw.barnard.edu/wp-content/nfs/reports/NFS5-Valuing-Domestic-Work.pdf. Accessed 2 September 2018.

Naismith, Gaye. "Tales from the Crypt: Contamination and Quarantine in Todd Haynes' [*Safe*]." *The Visible Woman: Imaging Technologies, Gender, and Science*, edited by Paula A. Treichler, Lisa Cartwright, and Constance Penley, New York University Press, 1998, pp. 360–388.

Nathanson, Elizabeth. *Television and Postfeminist Housekeeping: No Time for Mother*. Routledge, 2013.

"National Statistics." *The National Coalition Against Domestic Violence*, https://ncadv.org/statistics. Accessed 3 March 2017.

"NCDVA Denounces President Trump's FY'19 Budget Request." *National Coalition Against Domestic Violence Blog*, 20 February 2018, https://ncadv.org/blog/posts/ncadvdenounces-president-trumps-fy19-budget-request. Accessed 9 June 2018.

Needham, Gary. "*Transamerica* (2005): The Road to the Multiplex After New Queer Cinema." *Feminism at the Movies: Understanding Gender in Contemporary Popular Cinema*, edited by Hilary Radner and Rebecca Stringer, Routledge, 2011, pp. 51–64.

Negra, Diane. *What a Girl Wants?: Fantasizing the Reclamation of Self in Postfeminism*. Routledge, 2008.

Neimark, Jill. "Extreme Chemical Sensitivity Makes Sufferers Allergic to Life." *Discover*, November 2013, http://discovermagazine.com/2013/nov/13-allergic-life. Accessed 21 September 2015.

"New World Coming." *Transparent*, created by Jill Soloway, Amazon Studios, 11 December 2015,.

Newman, Emily L., and Emily Witsell. *The Lifetime Network: Essays on "Television for Women" in the 21st Century*. McFarland, 2016.

"Night." *The Handmaid's Tale*, season 1, episode 10, 14 June 2017, *Hulu*.

"No Looking Back." *MTV*, 9 March 2010, http://www.mtv.com/episodes/uz7isg/16-and-pregnant-chelsea-season-2-ep-4. Accessed 1 June 2018.

Nodelman, Perry. "Making Boys Appear: The Masculinity of Children's Fiction." *Ways of Being Male: Representing Masculinities in Children's Literature and Film*, edited by John Stephens, Routledge, 2009, pp. 1–14.

North, Anna. "Breaking Dawn: What to Expect When You're Expecting…A Vampire." *Jezebel*, 7 August 2008, https://jezebel.com/5034213/breaking-dawn-what-to-expect-when-youre-expecting-a-vampire. Accessed. 8 August 2008.

Nussbaum, Emily. "*Jane the Virgin* Is Not a Guilty Pleasure." *The New Yorker*, 12 March 2018, https://www.newyorker.com/magazine/2018/03/12/jane-the-virgin-is-not-a-guilty-pleasure. Accessed 15 March 2018.

———. "The Surprising Generosity of *Big Little Lies*." *The New Yorker*, 6 March 2017. https://www.newyorker.com/magazine/2017/03/06/the-surprising-generosity-ofbig-little-lies. Accessed 10 March 2017.

Obvious Child. Written and directed by Gillian Robespierre, performance by Jenny Slate, A24, 2014.

O'Connor, Flannery. "A Good Man Is Hard to Find." *A Good Man Is Hard to Find*, Harcourt Brace Jovanovich, 1955, 1977, pp. 1–24.

O'Dair, Sharon. "Horror or Realism? Filming Toxic Discourse in Smiley's *A Thousand Acres*." *Textual Practice*, vol. 19, no. 2, 2005, pp. 263–82.

Okin, Susan Moller. *Justice, Gender, and the Family*. Basic Books, 1991.

Oliver, Kelly. *Knock Me Up, Knock Me Down: Images of Pregnancy in Hollywood Films*. Columbia University Press, 2012.

O'Meara, Jennifer. "A Shared Approach to Familial Dysfunction and Sound Design: Wes Anderson's Influence on the Films of Noah Baumbach." *The Films of Wes Anderson: Critical Essays on an Indiewood Icon*, edited by Peter Kunze, Palgrave Macmillan, 2014, pp. 109–124.

"Once Bitten." *Big Little Lies*, season 1, episode 5, HBO, 19 March 2017.

"Open House." *American Horror Story: Murder House,*,season 1, episode 7, FX, 16 Nov. 2011.

"Oscillate." *Transparent*, season 2, episode 8, 11 December 2018, *Amazon Studios*.

"Other Women." *The Handmaid's Tale*, David E. Kelley, Hulu, 9 May 2018.

"Paris Is Burning." *Gilmore Girls*, created by Amy Sherman-Palladino, The WB, 11 January 2011.

Patten, Eileen, and Gretchen Livingston. "Why Is the Teen Birthrate Falling?" *Pew Research Center*, 29 April 2016, http://www.pewresearch.org/fact-tank/2016/04/29/whyis-the-teen-birth-rate-falling/. Accessed 1 June 2018.

Patterson, Robert J. "'Woman Thou Art Bound': Critical Spectatorship, Black Masculine Gazes, and Gender Problems in Tyler Perry's Movies." *Black Camera*, vol. 3 no. 1, 2011, pp. 9–30. *Project MUSE*, muse.jhu.edu/article/453481.

Pearce, Diana. "The Feminization of Poverty: Women, Work and Welfare." *The Urban and Social Change Review*, vol. 11, no. 1–22, 1978, pp. 28–36.

Peoples, Whitney. "(Re)Mediating Black Womanhood: Tyler Perry, Black Feminist Cultural Criticism, and the Politics of Legitimation." *Womanist and Black Feminist Responses to Tyler Perry's Productions*, edited by LeRhonda S. Manigault-Bryant, Tamura A. Lomax, and Carol B. Duncan, Palgrave MacMillan, 2014, pp. 147–162.

Peretz, Evgenia. "Inside the Trump Marriage: Melania's Burden." *Vanity Fair*, 21 April 2017, https://www.vanityfair.com/news/2017/04/donald-melania-trump-marriage. Accessed 8 September 8, 2017.

Perkins, Claire. "Kicking and Screaming: Altmanesque Cynicism and Energy in the Work of Paul Thomas Anderson and Noah Baumbach." *A Companion to Robert Altman*, edited by Adrian Danks, John Wiley and Sons, 2015, pp. 480–500.

"Perpetrators of Sexual Violence." *RAINN*, 2018, https://www.rainn.org/statistics/perpetrators-sexual-violence. Accessed 1 June 2018.

Perry, Tyler. *Madea's Family Reunion—The Play*. Lionsgate, 2005.

Persley, Nicole Hodges. "Bruised and Misunderstood: Translating Black Feminist Acts in the Work of Tyler Perry." *Palimpsest: A Journal on Women, Gender, and the Black International*, vol. 1 no. 2, 2012, pp. 217–236. *Project MUSE*, muse.jhu.edu/article/500174.

Personal Velocity. Directed by Rebecca Miller, performance by Kyra Sedgwick, United Artists, 2002.

"Pesticides: The Price for Progress." *Time*, vol. 28, September 1962, http://content.time.com/time/subscriber/article/

0,33009,940091-4,00.html. Accessed 21 June 2017.

Petersen, Anne Helen. "The Cult of Connie Britton." *Buzzfeed*, 9 November 2014, https://www.buzzfeed.com/annehelen petersen/the-cult-of-connie-britton. Accessed 5 May 2018.

The Philadelphia Story. Directed by George Cukor, performances by Cary Grant, Katharine Hepburn, and James Stewart, Metro-Goldwyn-Meyer, 1940.

Piercy, Marge. *Woman on the Edge of Time*. 1976. Ballantine Books, 1997.

"Pilot." *American Horror Story: Murder House*, created by Brad Falchuk and Ryan Murphy, FX, 5 Oct. 2011.

_____. *Gilmore Girls*, created by Amy Sherman-Palladino, The WB, 5 October 2000.

_____. *Parenthood*, developed by Jason Katims, NBC, 2 March 2010.

_____. *Transparent*, created by Jill Soloway, Amazon Studios, 6 February 2014.

Pimpare, Stephen. *Ghettos, Tramps, and Welfare Queens: Down and Out on the Silver Screen*. Oxford University Press, 2017.

Plant, Rebecca Jo. *Mom: the Transformation of Motherhood in Modern America*. University of Chicago Press, 2010.

Platz, Jenny. "Subversion of the Final Girl in Rape Revenge Narratives and the Normalization of Violence Against Women in *The Tenth Circle* and *The Assault*." *The Lifetime Network: Essays on "Television for Women" in the 21st Century*, edited by Emily L. Newman and Emily Witsell, McFarland, 2016, pp. 151–170.

Pollitt, Katha. *Pro: Reclaiming Abortion Rights*. Picador, 2015.

_____. "Wisconsin GOP Legislators Go After Single Mothers." *The Nation*. 26 March 2012, https://www.thenation.com/article/wisconsin-gop-legislators-go-after-single-mothers/. Accessed September 23, 2013.

"Postpartum." *The Handmaid's Tale*, created by Bruce Miller, Hulu, 4 July 2018.

Potter, Susan. "Dangerous Spaces: Safe." *Camera Obscura*, vol. 57, no. 19, 2004, pp. 125–155.

Precious. Directed by Lee Daniels, performances by Gabourey Sidibe and Mo'Nique. Lionsgate, 2009.

Press, Joy. *Stealing the Show: How Women Are Revolutionizing Television*. Atria Books, 2018.

Pretty Woman. Directed by Garry Marshall, performances by Julia Roberts and Richard Gere, Buena Vista Pictures, 1990.

Provencher, Ashley, and Audrey Sabatini. "Evaluating the Poverty Status of Single Parent Families: Evidence of the Feminization of Poverty." *Proceedings of the New York State Economics Association*, edited by Richard Vogel, vol. 7, 2014, pp. 159–169.

The Public Enemy. Directed by William A. Wellman, performance by James Cagney, Warner Brothers, 1931.

Pupa, Francesco. "Genetics, Birth, and the Biological Revolution." Nassau Community College, 1 August 2018. PowerPoint Presentation.

Quigley, Paula. "When Good Mothers Go Bad: Genre and Gender in *The Babadook*." *Irish Journal of Gothic and Horror Studies*, vol. 15, Autumn 2016, pp. 57–75.

Rabinovitz, Lauren. "Sitcoms and Single Moms: Representations of Feminism on American T.V." *Cinema Journal*, vol. 1, 1989, pp. 3–19.

Radner, Hilary. *Neo-Feminist Cinema: Girly Films, Chick Flicks, and Consumer Culture*. Routledge, 2011.

_____. *The New Woman's Film: Femmecentric Movies for Smart Chicks*. Routledge, 2017.

_____, and Rebecca Stringer. *Feminism at the Movies: Understanding Gender in Contemporary Popular Cinema*. Routledge, 2011.

Raging Bull. Directed by Martin Scorsese, performance by Robert DeNiro, United Artists, 1980.

Raposo, Jacqueline. "GMOs Are Haunting in the New Thriller *Consumed*." *The Village Voice*, 9 December 2015, http://www.ellinghuysen.com/article/20151210_consumed_antigmo_drama/ellinghuysen. Accessed 15 March 2017.

Reger, Jo. *Everywhere and Nowhere: Contemporary Feminism in the United States*. Oxford University Press, 2012.

Reidy, Dennis E., et al. "Man Enough? Masculine Discrepancy Stress and Intimate Partner Violence." *Personality and Individual Differences*, vol. 68, 2014, pp. 169–164.

"Remember Me, I'm the One Who Loves You." *Parenthood,* developed by Jason Katims, NBC, 21 February 2012.

Rich, Adrienne. *Of Woman Born: Motherhood as Experience and Institution.* W.W. Norton and Company, 1976. Reprint. 1995.

Rich, B. Ruby. *The New Queer Cinema: the Director's Cut.* Duke University Press, 2013.

Richardson, Sarah S. "Don't Blame the Mothers: Careless Discussion of Epigenetic Research on How Early Life Affects Health Across Generations Could Harm Women, Warn Sarah S. Richardson and Colleagues." *Nature,* vol. 512, no. 7513, 2014, p. 131+.

Riggs, Damien W. "What Makes a Man?: Thomas Beatie, Embodiment, and 'Mundane Transphobia'" *Feminism and Psychology,* vol. 24, no. 2, pp. 157–171.

Rogers, Anna Backman, et al., editors. "Lena Dunham's Girls: Can-Do Girls, Feminist Killjoys, and Women Who Make Bad Choices." *Feminisms: Diversity, Difference and Multiplicity in Contemporary Film Cultures,* Amsterdam University Press, 2015, pp. 44–53, JSTOR, www.jstor.org/stable/j.ctt16d6996.8.

Romero, Ariana. "CBS Has a Brogramming Problem—& You Can Blame Les Moonves." *Refinery 29,* 31 July 2018, https://www.refinery29.com/en-us/2018/07/205842/les-moonves-cbs-sexism-men-women-tv-programming. Accessed 12 December 2018.

Royce, Tracy. "Unfit Mothers? Mother-Blame and Moral Panic Over Obesity." *The Mother-Blame Game,* edited by Vanessa Reimer and Sarah Sahagian, Demeter Press, 2015, pp. 52–64.

"Rubber Man." *American Horror Story: Murder House,* created by Brad Falchuk and Ryan Murphy, FX, 21 November 2011.

Rudrappa, Sharmila. "India Outlawed Commercial Surrogacy—Clinics Are Finding Loopholes." *The Conversation,* 23 October 2017, http://theconversation.com/india-outlawed-commercial-surrogacy-clinics-are-finding-loopholes-81784. Accessed 8 September 2018.

Russo, Nancy Felipe. "The Motherhood Mandate." *Journal of Social Issues,* vol. 32, no. 3, 1976, pp. 143–153.

Safe. Directed by Todd Haynes, performance by Julianne Moore, Good Machine, 1995.

Saint Hoax. "When Did He Stop Treating You Like a Princess?" Sainthoax.com, 2017. Accessed 15 January 2017.

Salaky, Kristen. "People Can't Stop Shaming Moms, and It's Causing 'maternal Anxiety.'" *Business Insider,* 20 June 2017, http://www.businessinsider.com/author/kristin-salaky/date/asc?page=2. Accessed 8 September 2017.

Sapphire. *The Kid: A Novel.* Penguin Books, 2011.

———. *Push: A Novel.* Vintage, 1996.

Sava, Oliver. "Adapting a Telenovela with *Jane the Virgin* Showrunner Jennie Urman." *The AV Club,* 14 December 2014, https://tv.avclub.com/adapting-a-telenovela-with-jane-thevirgin-showrunner-j-1798274690. Accessed 1 June 2018.

Schapiro, Mark. *Exposed: The Toxic Chemistry of Everyday Products and What's at Stake for American Power.* Chelsea Green Publishing, 2007.

Sconce, Jeffrey. "Irony, Nihilism and the New American 'Smart' Film." *Screen,* vol. 43, no. 4, 1 December 2002, pp. 349–369.

Scott, Dayna N., Lauren Rakowski, and Laila Zahra Harris. "The Production of Pollution and the Consumption of Chemicals in Canada." *Our Chemical Selves: Gender, Toxics and Environmental Health,* 2015.

"Season 8 *Teen Mom 2* Reunion." *Teen Mom 2,* created by Lauren Dolgen, MTV, 13 August 2018.

"Second National Report on Human Exposure to Environmental Chemicals." *Centers for Disease Control and Prevention (CDC),* Department of Health and Human Services. NCEH Pub, no. 02-0716, 2003, pp. 1–257.

Seidel, Linda. *Mediated Maternity: Contemporary American Portrayals of Bad Mothers in Literature and Popular Culture.* Lexington Books, 2013.

Sélavy, Virginie. "*The Babadook*: An Interview with Jennifer Kent." *Electric Sheep: A Deviant View of Cinema,* 24 October 2014, http://www.electricsheepmagazine.co.uk/features/2014/10/24/the-babadook-interview-with-jennifer-kent/. Accessed 1 November 2017.

Seltzer, Sarah. "The Imminent Whitewashing of the *Hunger Games* Heroine." *Jezebel,* 14 March 2011, https://jezebel.com/5781682/the-imminent-whitewashing-of-the-hunger-games-heroine. Accessed 27 July 2017.

Serano, Julia. *Excluded: Making Feminist and Queer Movements More Inclusive.* Seal Press, 2013.

Shachar, Hila. "A Post-Feminist Romance: Love, Gender, and Intertextuality in Stephenie Meyer's Saga." *Theorizing Twilight: Critical Essays on What's at Stake in a Post-Vampire World,* edited by Maggie Park and Natalie Wilson, McFarland, 2011, pp. 147–164.

Shahvisi, Arianne. "Hermeneutical Injustice and Outsourced Domestic Work." *Women's Studies International Forum,* vol. 69, 2018, pp. 18–25.

Sharrow, Elizabeth A., et al. "The First-Daughter Effect: The Impact of Fathering Daughters on Men's Preference for Gender-Equality Policies." *Public Opinion Quarterly,* vol. 82, no. 3, 18 October 2018, pp. 493–523.

Sheppard, Samantha N. "Lion and Lamb—The Strong Black Woman Gets Abused: 'Afflictions of Specialness' in Post-Feminist and Post-Civil Rights Film." *Thinking Gender Papers from UCLA Center for the Study of Women,* 1 February 2009.

"Shout Your Abortion." Shoutyourabortion.com. Accessed 15 November 2017.

Showalter, Elaine. *Hystories: Hysterical Epidemics and Modern Media.* Columbia University Press, 1997.

Silbergleid, Robin. "Hip Mamas: *Gilmore Girls* and Ariel Gore." *Mommy Angst: Motherhood in American Popular Culture,* edited by Anna C. Hall and Mardia J. Bishop, Praeger, 2009, pp. 93–112.

Silver Linings Playbook. Directed by David O. Russell, performance by Bradley Cooper, the Weinstein Company, 2012.

Silverstein, Melissa. "Interview with Lena Dunham Writer/Director of *Tiny Furniture.*" *The Huffington Post,* 12 November 2018, https://www.huffingtonpost.com/melissasilverstein/interview-with-lena-dunha_b_782760.html. Accessed June 28 2017.

Slaughter, Ann Marie. *Unfinished Business: Women Men Work Family.* Random House, 2016.

———. "Why Women Still Can't Have It All." *The Atlantic,* July/August 2012, https://www.theatlantic.com/magazine/archive/2012/07/why-women-still-cant-have-it-all/309020/. Accessed 28 August 2013.

Sleeping with the Enemy. Directed by Joseph Rubin, performance by Julia Roberts, Twentieth Century–Fox, 1991.

"Smart Power." *The Handmaid's Tale,* created by Bruce Miller, Hulu, 13 June 2018.

Smith, Michael B. "'Silence, Ms. Carson!': Science, Gender, and the Reception of *Silent Spring.*" *Feminist Studies,* 2001, vol. 27, no. 3, pp. 733–752.

"So Much to Lose." *Teen Mom 2,* created by Lauren Dolgen, MTV, 18 January 2011.

"Somebody's Dead." *Big Little Lies,* created by David E. Kelley, HBO, 19 February 2017,.

Stabile, Carol. "'First He'll Kill Her Then I'll Save Her': Vampires, Feminism, and the Twilight Franchise." *Journal of Communication,* vol. 61, 1 February 2011, pp. E4–E8.

Stark, Jeff. "Personal Velocity." *Salon,* 27 November 2002, https://www.salon.com/2002/11/27/velocity/. Accessed 10 April 2017.

Stasia, Cristina Lucia. "'Wham! Bam! Thank You Ma'am': The New Public/Private Female Action Hero." *Third Wave Feminism: A Critical Exploration,* edited by Stacy Gillis, Gillian Howie, and Rebecca Munford, Palgrave MacMillan, 2004, pp. 175–184.

"The Status of Women in the U.S. Media 2017." *The Women's Media Center Reports,* 21 March 2017, https://www.womensmediacenter.com/reports/the-status-of-women-in-u.s.media-2017. Accessed 1 May 2018.

Stewart, Melanie Ann. "Sensationalizing the Sentimental: National Culture and Futurity." *MTV and Teen Pregnancy: Critical Essays on* 16 and Pregnant *and* Teen Mom, edited by Letizia Guglielmo, Scarecrow Press, pp. 93–108.

Stoneman, Scott. "Ending Fat Stigma: *Precious,* Visual Culture, and Anti-Obesity in the 'Fat Moment.'" *Review of Education, Pedagogy, and Cultural Studies,* vol. 34, no. 3–4, 2012, pp. 197–207.

Stringer, Rebecca. "From Victim to Vigilante: Gender, Violence, and Revenge in *The Brave One* (2007) and *Hard Candy* (2005)." *Feminism at the Movies: Understanding Gender in Contemporary Popular Cinema*, edited by Hilary Radner and Rebecca Stringer, Routledge, 2011, pp. 268–282.

———. "Rethinking the Critique of Victim Feminism." *Victim No More: Women's Resistance to Law, Culture and Power*, edited by Ellen Faulkner and Gayle MacDonald, Fernwood Publishing Company, 2009, pp. 20–27.

Swiffer Bissel. "Feel the Power." 2013.

"Switching Teams." *CBS News*, 10 April 2016, https://www.cbsnews.com/videos/switching-teams/. Accessed 15 May 2017.

Taddeo, Julie Ann, and Ken Dvorak. Introduction. *The Tube Has Spoken: Reality TV and History*, University Press of Kentucky, 2009, pp. 1–10.

Takeda, Allison. 2013. "Dr. Drew Pinsky on Farrah Abraham: Farrah Is Making 'Horrible, Horrible Choices.'" *US Magazine*, 4 May 2013, https://www.usmagazine.com/celebrity-news/news/dr-drew-pinsky-farrah-abraham-is-making-horrible-horrible-choices-201345/. Accessed 15 June 2015.

Tanenbaum, Leora. *I Am Not a Slut: Slut-Shaming in the Age of the Internet*. Harper Perennial, 2015.

Taormino, Tristan. "The Rise of MILFS and Mommies in Sexual Fantasy Materials." *The Village Voice*, 30 October 2014, https://archive.li/LknEy. Accessed 28 May 2014.

Tasker, Yvonne, and Diane Negra. *Interrogating Postfeminism: Gender and the Politics of Popular Culture*. Duke University Press, 2007.

Taubin, Amy. "Nowhere to Hide." *Sight and Sound*, vol. 5, 1996, pp. 32–34.

Taylor, Dorceta E. "Women of Color: Environmental Justice, and Ecofeminism" *Ecofeminisim: Women, Culture, Nature*, edited by Karen J. Warren, Indiana University Press, 1997, pp. 38–81.

"Teach Me Tonight." *Gilmore Girls*, created by Amy Sherman-Palladino, The WB, 30 April 2002.

Teeman, Tim. "Why Are So Many Transgender Women of Color Being Killed in America?" *The Daily Beast*, 4 August 2017, https://www.thedailybeast.com/why-are-so-many-trans-women-of-color-being-killed-in-america. Accessed 1 May 2018.

"Teen Pregnancy, Poverty, and Income Disparity." *The National Campaign to Prevent Teen Pregnancy*, 2010, Teenpregnancy.org. Accessed 1 May 2017.

Thau, Barbara. "Will 'Record High' Mother's Day Spending Give Ailing Retail Sector a Much Needed Boost?" *Forbes*. 2 May 2017, https://www.forbes.com/sites/barbarathau/2017/05/02/will-record-high-mothers-day-spending-give-ailing-retail-sector-a-much-needed-boost/#185992ce12de. Accessed 27 September 2017.

Thomason, Linda Bloodworth. "*Designing Woman* Creator Goes Public with Les Moonves War: Not All Harassment Is Sexual." *The Hollywood Reporter*, 12 September 2018, https://www.hollywoodreporter.com/news/designing-women-creator-les-moonves-not-all-harassment-is-sexual-1142448. Accessed 1 December 2018.

Tiny Furniture. Directed by Lena Dunham, performances by Lena Dunham and Laurie Simmons, IFC Films, 2010.

"A Tittin' and a Hairin.'" *Orange Is the New Black*, created by Jenji Kohan, Netflix, 11 June 2015.

"To Sardines and Back." *Transparent*, created by Jill Soloway, Amazon Studios, 23 September 2015.

Tomkins, Calvin. "A Doll's House: Laurie Simmons's Sense of Scale." *The New Yorker*, 2 December 2012, https://www.newyorker.com/magazine/2012/12/10/a-dolls-house-2.

"Tongue-Tied." *Orange Is the New Black*, created by Jenji Kohan, Netflix, 11 June 2015.

Torkelson, Anne. "Violence, Agency, and the Women of *Twilight*." *Theorizing Twilight: Critical Essays on What's at Stake in a Post-Vampire World*, edited by Maggie Park and Natalie Wilson. McFarland, 2011, pp. 209–223.

Toscano, Margaret M. "Mormon Morality and Immortality in Stephenie Meyer's *Twilight* Series." *Bitten by Twilight: Youth Culture, Media, and the Vampire Franchise*, edited by Melissa A. Clark, Jennifer Stevens Aubrey, and Elizabeth Behm-Morawitz, Peter Lang, 2010, pp. 21–36.

"Toxic Waste and Race at Twenty." *United*

Church of Christ, 2007, http://www.ucc.org/environmental-ministries/environment/toxic-waste-20.html. Accessed 1 May 2009.

Transamerica. Directed by Duncan Tucker, performances by Felicity Huffman and Kevin Zegers, IFC Films, 2005.

Trier-Bieniek, Adrienne. Introduction. *The Beyoncé Effect: Essays on Sexuality, Race and Feminism*, McFarland, 2016, 1–10.

Tully. Directed by Jason Reitman, written by Diablo Cody, performances by Charlize Theron, Mackenzie Davis, and Ron Livingston, Focus Features, 2018.

The Twilight Saga: Breaking Dawn, Part I, Directed by Bill Condon, performances by Kristen Stewart and Robert Pattinson, Summit Entertainment, 2011.

The Twilight Saga: Breaking Dawn, Part II, Directed by Bill Condon, performances by Kristen Stewart and Robert Pattinson, Summit Entertainment, 2012.

The Twilight Saga: Eclipse. Directed by David Slade, performances by Kristen Stewart and Robert Pattinson, Summit Entertainment, 2010.

The Twilight Saga: New Moon. Directed by Chris Weitz, performances by Kristen Stewart and Robert Pattinson, Summit Entertainment, 2009.

The Twilight Saga: Twilight. Directed by Catherine Hardwicke, performances by Kristen Stewart and Robert Pattinson, Summit Entertainment, 2008.

"The 2017 GLAAD Studio Responsibility Index." GLAAD.org, 2017, https://www.glaad.org/sri/2017. Accessed 1 May 2018.

"The 2017 Hollywood Diversity Report: Setting the Record Straight." *Ralph J. Bunche Center for African American Studies at UCLA*, 2017, https://bunchecenter.ucla.edu/wp-content/uploads/sites/82/2017/04/2017-Hollywood-Diversity-Report-2-21-17.pdf. Accessed 1 May 2018.

Tyler, Imogen. "Pregnant Beauty: Maternal Femininities Under Neoliberalism." *New Femininities: Postfeminism, Neoliberalism, and Subjectivity*, edited by Rosalind Gill and Christina Scharff, Palgrave Macmillan, 2011.

"Unwomen." *The Handmaid's Tale*, created by Bruce Miller, Hulu, 25 April 2018.

Vagianos, Alanna. "30 Shocking Domestic Violence Statistics That Remind Us Its an Epidemic." *The Huffington Post*, 13 February 2015, https://www.huffingtonpost.com/2014/10/23/domestic-violence-statistics_n_5959776.html. Accessed 3 March 2017.

Vandenberg-Daves, Jodi. *Modern Motherhood: An American History*. Rutgers University Press, 2014.

Vavrus, Mary Douglas. "Unhitching from the 'Post' (of Postfeminism)." *Communication Studies*, vol. 34, 2010, pp. 222–227.

Vered, Karen Orr, and Sal Humphreys. "Postfeminist Inflections in Television Studies." *Continuum*, vol. 28, no. 2, 2014, pp. 155–163.

Villarreal, Yvonne. "*Jane the Virgin*: *Ugly Betty* Meets *Gilmore Girls*, Co-Creator Says." *LA Times*, 18 July 2014, https://www.latimes.com/entertainment/tv/showtracker/la-et-st-jane-the-virgin-ugly-betty-meets-gilmore-girls-20140718-story.html. Accessed 1 June 2018.

Vinson, Jenna. *Embodying the Problem: The Persuasive Power of the Teen Mother*. Rutgers University Press, 2017.

"Waiting to Be Ashamed of What You'll Probably Do This Weekend." *Obvious Child Tumblr*, http://obviouschildmovie.tumblr.com/post/89272729185. Accessed 1 June 2018.

Waitress. Written and directed by Adrienne Shelley, performance by Keri Russell, Fox Searchlight Pictures, 2007.

Walker, Alice. *The Color Purple*. Harcourt Brace Jovanovich, 1982.

Walsh, Matt. "Bruce Jenner Is Not a Woman. He Is a Sick and Delusional Man." *The Blaze*, 27 April 2015, http://www.theblaze.com/contributions/bruce-jenner-is-not-a-woman-he-is-a-sick-and-delusional-man/. Accessed 4 November 2015.

Wang, Wendy, Kim Parker, and Paul Taylor. Pew Research, "Breadwinner Moms." Last modified 29 May 2013, http://www.pewsocialtrends.org/2013/05/29/breadwinner-moms/. Accessed 20 August 2013.

"We Have Had Abortions." *Ms*, Spring, 1972, pp. 34–35.

Weber, Brenda R., and Jennifer Lynn Jones. "Sperm Receptacles, Money-Hungry Monsters and Fame Whores: Reality Celebrity Motherhood and the Transmediated Grotesque." *The Sage Handbook of Television Studies*, edited by Manuel Alvardo, et al., Sage Reference, 2015, pp. 325–226.

Weiss, Suzannah. "YES: The Majority of Teens Now Identify as Feminists." *Glamour*, 4 August 2017, https://www.glamour.com/story/majority-teen-girls-feminists. Accessed 1 May 2018.

Wendell, Susan. *The Rejected Body: Feminist Philosophical Reflections on Disability*. Routledge, 1996.

"What Happens When the Abusive Relationship Ends?" *National Coalition Against Domestic Violence*. https://ncadv.org/learn-more. Accessed 9 June 2018.

"What Is Domestic Violence?" *National Coalition Against Domestic Violence*, https://ncadv.org/learn-more. Accessed 1 June 2017.

What to Expect When You're Expecting. Directed by Kirk Jones, performances by Jennifer Lopez, Cameron Diaz, and Elizabeth Banks, Lionsgate, 2012.

"What's Goin' on Down There?" *Parenthood*, developed by Jason Katims, NBC, 13 April 2010.

Wheeler, Duncan. "The Representation of Domestic Violence in Popular English-Language Cinema." *New Cinemas: Journal of Contemporary Film*, vol. 7 no. 2, 2009, pp. 155–175.

"Where My Dreidel At." *Orange Is the New Black*, created by Jenji Kohan, Netflix, 11 June 2015.

"Why a Women's Organization." *Women's Voices for the Earth*, 2017, https://www.womensvoices.org/about/why-a-womens-organization/. Accessed 1 December 2016.

Williams, Cristan. "Gender Critical Feminism, the Roots of Radical Feminism, and Trans Oppression." *The Advocate*, 8 December 2014, http://transadvocate.com/gender-critical-feminism-the-roots-of-radical-feminism-and-trans-oppression_n_14766.htm. Accessed 1 May 2018.

_____. "Radical Inclusion: Recounting the Trans Inclusive History of Radical Feminism." *Transgender Studies Quarterly*, vol. 3, 2016, pp. 1–2, 254–258.

Williams, Florence. *Breasts: an Unnatural History*. W.W. Norton and Company, 2013.

The Wizard of Oz. Directed by Victor Fleming, performance by Judy Garland, Metro-Goldwyn-Meyer, 1939.

"Women's Work." *The Handmaid's Tale*, created by Bruce Miller, Hulu, 6 June 2018.

Won, Brittany. "17 of the Most Absurd Things Donald Trump Has Said About Marriage." *The Huffington Post*, 23 June 2016. https://www.huffingtonpost.com/entry/marriagerules-according-to-donald-trump_us_576c3886e4b0dbb1bbb9e5a8. Accessed 27 September 2017.

"Words from Prison—Did You Know?" *ACLU*, https://www.aclu.org/other/words-prison-did-you-know. Accessed 15 April 2017.

Wyeth, Andrew. *Christina's World*. 1948. The Museum of Modern Art, New York.

Yakas, Lisa. "Nasty Germs Are Lurking in Your 'Clean' Home." *Bottom Line Inc.*, 23 June 2017, https://bottomlineinc.com/life/germs/nasty-germs-lurking-clean-home. Accessed 25 June 2017.

Yelling to the Sky. Written and directed by Victoria Maloney, performance by Zoë Kravitz, MPI Media Group, 2011.

"You Get What You Need." *Big Little Lies*, created by David E. Kelley, HBO, 2 April 2017.

Young, Iris Marion. "The Five Faces of Oppression." *The Philosophical Forum*, vol. xix, no. 4, Summer 1998, pp. 270–290.

_____. *On Female Body Experience: "Throwing Like a Girl" and Other Essays*. Oxford, 2005.

Zeisler, Andi. *We Were Feminists Once: From Riot Girl to Cover Girl®, the Buying and Selling of a Political Movement*. Public Affairs, 2017.

Zuckerman, Esther. "'Obvious Child' Director Gillian Robespierre on Choosing the Song 'The Obvious Child.'" *The Atlantic*, 5 June 2014, https://www.theatlantic.com/entertainment/archive/2014/06/obvious-child-director-gillian-robespierre-on-choosing-the-song-the-obvious-child/372224/. Accessed 21 August 2017.

Index

Numbers in **_bold italics_** indicate pages with illustrations

abortion 22, 65–66, 103, 130–133, 137–140
Abraham, Farrah 52–53
advanced reproductive technology (ART) 144, 157–159, 196n3
Ahmed, Sarah 187n2
Aho, Tanja 190n22
Akin, Stephanie 88
Alghrani, Amel 197n7
Alice Doesn't Live Here Anymore 94, 102, 126
Al Kramden 94
Allmark, Panizza 38
Al Odhayani, Abdulaziz 188n8
Als, Hilton 195n8
American Horror Story 2, 20, 21–25
Ames, Melissa 9, 187n9
Anderson, Lisa Arrindell **_116_**
androgenesis 157–158
Apted, Michael 7, 91, 93, 110
Armstrong, Evan Read 198n14
Arthurs, Jane 196n6
Ashcraft, Diana Musialowski 57
Atwood, Margaret 152
Aytes, Rochelle 115–**_116_**

The Babadook 12, 20, 25–31, 32, 33
Baby Boom 126
Baby Mama 142
Bacchiocchi, Gina 51
Bachmann, Michele 5
Bad Moms 35, 41
A Bad Moms Christmas 35
Bailar, Schuyler, 174–176
Barry, Doug 189n2
Baumbach, Noah 7, 125, 127–130
Baumgardner, Jennifer 5, 136, 182
Beam, Cris 35
Bean, Anna 196n8
Beatie, Thomas 99n23
Bechdel test 183–184, 199n5

Beltràn, Mary 178, 199n2
Benard, Stephen 23
benevolent patriarch 44–46, 53–54, 91, 100–101, 102, 104–106, 109, 126
Bennett, Jessica 141
Bettcher, T.M. 162
Bewley, Alison L. 191n4
Big Little Lies 14, 119–123, 124
Bledel, Alexis **_40_**
Bloom, Ester 196n1
Bonner, Mehera 53
Bouchard, Danielle 84, 193n10
Brady, Anita 73, 198n15
breastfeeding 149, 154; chestfeeding 176
Briefel, Aviva 29
Britton, Connie 21, **_24_**
Broad, Katherine R. 62
Brockington, Ariana 181
Brody, Richard 147, 197n8
Brown, Angela 92–93
Brunsdon, Charlotte 8, 187n8, 192n13
Buell, Laurence 73, 86
Bullard, Robert D. 193n9
Bullock, Charlotte 81
Bumiller, Kristin 109–110, 113, 123
Burcon, Sarah 9, 187n9
Burke, Tarana 179
The Burning Bed 90, 94
Burns, Katelyn 198n4
Burns, Kellie 173, 198n15
Butler, Jess 138, 188n10, 196n11
Butler, Judith 161
Butsch, Richard 189n7

Caldwell, Maggie 196n1
Camil, Jaime 177
"canary in the coal mine" 71–72, 89
Cannon, Robin 81
Caplan, Paula 69

Capuzza, Jamie 162
Carline, Anna 106
Caron, Christina 197n6
Carson, Rachel 73–74, 88
Carter, Darla 193n2
Catastrophe 146
Chase and Sanborn coffee 94–**95**
Chidgey, Red 9–11
childcare (lack of affordable) 16, 23, 51, 66, 68–69, 125, 143–44, 147–150, 188n5
class exploitation film 31
Clinton, Hillary 181
Clorox **72**
Cody, Diablo 146, 184, 197n5
Coll, Ivonne **185**
Collins, Suzanne 55–63, 191n4, 191n5, 192n9
The Color Purple 115, 195n7
Concerned Citizens of South Central Los Angeles 81
Condit, Deirdre M. 157–158
Consumed 13, 72–74, 85–89
Conway, Kellyanne 123
Coontz, Stephanie 43, 71, 90
Cooper, Britney 11, 195n4
Cooper, Richard 197n8
Correll, Shelley J. 23
Coulter, Ann 5
Couric, Katie 175
Covert, Bryce 183
Cox, Jamieson 198n15
Cox, Laverne 138, 165, 175, 198n15, 199n22
Crenshaw, Kimberlé 117–118
Crews, Terry 184
Crispin, Jessa 5
Crothers, Lane 187n7

Daniels, Lee 30–31
Davies, Cristyn 173, 198n15
Davis, Devra 74, 193n3
Davis, Essie 26, **30**
Davis, Mackenzie 146
DeaVault, Rodney M. 61
DeBoer, Chelsea (Houska) 46–48, 191n25
Dervasula, Shreya 183
Desai, Jigna 84, 193n10
Devries, Karen 95
Di Chiro, Giovanna 81
disability studies 73, 193n8
Dolgen, Lauren 190n21
domestic violence 6, 13–14, 49, 52, 90–106, 109–124, 126, 194n3, 194n8, 194n13, 194n15, 195n9
domestic worker 80–81, 143–144, 146–151, 156–7, 196n1, 197n4
Douglas, Susan, 23, 126–127, 187n4, 189n11, 195n1
drag 117, 195n6
Draper, Polly 130, **132**
Drucker, Zachary 173
Dubrofsky, Rachel E. 60
Dunham, Lena 7, 125, 133–137, 184
Dunn, Stephen 195n6
Dvorak, Ken 189n7

Easteal, Patricia 95, 105–106, 194n13
Edwards, Leigh H. 190n19
Eligon, John 88
Elman, Julie Passanante 66
Emanuel, Ezekiel 193n3
Enough 14, 90–91, 93–102, 105–106, 110–111, 114, 116, 121, 126
environmental illness 71, 73–76, 81–83, 193n4
epistemic injustice 13, 19, 83, 86
Ergas, Yasmine 144–145
Erin Brockovich 74, 87
Eschner, Kat 71
Evans, Jenelle 48–52, 191n26
Evil Nanny 149

fairy godmother 100, 121
fairy tales 56, 90–94, 96, 100–101, 104, 106, 118, 121
Fallas, Jennifer A. 47, 191n27
Faulkner, Ellen 194n2, 195n14
Feasey, Rebecca 43, 187n4
Feldman, Dana. 186
The Feminine Mystique 90, 138
Feminist International Network of Resistance to Reproductive and Genetic Engineering (FINNRAGE) 196n2
feminization of poverty 69
Ferraro, Kathleen 195n1
Finley, Laura L. 90, 194n12
Firestone, Shulamith 66, 144, 157
Flaherty, Colleen 198n5
Flint, Michigan water crisis 88–89
Fricker, Miranda 83, 86
Friedman, May 49
Fuller, Bonnie 48

Gadsby, Hannah 180
Gandal, Keith 31
Garcia, Sandra E. 179
Garcia-Moreno, C. 95
Garland-Thomson, Rosemary 73, 193n8
Garlinghouse, Rachel 192–193n22
Garner, Julia 137–138
Gay, Roxane 5
Gay & Lesbian Alliance Against Defamation (GLAAD) 180
gender critical feminists 138–139, 162, 167, 172, 196n14, 198n5
genetically modified organisms (GMOs) 72, 85–87
Genius, Stephen J. 75
Gibbs, Lois 72, 74, 76–77
Gill, Rosalind 9, 39, 51, 187n4, 189n9, 193n12, 196n7
Gilman, Charlotte Perkins: "The Yellow Wallpaper" 23

Gilmore Girls 12–13, 37–41, 43–45, 63
Girls 133–134, 135, 136
Girls' Trip 189n14
"girly mom" 37–38, 43–45, 49, 53–54, 63
Gitlin, Todd 187n9
Glynn, Sarah Jane. 69
Goldberg, Leslie. 199n20
Goldberg, Michelle 198n6
Good Will Hunting 90
Gotlib, Anna 193n23
Graham, Lauren 37–**40**, 44
Grandma 14, 125, 127, 137–141
Gregson, Joanna 49
"ground zero" 88

Hamilton, Cynthia 81
The Hand That Rocks the Cradle 149
The Handmaid's Tale (Hulu series) 14–15, 142–143, 151–156, 158–159
Harden, Marcia Gay 137
Harris, Laila Zahra 71
Harrison, Laura 144, 197n9
Harvey, David 188n10
Haynes, Todd 7, 73, 82–84, 193n10, 193n13
Hazlett, Maril 73
Heder, Sean 165
Heitler, Susan 28
Heller, Dana 45
Heller-Nicholas, Alexandra 194n12
Hempel, Evan 176
Henry, Astrid 198n16
Hicks, Hope 123
Hinckley, David. 189n6
Hines, Sally 196n14, 198n2
Hobson, Jenelle 84
Holderness, Colbie 123
Holland, Kate 95, 105–106, 194n13
Hollows, Joanne 8, 184
Holm, Elizabeth 196n8
Hooker Chemical 193n6
hooks, bell 188n14
Horne, Rebecca N. 197n7
Hosey, Sara 193n8
housewife (representations of) 71–72, 74–77, 80, 86
How to Live with Your Parents (for the Rest of Your Life) 190n18
Huffman, Felicity 162
Humphreys, Sal 3
The Hunger Games (film franchise) 13, 55–64, 70, 124; *Catching Fire* 60; *Mockingjay, Part I* 60–61; *Mockingjay, Part II* 62
The Hunger Games (novel) 55, 59; *Mockingjay* 61, 63, 69
Hunting, Kyra 196n15
hysteria 73, 75–76, 78–79, 82, 85–86

immigration 181–182
The Incredible Shrinking Woman 13, 71–73, 74–81, 85–89

independent film 127, 195n2
intimate partner violence *see* domestic violence
in vitro fertilization (IVF) *see* advanced reproductive technology
Ira, Stephen 162

Jacobo, Julia 88
Jane the Virgin 3, 177–186
Janicker, Rebecca 21
Jarman, Michelle 188n9
Jefferson, J'na 179
Johnson, Mark 73
Johnston, Derek 188n6
Jones, Jennifer Lynn 53
Juffer, Jane 69

Kaplan, Amy 88
Kardashian, Kim 141
Karlyn, Kathleen Rowe 56, 131
Kawash, Samira 197n14
Keegan, Cael 198n7
Keetley, Dawn 25, 188n4
Kelley, David E. 119
Kelly, Casey Ryan. 64, 68, 192n17, 192n19
Kent, Jennifer. 25–26, 27–28, 30
Keziah, Judd 95, 105–106, 194n13
Khazan, Olga 197n7
The Kid 34
Kidd, Briony 27
Kidman, Nicole 119, 127
Kimmel, Michael 194n14
King, Geoff 196n2
King, Stephen 188n4
Knopper, Melissa 193n1
Knowles, Beyoncé 11, 184, 188n14
Kohan, Jenji 173, 179, 198n19
Kozol, Wendy 194n8, 195n1
Kramer vs. Kramer 126, 196n3
Kravitz, Zoë 120
Kunis, Mila 35

Lakoff, George 73
Latimer, Heather 220
Lauzen, Martha 160, 198n1
Law, Victoria 194n15
Lawrence, Jennifer 55–**62**
Leonard, Suzanne 125, 126–127, 196n5
The Let Down 146
Levy, Ariel 136, 199n17
The Lifetime Network 122, 149, 194n1
Light, Judith 160, 177
Lindner, Emilee 141
Lister-Jones, Zoe 85–86, 193n14
Littler, Jo 39
Longoria, Eva 181
Lopez, Jennifer 93, 106, 194n7
Lorde 141
Lotz, Amanda D. 199n18
Loudermilk, Kim 96, 187n1

Index

Love Canal *see* Gibbs, Lois
Lublin, Nancy 196*n*2
Lyle, Timothy 117

MacDonald, Gayle 194*n*2, 195*n*14
Madea's Family Reunion (film) 14, 114–119, 121, 123, 124
Maher, Jennifer 154
Maid in Manhattan 93
Maine, Kate 196*n*8
Mak, J.Y. 95
makeover sequence 82–83
Malatino, Hilary 198*n*10
Manchester by the Sea 196*n*4
Manne, Kate 156
Margot at the Wedding 14, 125, 127–130, 133
Martin, Nina 69
Martinez, Diane, 181
Matheson, Richard 193*n*7
matrophilia 14, 124–125
matrophobia 13–14, 56, 69, 125
matrophor 137, 172, 198*n*16
Mazziotta, Julie 176
McCuller, Michael 142
McDonald, Brian 60
McDonough, Kate 199*n*22
McRobbie, Angela 9, 31, 57
Mead, Rebecca 133
Meloy, Michelle L. 92–93
Mendez, Anthony 181
Messer, Leah 47–48
metaphorization 73, 79, 85
#metoo 1, 179
Mey 173, 199*n*21
Meyer, Stephanie 63–67, 192*n*11, 192*n*14
Michaels, Meredith W. 23, 189*n*11, 195*n*1
M.I.L.F. 39
Miller, C. 69
Miller, Cynthia 75
Miller, D. 86
Miller, J. Howard 9
Miller, Laura 61
Miller, Melissa 192*n*11
Miller, Rebecca 7, 110
Miller, Susan L. 92–93
Mr. and Mrs. Smith 101
Mitchell, David 193*n*8
Mock, Janet 175
"mom" 140–141
Monàe, Janelle 184
Mo'Nique 31
Moonves, Les 179
Moore, Demi 188*n*3
Moore, Julianne 58, 80
Moras, Amanda 143–144
Moreno, Carolina 181–182
Moriarty, Liane 195*n*13
Moselely, Rachel 8
Moss, Elisabeth 152
"motherhood mandate" 57, 62, 70, 192*n*23

"motherhood penalty" 68; motherhood wage gap 69, 70
Ms. 133
multiple chemical sensitivity *see* environmental illness
Murdock, Catherine Gilbert 191*n*3
Murkerjea, Ananya 192*n*15
Murphy, Caryn 51, 191*n*28
Murphy, Mekado 27
My Super Sweet 16 46–47

Nadasen, Premila 143
Naismith, Gaye 84, 192*n*13
"narrowcasting" 198*n*18
Nathanson, Elizabeth 187*n*4
National Coalition Against Domestic Violence (NCADV) 6
Navedo, Andrea 185
Needham, Gary 198*n*8
Negra, Diane 9, 16, 37–38, 187*n*4, 188*n*12, 196*n*7
"neoliberal mothering" 23
Newman, Emily L. 194*n*1, 194*n*11
9/11 attacks 89
Nodelman, Perry 59
North, Anna 192*n*14
Nussbaum, Emily 119, 122, 181

Obvious Child 14, 125, 127, 130–133
O'Connor, Flannery 116
O'Dair, Sharon 193*n*11
Okin, Susan Moller 157
Oliver, Kelly 21
O'Meara, Jennifer 129
Orange Is the New Black 7, 11, 15, 141, 161, 164–169, 172–173, 176, 199*n*19
outsourcing 142–159; *see also* domestic labor

Paik, In 23
Pais, Zane 128
Parenthood 12–13, 37, 41–45
patriarchal medicine 22, 23, 25, 76, 86
Patterson, Robert J. 114
Pearce, Diana 69
Peoples, Whitney 195*n*7
Perkins, Claire 127, 196*n*2
Perry, Tyler 7, 114–115, **116**, 117–119, 195*n*4, 195*n*5, 195*n*7, 195*n*11
Persley, Nicole Hodges 118
Personal Velocity (film) 14, 110–114, 123
Petersen, A.H. 21
The Philadelphia Story 7, 94
Piercy, Marge 158; *Woman at the End of Time* 197*n*16
Pimpare, Stephen 31, 189*n*12
Pinsky, Drew 46, 52–54, 190*n*22
Plant, Rebecca Jo 74
Platz, Jenny 194*n*11
Pollitt, Katha 190*n*12, 196*n*13
Porter, Rob 123

postfeminism 5–12, 21–25, 37–39, 43–44, 57, 65–68, 91, 99, 106, 108, 119, 124–127, 133, 138, 145, 147, 175, 181–182, 183n3, 189n7, 189n9, 193n13, 196n7
Potter, Susan 193n10
Precious 12, 20, 30–35
pregnancy 20–23, 31, 33, 38, 44, 46–51, 63, 66, 69, 102–103, 127, 130–132, 144–145, 148, 154, 158, 175, 188n2, 188n3, 190n21, 190n22, 191n28, 192n14, 197n20, 199n23
Press, Joy 11, 165, 178–179, 189n1, 199n21, 199n5
Provenchar, Ashley 69
The Public Enemy 194n9
Pupa, Francesco 144

Quigley, Paula 26, 27, 29–30

Rabinovitz, Lauren 189n3
Radner, Hillary 12, 172, 187n4, 194n7, 196n7, 198n8
Rae, Issa 179, 184
Raging Bull 90, 194n10
Raising Helen 126
Rakowski, Lauren 71
Ralph C. Bunche Center for African American Studies 179–180
Rape and Incest National Network (RAINN) 6
"rape-and-revenge" plot 96, 194n11, 194n12
Raposo, Jaqueline 86
Reger, Jo 5
Reidy, Dennis E. 194n5
Reitman, Jason 7, 142–143, 146, 197n5
Rich, Adrienne 13, 14, 39, 56, 69, 125, 138
Rich, B. Ruby 12, 180
Richards, Amy 5, 182
Richardson, Sarah S. 192n21
Riggs, Damien 161, 167, 199n23
Robespierre, Gillian 126, 130–132, 196n8
Rodriguez, Gina 177, 181, 182, 184, **185**
Rogers, Anna Backman 133
Romero, Ariana 179
Roseanne 189n8
Rosemary's Baby 21
Rosie the Riveter 9–11
Royce, Tracy 189n10
Rudrappa, Sharmila 145
Russell, Kerri 102
Russo, Nancy Felipe 57, 188n16
Ryalls, Emily D. 60

Sabatini, Audrey 69
Safe 13, 72–75, 80–87
Saint Hoax 91, **92**, 93, 194n4
Salaky, Kristen 193n22
Sasot, Sass Rogando 175
Sava, Oliver 181
Schapiro, Mark 78
Sconce, Jeffrey 196n2

Scott, Dayna N. 71
Sedgwick, Kyra 110
Seidel, Linda, 23, 34, 69, 147, 188n5, 189n13
Sélavy, Virginie 27
Seltzer, Sarah 191n5
Serano, Julia 174, 198n3
Shachar, Hila 192n18
Shahvisi, Arianne 143–144
Shelley, Adrienne 102
Sheppard, Samantha N. 115, 117
Sherman-Palladino, Amy 41
"Shout Your Abortion" 133
Showalter, Elaine 93n5
Sidibe, Gabourey 31
Silbergleid, Robin 44
Silkwood 74, 85
Silver Linings Playbook 94
Silverstein, Melissa 135
Simmons, Laurie 133, 137, 196n10
single mother 3, 12, 26–28, 30, 34, 37–39, 43–45, 50–51, 69, 85, 104, 120, 126, 142, 149, 163, 189n3, 190n12, 190n18; welfare 30–34
16 and Pregnant 12–13, 46–47
Slate, Jenny 130, **132**
Slaughter, Anne Marie 195n1
Smith, Michael B. 73
social services 14, 20, 28–29, 32, 34, 43–44, 51, 68, 90–91, 96, 98, 105, 109–110, 113
social workers 28–29, 32, 33, 113, 189n12
Soloway, Jill 8, 160, 173–174, 179, 184
Spencer, Leland G. 162
The Squid and the Whale 129
Stabile, Carol 192n13
Stahl, Lesley 174–176
Stark, Jeff 195n3
Stasia, Cristina Lucia 101, 194
Stevenson, Betsey 15–16
Stewart, Kristen 55
Stewart, Melanie Ann 51, 191n30
Stoneman, Scott 189n10
Strahovski, Yvonne 153
Stringer, Rebecca 12, 105, 187n4, 194n2, 195n4, 196n7, 198n8
Sukenick, Lynn 56, 125
surrogacy, 142–146, 152–159, 196n3, 197n9; *see also* advanced reproductive technology
Swiffer 9–**10**

Taddeo, Julie Ann 189n7
Takeda, Allison 52, 53
Tamblyn, Amber 184
Tambor, Jeffrey 165, **169**, 199n20
Tanenbaum, Leora 196n12
Tasker, Yvonne 9, 16, 187n4, 188n12, 196n7
Taubin, Amy 192n14
Taylor, Dorceta E. 193n9
Teen Mom 12–13, 25, 46–54
teen pregnancy 31, 38, 43–44, 46–47, 190n12, 192n14
telenovela 181, 185–186

testimonial injustice *see* epistemic injustice
Thau, Barbara 68
Theron, Charlize 146
Thomason, Linda Bloodworth 179
"time scarcity" 67, 70
Tiny Furniture 14, 125, 127, 133–137
Tomkins, Calvin 137
Tomlin, Lily 72, 77, 137
Torkelson, Ann 192n11
Toscano, Margaret 192n16
toxic discourse 13, 73–75, 86
toxic induced loss of tolerance (TILT) *see* environmental illness
Transamerica 161–164, 170, 198n8
transgender 15, 198n7, 198n14, 198n15; trans-misogyny and discrimination 162–164, 168, 198n4
Transparent 15, 160, 164–165, 168–174, 176, 177–178
Trier-Bienick, Adrienne 188n13
Trump, Donald 68, 106, 123, 181, 192n20, 199n5
Tucker, Duncan 162
Tully 14–15, 142–143, 146–152, 156–159
Twilight (film franchise) 13, 55, 63–68; *Breaking Dawn, Part I* 65; *Breaking Dawn, Part II* 66; *Twilight* 55–57, 63–70
Twilight (novel series) 55, 63–68; *Breaking Dawn* 65; *Eclipse* 67; *Twilight* 63–64, 67
Tyler, Imogen 31

United Church of Christ 193n9
Urman, Jenni Snyder 179, 181–182
uterine transplant 197n17, 197n18, 197n19; *see also* advanced reproductive technology

Vagianos, Alanna 90
Valdivia, Angharad 43
Vandenberg-Daves, Jodi 35, 66, 68, 144
Vavrus, Mary Douglas 15–16
Vered, Karen Orr 3
"victim" label 14, 50, 98, 119, 122–123, 194n2, 195n14
Vinson, Jenna 43

Waitress 14, 90–91, 102–106, 121, 126
Walsh, Matt 161
Walters, Lee Ann 88
Wang, Wayne 93
Watson, Lindsay 188n8
Watson, William J. 188n8
Weber, Brenda R. 53
Wein, Darren 72, 86, 193n14
Weinstein, Harvey 179
Weissman, Anna L. 197n15
Weitz, Paul 137–141
Wendell, Susan 75–76
What to Expect When You're Expecting 19–20, 22, 35, 188n1, 118n2
Wheeler, Duncan 110, 194n10
White, Armond 31
Will, George 190n12
Williams, Cristan 143, 196n14, 198n5
Williams, Florence 187n6
Williams, Tiffany 143
Wiseman, Noah 26, **30**
Witsell, Emily 194n1, 194n11
The Wizard of Oz 121, 150
Wolfers, Justin 15–16
Women's Media Center 179
women's shelters 98, 102, 109, 113, 117–118, 126
Women's Voices for the Earth 193,n1
working mother 10, 23, 43, 68, 72, 125–127, 147
"worldly girl" 38, 45–51, 53–54, 63
Wyeth, Andrew 62

Yakas, Lisa 193n2
Young, Iris Marion 20, 25, 151

Zegers, Kevin 162
Zeisler, Andi 5
Zuckerman, Esther 130